D0148616

Autonomy and Power

University of Pennsylvania Press
THE ETHNOHISTORY SERIES

A complete list of the books in this series
appears at the back of this volume.

Autonomy and Power

The Dynamics of Class and Culture in Rural Bolivia

Maria L. Lagos

University of Pennsylvania Press

Philadelphia

Copyright © 1994 by Maria L. Lagos
All rights reserved
Printed in the United States of America

Library of Congress Cataloging-in-Publication Data

Lagos, Maria L.
    Autonomy and power: the dynamics of class and culture in rural
Bolivia / Maria L. Lagos.
        p.   cm.—(Ethnohistory series)
    Includes bibliographical references and index.
    ISBN 0-8122-3213-5 (cloth).—ISBN 0-8122-1500-1 (paper)
    1. Indians of South America—Bolivia—Tiraque (Cordillera)—
Politics and government. 2. Indians of South America—Bolivia—
Tiraque (Cordillera)—Land tenure. 3. Indians of South America—
Bolivia—Tiraque (Cordillera)—Social conditions. 4. Peasantry—
Bolivia—Tiraque (Cordillera) 5. Rural poor—Bolivia—Tiraque
(Cordillera) 6. Tiraque (Cordillera, Bolivia)—History. 7. Tiraque
(Cordillera, Bolivia)—Social conditions. 8. Tiraque (Cordillera,
Bolivia)—Politics and government. I. Title. II. Series:
Ethnohistory series (Philadelphia, Pa.)
F3319.1.T56L34   1994
307.7'2'098423—dc20   93-48809
                                                           CIP

Contents

Illustrations

Abbreviations

AAT	Archivo Alcaldía Tiraque
AHM	Archivo Histórico Municipal
JT	Juzgado Tiraque
PC	Prefectura de Cochabamba
RDR	Registro de Derechos Reales
SNRA	Servicio Nacional de Reforma Agraria

Preface

Understanding the concept of peasantries was probably one of the most difficult tasks I confronted in my graduate studies. I vividly remember my confusion and doubt over the seemingly endless debates about the definition of peasantries, their class position, their politics and cultures, and the controversies over whether they had been doomed or created by capitalism. Every new article or book I read raised new questions and caused greater confusion. As I began to understand, I decided to undertake research in rural Bolivia. Armed with what I thought was a fairly sophisticated conceptual apparatus, I ventured into the "field" in January 1982 to study the transformation of agrarian class relations in Tiraque, a province in Cochabamba. But when I saw the women and men who were to become the subjects of my research, I was even more confused: none of them carried self-identifying class or ethnic tags that would help me make sense of the complex reality I was beginning to perceive. I encountered men and women who called themselves *campesinos* (peasants) when in fact they were not; people who showed no obvious phenotypic distinctions, but who referred to themselves or others as Indians, *cholos*,[1] or whites. Furthermore, political confrontations and alignments, as well as cultural practices, united and divided them in ways I had not anticipated. These paradoxical identifications of self and others, which shifted as the contexts and audiences changed, puzzled and frustrated me.

During three consecutive years of ethnographic and archival research, and in short visits during the summers of 1980, 1985, 1988, and 1989, I began to comprehend the reasons for my initial puzzlement. I was looking for certain essential cultural and political symbols and practices that would allow me to frame a reality that was fluid and ever changing. Prolonged contact and observation of the daily lives of Tiraqueños forced me to move away from fixed social categorizations and concentrate instead on the ambiguities, confusions, and paradoxes of daily life—on the ways in which they experienced, negotiated, and represented changing social relations. They thus not only taught me about their lives and histories, but also helped me to reconceptualize many theoretical concerns and to refine my understanding of the intersecting dynamics of class and culture, which is the central theme of this book.

Tiraqueños also made me realize the importance of doing field research: of being present when crises occurred and when actors were forced to take sides and to choose between competing identities and loyalties, or when others just did not get directly involved; to hear what they said in public and in private, and to whom. More than once, I was also pressed to take a stand, to deny or corroborate whether I supported one faction or the other, or to explain the reasons why I would leave the town to spend several days in the houses of "Indians" in the villages. It was not always easy, especially because I was straddling the invisible yet tension-ridden lines between town and villages, campesinos and *vecinos* (townsfolk), "whites" and "Indians." And, after all, I was living in a small town, one which Tiraqueños referred to as a "small town, big hell," and where everyone, including the anthropologist, could be the target of gossip and character assassination. I also learned that these seemingly parochial struggles and debates of daily life, in which it mattered how each actor defined himself and herself vis-à-vis others, were always engulfed within a much larger field of force and encoded within a hegemonic discourse, both shaping, as it were, the issues and discourse of political and cultural debate and negotiation as well as intra- and interclass alliances and oppositions. Thus another central aim of this study is to capture the dynamic interplay of the global and the particular in their historical and sociocultural specificity.

Life in Tiraque was not always mired in animosity and conflict. Most of the time everyone went quietly about the daily chores of livelihood, which involved both work and leisure, including drinking and dancing during celebrations of life and death and in the many ritual festivities that marked distinct phases in the annual cycle. I tried to participate in as many of these activities as far as it was possible for a *gringa* (foreigner) urbanite who could not properly peel potatoes nor dance the *cueca* (folkloric dance) well. Much of what I know about Tiraque and its people I learned through intensive participant observation and through casual conversations and gossip in private homes in Tiraque and in the city of Cochabamba, in markets, in social, religious, and political gatherings, and while traveling on trucks. I also spent time drinking, chatting, and dancing in *chicherías*,[2] where most patrons wanted to show me their affection (or test my capacity to drink) by offering inexhaustible volumes of *chicha* (maize beer) and gossip. They provided a substantial amount of information about their daily lives and how their struggles, concerns, intrigues, and shifting alliances have shaped their histories as well as the region itself.

My understanding of Tiraque and Tiraqueños began in the "ethnographic present," reaching back into the near or more distant past only when it served to illuminate the present and, for this, I primarily relied on oral histories. Local archives in the town of Tiraque provided the material to corroborate oral histories and reconstruct the social history of the region; to construct and expand geneaologies as well as patterns of marriage and fictive kin relations; and to learn about sources of credit, lawsuits, and conflicts. The last censuses of Indian tributaries conducted between 1876 and 1880, together with general population censuses, provided information on official ethnic classifications in Tiraque, while the local parish records of births and marriages illustrated the changing nature of these categorizations, which often varied with family fortunes. Data collected in archives in the cities of Cochabamba and La Paz furnished a wealth of information on land transactions, mortgages, and land distribution and ownership prior to and after agrarian reform in Cochabamba. A regional survey and a census in two peasant villages complemented this information.

Research for this study was made possible by the Institute of Latin American and Iberian Studies at Columbia University, the Fulbright Foundation, the Inter-American Foundation, and the Research Foundation of the City University of New York. I want to express my sincere thanks to these foundations for their financial support.

Many people generously helped in the development of this study. First, I would like to thank the people of Tiraque, most of whom received me with warmth and patiently answered my often repetitious questions. They asked many questions, too. Without them and without their curiosity, this work could not have been possible. They wanted to know about my personal life, about potato cropping in the United States, and about U.S. policy in Latin America. Above all, they wanted to know how anthropologists make a living, given that in Tiraque, as Doña Hortensia, an elderly Tiraqueña, said of me, "Usted se pasa el tiempo visitando y hablando con la gente! Cuándo va a trabajar?" ("You spend your time just visiting and talking with people! When are you going to work?"). Although I tried to answer her question, I am not sure my explanation made much sense to her. Yet I am grateful for her frankness and for her constant reminders that "time is gold," as she used to tell me every time she saw me talking with people. I am also indebted to my *compadres* (coparents) Eva and Hilarión, my *ahijados* (godchildren) Leonor and Exipión, my special friends Don Roberto, the late Doña Florita, Don Sandalio, and the many other friends I made in the villages, the town, and the city. Eucarpio Montaño was an excellent part-time assistant and good friend. His good nature and warmth toward all people were critical for opening doors in the villages. I also wish to thank all those non-Tiraqueños who helped me settle in Tiraque and assisted me there. Fathers Esteban Avellí and Javier Baptista and the *hermanitas* (little sisters) were most supportive throughout my stay. To those dedicated and committed Belgian volunteers Rita Cloet, Ian Herteleer, Inés and Wilfredo Marcelo, and the Bolivians who worked with them, in particular, María Manzano, I owe special thanks for their friendship and support.[3]

In the course of my research, I have accumulated many other debts in Bolivia. I would like to thank the staff of Registro de Derechos Reales, especially Dr. César Fiorillo, who did not seem to mind my presence in those busy offices; Archivo Histórico Municipal; Servicio Nacional de Reforma Agraria; Notaría de Hacienda and Tesoro de Hacienda at the Prefectura of Cochabamba; Centro de Estudios de la Realidad Económica y Social; and Centro de Investigación y Promoción del Campesinado. Fernando Calderón, Jorge Dandler, Roberto Laserna, Rosario León, Alberto Rivera, Juan Torrico, Carlos de la Riva, and Germán Ustariz not only shared ideas and information but also provided valuable support. Many friends also contributed to my stay in Bolivia and provided constant assistance and support as well as occasional criticism: Xavier Albó, the late Brian Anderson, Vicente Cuellar, Xavier Izko, Domingo Mendoza, Colin Sage, and Rose Marie Vargas. I am particularly indebted to Nancy Velarde for her hospitality during my overextended stay at her house in Cochabamba and to Phillip Blair for opening the doors of his house to every investigator who went to La Paz, where many of us weathered General García Meza's coup in 1980. I am grateful to Elba Luppo and Julio Zubieta for their help with statistical analysis as well as for their friendship.

There are also many people—too many to remember—who contributed, directly or indirectly, to my development as an anthropologist. I owe special gratitude to Joan Vincent, who, in the twenty years I have known her, has not only taught me anthropology but has been, and still is, a constant source of inspiration, encouragement, and support. I am also indebted to Herbert Klein for introducing me to the Andes and for helping me in many ways. Many other anthropologists and historians influenced my thinking, in particular, Arturo Warman, who I was fortunate to have as a visiting professor at Columbia University, and whose lectures were always a source of inspiration and commitment. Through his teachings and the writings of Eric Wolf, I began to understand peasantries.

In the course of writing several drafts of this manuscript, I benefited from the comments and support of many people: my friend Concepción Martínez, whose prodding questions led me to rethink much of my research material; and Xavier Albó, Lesley Gill, Brooke Larson, and Gavin Smith, who also provided thoughtful criticisms on earlier versions of this book. They, as well as many other friends, in particular Rodolfo Aiello, Michael Goodman, and June Nash, gave me continued support and encouragement. I owe a special debt of gratitude to Gerald Sider for his support and the many theoretical discussions we had while I was writing the first version of this work. The final version of this study also benefited from the comments provided by the anonymous readers as well as by the helpful editorial suggestions made by the project editor, Mindy Brown, and the copyeditor, Jacquelyn Coggin. Their colleague, acquisitions editor Patricia Smith, provided continuous, enthusiastic support for which I am also most grateful. Finally, my parents and my family encouraged me from a distance and in my infrequent, though much desired, trips to Argentina.

Several years have now passed since I started this project, yet Doña Hortensia's words still ring in my ears. For her sake, as well as for that of all Tiraqueños, mentors, and friends, I hope I have not wasted their time.

Introduction

On June 16, 1953, the exasperated mayor of Tiraque, a province in the highlands of Cochabamba, wrote a letter to the *prefecto* (governor) of the department of Cochabamba to inform him that:

Indian agitators . . . have dared to disavow the resolutions of this council, declaring that they are not dependent on any authority; that they are now their own masters and lords acting on their own free-will, and that they do not recognize any authority above them. Since this and even worse abuses are taking place in different parts in the department, it is most urgent that you take the necessary measures to avoid further excesses that could undermine the public order. I also want to inform you . . . [that] more than 300 men, who were supposed to repair the main roads, have not paid attention to the orders given by the Intendant and have decided, instead, to work on their own, repairing pathways of no importance, doing only what they please. If this continues and no steps are soon taken, your honor, next year no one will work and all the roads will further deteriorate. (AAT: Correspondencia)[1]

The mayor's letter reflects not only his dismay at the "Indian" agitators' lack of recognition for his authority, but also his impotence and, possibly, fear. He had two goods reasons to be afraid. The first was triggered by the militant actions of the rural poor who, soon after the National Revolution of 1952, organized in armed rural militias in Tiraque, as well as in other regions of Bolivia, seized hacienda lands, and arrested and terrorized hacendados and those considered enemies of the revolution. The second cause of deep concern to the mayor was that the revolution had awakened the "lazy, ignorant, and untrustworthy Indians," who now even dared to challenge his authority. To him and to many other Bolivians, "Indians" were both a living symbol of and the cause for Bolivia's underdevelopment, and the fact that they wielded so much power in the countryside raised the specter of chaos.

To the "Indians," the seizure of land was one important victory in a long struggle toward becoming "their own masters and lords," no longer subject to power holders but able to excercise "their own free will." This deep-seated and persistent ideal that underlies the desire for freedom has indeed moved people to struggle in Bolivia as well as in many other parts of the world. As the historical and ethnographic records show, subordinate groups have fought this battle on many fronts and with diverse strategies. In the central valleys and surrounding highlands of Cochabamba, *vallunos*, as the people from this region are called, adopted both private and collective forms of resistance. To avoid tribute exactions and forced labor drafts imposed on the indigenous population by Viceroy Toledo in the sixteenth century, many men and women abandoned their villages and settled in other villages, rural towns, and on the expanding haciendas. Many also "passed" into the mestizo category, which was an arbitrary and ambiguous status occupying the interstices of colonial society. They thus subverted the colonial project which was based on a rigid, but not impermeable, hierarchy of "castes." Several efforts on the part of the colonial state to incorporate the growing mestizo population in the Crown's tribute rolls were never successful and were often violently resisted (Larson 1988).

In the course of these struggles, however, vallunos lost their lands to the point that, by the eighteenth century, no Indian communities existed on the valley floor and much of the highlands, having been replaced by haciendas populated with landless Indians and mestizos. As *colonos* (hacienda tenants) and sharecroppers, they challenged the power of hacendados who were able neither to tie them permanently to their estates nor to avoid their aggressive competition in the market. Some were able to buy small plots of land and become *piqueros* (landowning peasants), gnawing, bit by bit, at the lands of debt-burdened hacendados. When vallunos seized hacienda lands after the revolution of 1952, claiming that they had rights over these lands because they worked them and because the lands had belonged to their ancestors "since time immemorial," they were at the vanguard of rural mobilization in Bolivia and were one of the major forces pressuring the revolutionary government to pass, in 1953, one of the most radical agrarian reforms in Latin America. Through these actions and their organization in rural unions, "Indians," now turned *campesinos* (peasants), were also able to re-create rural "communities" in the central valleys and highlands of Cochabamba as "aspects of struggle" (Williams 1973) during the years of revolution and agrarian reform.[2] Possibly what led the "Indian agitators" to defy the resolutions of the mayor of Tiraque, declaring instead that they could do as they pleased, was that they must have felt the immediate satisfaction of having an unprecedented degree of control over their livelihoods. It did not take too long, however, for them to rediscover that direct access to land made them vulnerable to new forms of exploitation and domination. How this happens is what this study seeks to recount.

This book also tries to show the complex ways in which the transformation of agrarian class relations interweaves with political practices, culture, and discourse. Therefore, I set out to examine two fundamental processes that seem to move in different and opposing directions: first, the emergence and persistence of a land-owning peasantry—a process that began in the 1800s and took on particular force after the revolution of 1952; and second, the emergence of a rural merchant class extracting surplus from this peasantry by a combination of alliances in production and a reliance on "traditional" practices—such as reciprocity, coparenthood, and "community"—to consolidate its hold over production. Paradoxically, it has been these same cultural practices and customs that peasants have used in an attempt to maintain a certain degree of autonomy from merchant-class control. This apparent contradiction, I argue, is inherent in the ideology and practice of autonomy. As an ideal, autonomy involves a yearning for freedom from power holders; as a practice, autonomy simultaneously generates the dependence of households on intimate relations of work and production with other households. In essence, the ideology of autonomy intertwines with the ideology of "community," as inextricably related ideals that, in practice, delineate possible ways in which social relations can be negotiated and affected within and between households. My argument is that, over time, the reproduction of these sociocultural relations underwrites processes of social differentiation and transformation in rural hinterlands.[3]

As in other regions of the "third world," the transformation of agrarian class relations in Cochabamba was by no means a linear process but rather a complex and ambiguous one.[4] Historically, the various merchant classes that emerged in Tiraque accumulated wealth but did not, or could not, transform this wealth into capital in the region. The first group of merchant families studied emerged in the late nineteenth century, persisting until the agrarian reform of 1953, when they were replaced by other social climbers. In both cases, they accumulated wealth through speculative commercial, as well as usurious, relations with landowning peasants and artisans. They also accumulated land, extracting ground rent from landless peasants and, after the agrarian reform, from landowning peasants through the establishment of sharecropping agreements on the *peasants' land.* Although these relations of production are qualitatively different, neither has divorced producers from the means of production.

My purpose in this study is to understand how the rural poor get

caught up in larger processes of transformation and how they participate in giving shape and direction to these processes. The struggle of
peasants to gain direct access to land and to maintain a certain degree
of control over the labor process has enabled them to produce use
values outside the influence of the market. But, in order to preserve
this delicate autonomy, paradoxically, they have increased participation in well-developed markets for their labor, cash crops, chemical
fertilizer, and transport for their cash crops, even for the "traditional"
manure that many now obtain outside their farms. In producing, buying and selling, peasants are constrained by the practices of a new
dominant class of merchants, transporters, and usurers, who have
arisen from within rural villages and towns.

This book then explores the relationship of autonomy—as ideology
and as agency—and power. Although the term *ideology* has many
meanings (cf. Eagleton 1991), I understand this concept not as false
consciousness but as one form in which culture interweaves with
power (cf. Comaroff and Comaroff 1991; Hall 1988; Sider 1986; Williams 1985). More specifically, my concern is with the "active and
formative, but also transformational" aspects of this relationship (Williams 1989:113); with the ways in which subordinate groups continu-
ously seek to create autonomous sociocultural spaces and relations
and how these almost invariably give rise to new forms of exploitation
and domination. In fact, the pathways the "Indian" agitators built in
Tiraque instead of roads may serve as a metaphor for this recurrent
contradiction. Pathways lead to the relative security and intimacy of
the household and the village but they can also be traversed in the
opposite direction, toward a much wider and more difficult to control
field of forces. In the account that follows, I attempt to unravel from
a double perspective this apparent paradox.

On the one hand, I seek to convey the fluidity and ambiguity of
social life as it is experienced, interpreted, and elaborated by the protagonists themselves. On the other hand, I seek to objectify the subjective by analyzing social relations of production (involving relations
of work and appropriation) that both give rise to and shape class relations under changing conditions of production. Because these social
relations are not circumscribed within the boundaries of a household,
a village, or a confederation of households (G. Smith 1989), I cast a
wide net to encompass other social groups—the continuous presence
of the state, institutions of civil society, and hegemonic forms of domination. Class is, of course, an analytical concept that requires ab-
straction and generalization of key social relations through which rent
(or surpluses of labor and product) is transferred to powerholders.
As Warman (1980:186) so clearly states, "Class analysis does not seek

to classify people but to understand a social process." My goal in this study, to paraphrase Bourdieu (1990:26), lies with the "coincidence [or lack of coincidence] of objective structures and the internalized structures," that is, with subjective, yet social, understandings of lived experience—with "practical consciousness [of] what is actually being lived, and not only what it is thought is being lived" (Williams 1989:130–31).

In seeking to understand this double process, I explore the structural conditions that may force landowning peasants to establish intimate ties of dependence—as well as ties of domination and subordination—in capitalist social formations. My argument is that once the landless become owners of the land, land itself loses its importance and the monetary requirements *for production* take center stage. This is, as Marx (1894/1977) puts it, what subjects the small peasant to the moneylender or, more broadly, to those who will lend the basic necessities for livelihood. More recently, Wolf (1983:55) urged anthropologists and historians to pay more attention to "the effects of debt on the constitution and differentiation of peasantries . . . peasant needs for money and peasant indebtedness remain to be explored in further research." My analysis of the related emergence of both a landowning peasantry and a merchant class places emphasis on credit relations and sharecropping agreements, which proved to be an excellent analytical focus to examine the process of commoditization "on the ground" and to move beyond the market to unravel the manner in which peasants are exploited in production.[5] My study tries to show that the most significant and influential point in the process of merchant-class domination of a peasantry is not the market, or the culturally shaped unequal exchange relations they enter into by selling their cash crops cheap and paying dear for what they buy, or even their transport needs. Rather, the appropriation of peasant surplus begins in production itself, and is, or can be, extended through market and transport relations, particularly when the sharecropper or provider of credit is at the same time merchant and transporter. Most importantly, these are also the covillagers, fictive kin, or even kin of poorer villagers. And it is because practices and ideologies of reciprocity, "community," and coparenthood often underlie these relations of domination and subordination, as if these relations were indeed horizontal, that I find it necessary to distinguish between the objectivity of inequality and the subjectivity of equality (Bourdieu 1990).

In examining the manner in which Tiraqueños negotiated and represented changing social relations, I was always intrigued because, even though their lives were intricately intertwined, cultural and political practices and discourses united and divided them in ways that I had not anticipated. As I indicated in the preface and notwithstanding my theoretical understanding of the vast body of literature on peasantries, field research taught me that there was nothing essential in the ways in which Tiraqueños portrayed themselves and others, or in the ways in which they established intra- and inter-class alliances and oppositions. Rather, their identities and politics were defined and shaped by cultural constructions of class (campesino) and ethnicity.

Nowadays, to be a campesino in Cochabamba is to have access to land, to speak Quechua and, probably more importantly for men, to know how to drive the ox-drawn plow. But campesinos may also be recognized by the sandals and weathered feet and hands of men, women, and children; the rough homespun slacks and *corazas* (short ponchos) men wear over manufactured clothes when working in the fields or the ponchos they wear on cold days; the thick homespun polleras, shawls, and hats women wear on their braided hair. In both senses, however, the concept *campesino* is far from clear, for it encompasses several differentiated groups. Most campesinos live in villages, but some also live in towns, work the land, and raise animals; many also move to other regions and neighboring countries to work as wage laborers, colonizers, and traders. Thus, they all produce commodities, including their labor power, but they also produce use values. Some own more than one hundred hectares of land, have numerous sheep and oxen, own trucks, and are large-scale merchants and moneylenders; others have very little or no land, few animals, and little money. For the most part, they have to rely on share systems to raise animals and on sharecropping to produce cash crops. Most of them speak Quechua and many also speak Spanish, although an older generation of men and women as well as children, speak little, if any, Spanish. Furthermore, *vecinos* (townsfolk) share many social and cultural characteristics with campesinos. All vecinos speak Quechua, most have access to land, know how to plow, and some are members of *sindicatos campesinos* (peasant unions); many vecinas don polleras, shawls, and put their hair in braids. Unlike the concept *campesino*, which is an inclusive category glossing over class differences, ethnicity is an exclusive category distinguishing vecinos from villagers along cultural definitions of "race," that are, in turn, encoded within dominant images and associations of the countryside, and the people who live in it, with "Indianness" (cf. Wolfe 1991). What is important for this analysis is that the ambiguity of both concepts leaves them open for manipulation and contestation, and simultaneously, open for building shifting alliances in factional conflicts and in mobilizations against the state.

By focusing on the ambiguities and paradoxes of daily life, this study also addresses current concerns in the literature regarding conceptual definitions of peasantries,[6] their political practices, and discourse. While recent contributions to our understanding of peasant politics have called our attention to everyday forms of resistance (cf. Guha 1989; Scott 1985, 1990), this study suggests a more complex interpretation, one that seeks to relate culture to social transformations and takes into account the emergence of new social classes or class fractions and the displacement of others, as well as changing relations between the state and civil society (cf. Bayly 1988; Brass 1991; Isaacman 1990; Lagos 1993). My point is that the political practices of subaltern and dominant groups need to be analyzed within the context of particular social relations and specific hegemonic moments. In fine, what I argue is that an analysis of the dynamics of domination and resistance bears more directly on hegemony (Gramsci 1975), a process which "does not just passively exist as a form of dominance [or resistance]. It has continually to be renewed, recreated, defended, and modified [because] it is continually resisted, limited, altered, challenged" (Williams 1989:112). As I try to show in this study, this is a process that involves not only social but also cultural struggles over the daily lives of people and their culture, which, in the last analysis, revolves around the appropriation of surplus and efforts to make this appropriation more or less difficult, and takes a wide range of forms in specific historical contexts and cultural arenas (Hall 1981; Lagos 1993).

A final but necessary caveat is in order here. Although this study does not directly address the issue of gender, women are present throughout my discussion and analysis of processes of class formation and cultural transformations in Tiraque. As is true everywhere, women in Cochabamba play an important role in production and reproduction and, as in most regions in the Andes, women are conspicuous in urban and rural markets (Babb 1989; Seligmann 1989). But for some women, this double workload is heavier than it is for others, and their productive and exchange activities may result in very different outcomes: some households are barely able to reproduce, while others accumulate wealth. In this study, I give precedence to this form of inequality.

* * *

This book is organized into six chapters. In the first, I introduce the region of Tiraque as it existed at the time of research and its fluctuating relationship to a wider social field. Tiraque is not more representative than any other region in the Andes; rather my choice of this area as a research site was based on the usual practical considerations. I looked for a rural market town that was small enough to allow me use the "community" method of investigation, but was also the seat of a transporters' union.[7] Other important reasons for the selection of this area were the previous studies that other social scientists[8] had made in Tiraque and the contacts with some Tiraqueños that I had already established.

The narrative begins in Chapter 2, which covers the period from 1900 to 1952, marking two major transformations in Bolivia: the consolidation of the nation state and Bolivia's integration in the capitalist world market as a producer of minerals, and a revolution that ruptured the social fabric of the country. A practical reason for selecting 1900 as the starting date for this work is that it was the year Tiraque first elected officials who felt the need to record both social, political, and economic events as well as everyday occurrences. Tiraque had become, in 1900, the capital of an administrative district, and it was being taken, and was taking itself, more seriously. A more important reason is that I wanted to reconstruct the trajectories of those families and individuals who were still remembered in Tiraque at the time of research.

I set out to present the whole cast of characters in Tiraque[9] and analyze the formation of a landowning peasantry and its social counterpart, a merchant class. I examine the various ways in which social climbers profited from the expansion of the economic frontier into the tropical lowlands, from which coca and wood were exported to the expanding mines, and how the wealth they accumulated was then used to purchase land in the highlands of Tiraque and invested in speculative enterprises. The last part of the chapter (1932–52) focuses on the way generalized economic stagnation and political conflicts stemming from the world depression and Bolivia's disastrous defeat in a war with Paraguay were felt in Tiraque, and how different people with divergent interests and options coped with, or exacerbated, these problems in the region.

Chapter 3 deals with the revolution of 1952 and the mobilization of the rural poor in order to show how most of them were transformed into landowning campesinos, and how, through their organization into powerful and militant unions, they were able to seize hacienda lands and force the departure of hacendados from Tiraque. This newly gained power and autonomy, however, did not last long, since the departure of hacendados and the transformation of social relations left them vulnerable to state pressures and, particularly, to a new, emergent merchant class. The state has had a significant yet shifting and ambiguous role, since it dictated policies for rural development that did not lead to development but set new conditions for the accumulation of wealth, while at the same time it attempted to control the peasantry through its unions, populism, and direct force.

In Chapter 4, I analyze the organization of work and relations of production (which encompass both production and appropriation) in rural villages during the period of fieldwork in order to trace the process through which campesinos have developed new forms of production and new relations of dependency. By looking at the material base and social relations of the labor process, two aspects of village life become particularly salient: (1) the processes of internal differentiation and class formation within the peasantry, and (2) the ambiguities of collusion and resistance displayed by peasants and village elites in a context where the ideologies of "community" and reciprocity permeate most social relations.

In Chapter 5 I move from the village to the region to describe differences between regional town merchants and village merchants (by now composed of both fairly well-established and newly emergent wealthy families) and to show how, in spite of these differences, both rely on similar "traditional" values, institutions, and forms of exchange to extract surplus from the peasantry and to profit from unequal exchange. In this chapter, I focus on merchant-class competition in the appropriation of peasant surplus, and on the social and cultural strategies the town-based merchants use to maintain areas of operation and control over peasant households outside the reach of emergent merchants and transporters from the villages as well as from other towns.

Chapter 6 analyzes regional politicking, factional disputes, and social cleavages, focusing on the use of, and struggle over, divergent interpretations of cultural concepts that define class and ethnicity. At issue is the complex interweaving of class, politics, and culture, and how this shapes the political disputes, alliances, and antagonisms of emergent elites and their relations with peasants.

In the conclusion, I return to the larger issues of class formation and the persistence of a landowning peasantry to discuss how, in the final analysis, both merchant classes and peasantries are dependent on the state and on larger capitalist forces beyond the state. As both Warman (1978) and Wolf suggest, the state is the ultimate arbiter of peasant livelihood, since it is the "arena where major internal and international decisions affecting the relations of industry and agriculture are fought out" (E. Wolf 1983:75), and where the general conditions for appropriation from peasants are established. By focusing on processes of class formation and on the paradoxes of autonomy, power, and culture in a region in Bolivia, this analysis will show how these forces and processes of transformation are played out, reproduced, contested, and reshaped in peasant villages and rural hinterlands.

Chapter 1
An Introduction to Tiraque

The region of Tiraque, situated in the Department of Cochabamba, encompasses the rural town of Tiraque, the countryside immediately surrounding it, and a wider area. Located east of the capital city of the department, just beyond the central valleys of Cochabamba—long known as the granary of Bolivia and the center of commercial activity in the department—Tiraque is not an isolated backwater hinterland involved only in subsistence production but has been integrated into a market economy and a wider context since early colonial times. Today, international capital reaches campesino households in the form of credit and chemical fertilizers through state institutions and four private development organizations funded by European and North American agencies.

Because of their proximity to the central valleys, men and women from Tiraque have shared many experiences with *vallunos*, as their valley neighbors are called, and together they have shaped daily life in the central valleys of Cochabamba and beyond. By the mid-eighteenth century, the region had proportionally the lowest Indian and highest mestizo population of Alto Perú (later Bolivia); rural artisans and petty commodity producers competed with hacendados in the marketplace; and many were able to purchase lands and become *piqueros* (landowning peasants). Much later in 1952, vallunos took the vanguard in the mobilization of the rural poor for the enactment of an agrarian reform in Bolivia. Since early colonial times, vallunos have also been reputed for their geographical mobility and participation in events taking place within a much broader geographic and social context. Not only did they abandon their villages and "pass" into the mestizo category in order to escape colonial tribute and labor exactions, but the laboring poor also moved to and from Cochabamba's haciendas, coca plantations, rural towns, and the city, as well as to more distant mining camps. In the late nineteenth century, many men went to the Pacific coast to work in the nitrate mines, moving shortly thereafter to the mining camps in the highland plateau, where they imposed Quechua as the lingua franca amidst Aymara-speaking peasants. Since the mid-nineteenth century, they have colonized or moved as seasonal laborers to the eastern lowlands of Bolivia and, more recently, to and beyond Buenos Aires in Argentina. As traders and merchants, muleteers, truck and bus drivers, vallunos have also traveled far and wide in Bolivia. This movement of people reflects larger transformations affecting Bolivia as a whole and, at the same time, shapes the history and the boundaries of our area of study over time. But before we follow them in these journeys, we should begin by placing Tiraque within its larger spatial context.

Bolivia is a landlocked country of extreme ecological diversity, largely determined by the Andes mountain range to the west and by the Amazon river basin to the north and east. The national territory may be divided into three distinct ecological zones. In the west, the cold and arid highland plateau lies between the Cordillera Occidental and the Cordillera Real, or Oriental, at an altitude of approximately 4,000 meters above sea level. To the east, the intermontane valleys cutting across the slopes of the Cordillera Real are steep and rugged in the northern tropical *yungas,* or steep tropical valleys (altitudes ranging from 1,600 to 450 meters above sea level), and more open and temperate around the cities of Cochabamba, Sucre, and Tarija (2,500–1,950 meters above sea level). Finally, the eastern plains or the Oriente, at an altitude of about 200 meters above sea level, occupy 70 percent of the national territory (see Map 1).

The Cordillera Oriental stands as a massive barrier separating the Department of Cochabamba from the highland plateau. The climate in the cordillera is cold, with an average temperature range of 5–12 degrees centigrade. Very little, if any, vegetation covers the high mountains, but potatoes and other rootcrops grow, and sheep pasture on the mountain slopes and in the high valleys. The steep descent from this barren yet spectacular mountain chain opens onto the wide and long central valleys of Cochabamba made up of the Valle Bajo, Valle Central, and Valle Alto where a more temperate climate (an average temperature of 20 degrees centigrade) and irrigation turn these valleys into green and yellow oases of maize and wheat fields, vegetables, fruit trees, and fruit-bearing cacti. The departmental capital, the city of Cochabamba, and the three largest regional market towns— Quillacollo, Sacaba, and Punata—are centrally located in these valleys

Map 1. Ecological zones and the location of the department of Cochabamba in relation to other departments in Bolivia.

on the routes from La Paz to Santa Cruz and Chapare. Continuing east, the Valle Alto begins to climb up until it ends at the foot of the Cordillera of Cochabamba, a west–east chain of the Cordillera Real. The eastern flanks of the Cochabamba chain are less rugged, sloping down toward the oriental lowlands in the Department of Santa Cruz. The Cordillera of Cochabamba cuts the Department into two very distinct zones: to the south, the temperate valley system of Cochabamba, bounded by another massive mountain chain separating Cochabamba from the southern Department of Potosí; to the north, steep tropical yungas where plantations of coca, bananas, citrus, and other fruits cut into the tropical vegetation covering the mountain slopes. The river systems follow the west–east incline of Cochabamba, channeling their waters into the Upper Amazonian basin. Rivers flow down from the Cordillera, cutting the mountain slopes into deep gorges; generally empty during the dry season, these rivers irrigate the valleys after the rains.

Although mining and, more recently, cocaine production are the activities for which Bolivia is generally known in other parts of the world, Bolivia is a predominantly agrarian country with approximately 65 percent of its population engaged in agriculture. Yet the history of Bolivia has been shaped, to a large extent, by the growth and decline of silver mining in the colonial period and by the recovery of the mining economy in the late nineteenth century, leading to the growth, expansion, or decline of urban centers, haciendas and indigenous communal lands, patterns of population distribution, and the country's transport system.[1] Until recently, the highland plateau, with its rich mineral deposits, and the fertile intermontane valleys were economically the most important regions. About three-fourths of Bolivia's total population of approximately six million live in these regions, principally near lake Titicaca and the central valleys of Cochabamba, which have an average population density of 69 inhabitants per square kilometer. In contrast, the Oriente has an average population density of 0.8 inhabitants per square kilometer (Wennergren and Whitaker 1975). Since the National Revolution of 1952, export-oriented agricultural enterprises have developed in the eastern lowlands, attracting people from the more densely populated highland plateau and intermontane valleys. The coca-producing yungas of La Paz and Cochabamba have attracted people from other regions. In pre-colonial times, highland *ayllus* (Andean corporate kin groups) set up colonies in the yungas.[2] Another wave of colonizers began to arrive in the mid-nineteenth century, when these valleys reopened for colonization, and even larger groups of settlers were established there after the agrarian reform of 1953. Today the yungas of Chapare have become a major center of illegal cocaine paste production.

The distribution of languages in Bolivia roughly correlates to the geographical zones described above. Aymara is the predominant language in the highland plateau, Quechua in the intermontane valleys, and numerous languages are spoken by small groups of native Americans in the eastern lowlands. Spanish is, however, the official language of Bolivia, but it is primarily spoken in the urban centers, in the eastern regions, and in the Department of Tarija. While Aymara and Quechua still predominate in the countryside, internal migration has spread the autochthonous languages to the mining camps, urban centers, and the lowlands, where more and more people are now bilingual and, in some areas, trilingual. Monolingualism has thus declined in favor of bilingualism (Albó 1976).

Bolivia's transport system has been shaped by the country's topography, as well as its history. Until the turn of the century, large caravans of pack mules and llamas supplied the mines and towns with agricultural goods and transported minerals to the Pacific coast for shipment to Europe (Cobb 1949; Sánchez-Albornóz 1965). The recovery of the mining economy in the late nineteenth century stimulated railway construction. Since most of the railway lines were built by private capital to serve the interests of the mining industry, few extended east beyond the mining districts; the railroad reached the city of Cochabamba only in 1917. Motor vehicles were introduced for transport during the Chaco War (the Bolivian-Paraguayan war of 1932–35), when a rudimentary road network was built mainly for military purposes (Volmuller 1954). More recently, new roads, such as the all-weather road from La Paz to Cochabamba to Santa Cruz, were constructed to stimulate agricultural development in the eastern lowlands and to facilitate the transport of agricultural products to the cities.

The motor vehicle is today the most important means of transportation in Bolivia. While other forms of transportation such as pack animals, railways, planes, and water transport are used, it has been estimated that trucks transport 90 percent of all domestic freight and passengers (Cardona 1979). A powerful syndicate, the Confederación Sindical de Choferes de Bolivia, affiliating bus, truck, and taxi owners and drivers, largely controls and regulates road transport. By the time of the field research for this study, truckers played a crucial role in lacing together Bolivia's diverse regions and in giving shape to the productive activities of each region.

Tiraque in the 1980s

The term *Tiraque* has several meanings: it refers to the *Segunda Sección*, or second section, of the province of Arani, a territorial and administrative division of a province, encompassing under its jurisdiction the *cantones* (territorial subdivisions) of Tiraque, Vacas, and Vandiola[3] (see Map 2). In 1986, the administrative status of Tiraque was upgraded to that of a province, incorporating the cantones of Tiraque, Vandiola, and part of cantón Vacas. Tiraque is also a rural town, capital of the former Segunda Sección and present-day province. This study is mainly concerned with the cantones Tiraque and Vandiola, including Tiraque town. Some 1,400 people of an estimated total of 15,200 live in the town and the rest in fifty-eight campesino villages.[4] Two paved roads connect the region with the Valle Alto and its market towns, the cities of Cochabamba (60 kilometers away) and Santa Cruz, and with the neighboring Chapare province. Dirt roads link the town with the villages. Trucks transport passengers, agricultural products, animals, and wood out of the region and bring in other products such as cattle manure, vegetables, fruit not locally produced, and industrial and manufactured goods.

The region extends through the Cordillera of Cochabamba and may be divided into three zones: (1) the yungas of Vandiola where coca was produced until the plantations were abandoned in the 1960s, (2) the mountains, and (3) a high valley (3,300 meters above sea level) overlooking the Valle Alto of Cochabamba. The three zones occupy a total area of 6,000 square kilometers: 1,000 square kilometers are in the valley, 1,800 in the mountains, and 3,200 in the yungas (Cajka 1979:10). At present, the estimated total cultivable lands extend to 20,000 hectares, 95 percent of which are without irrigation. The average annual temperature in the region is 12 degrees centigrade, varying with altitude and season. During the long dry season, which begins in March and ends in November, the temperature is lower than in the rainy season, which begins in November and lasts until February. The weather on the mountains is generally cold and windy; occasional night snowstorms leave behind a thin layer of snow on the ground until the strong sunlight melts it down by mid-morning. Few trees grow in this harsh environment, but rootcrops—potatoes, oca (*Oxalis tuberosa*), and papalisa (*Ullucus tuberosus*)—grow on the mountain slopes. Other crops such as oats, barley, tarwi (*Lupinus mutabilis*), and quinoa (*Chenopodium quinoa*) may be planted on the slopes of deep gorges or in small valleys where they are protected from the cold and winds. Rudimentary irrigation canals water some cultivable lands, allowing for the planting of broad beans (*Vicia faba*), peas,

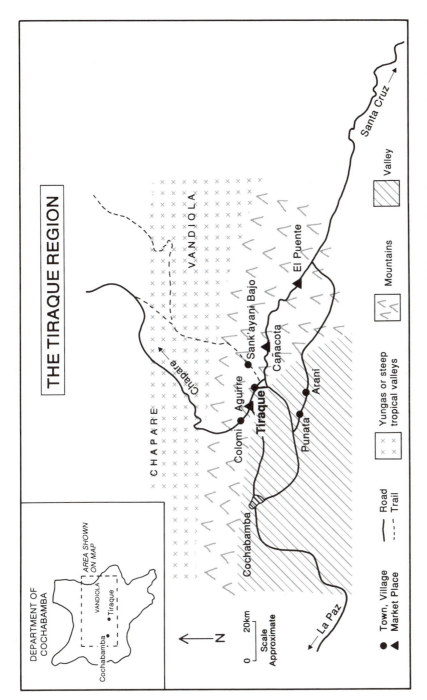

Map 2. The Tiraque region. Roads and trails shown connect the town of Tiraque with other towns, market places, and villages mentioned in the text.

and wheat for household consumption, as well as two or three potato crops.

In the valley of Tiraque the climate is milder than on the mountains. A large proportion of the land is irrigated with the waters from the Millumayo and Tiraque rivers and from several irrigation canals coming down from dams built on high mountain lakes. These conditions allow for the more intensive cultivation of potatoes, barley, tarwi, broad beans, peas, wheat, and maize. Eucalyptus and a few fruit trees grow alongside the rivers and on the slopes of hills. The mountains and, beyond them, the high cordillera, surround the valley from the northwest to the northeast. For the traveler, walking north from the valley of Tiraque and crossing the mountain peaks on an abandoned mule trail under the watchful eye of high-flying condors, the barren landscape opens onto a wood of cinchona trees. After an hour's walk, ferns and other tropical plants and birds begin to populate the landscape, turning into a thick tropical forest watered by low-lying clouds and numerous waterfalls on the steep mountain slopes.

The town of Tiraque, sitting against the mountains on the valley floor, is the administrative and commercial center of the region. The main road leads into the square—the center of town—which is surrounded by the *alcaldía* (city hall), the police station, the church and the parish house, and nearby, the courthouse. Around the square and in its immediate vicinity are the houses of prominent vecinos,[5] or townsfolk. Further away, on the outskirts of town, live poor vecinos and campesinos who have recently moved to town, although some rich campesinos, fresh from the countryside, also live on or close to the square. Most campesinos, however, live in nucleated or dispersed settlement villages located in the valley and the mountains.

Agriculture is the main activity of Tiraqueños, including most townsfolk. Potatoes are the main subsistence and cash crop.[6] Its productive cycle marks the rhythm of life in this agrarian society, regulating rotation cycles, peak times of agricultural work, the influx of merchants, commerce, and social activity in general. Cropping is generally undertaken on small farms with an average size of three hectares. The fragmentation of land is more acute in the valley than on the mountains, but in both areas fragmentation has led to shorter fallow periods, intensification of production, reduction of grazing lands, and erosion. On average, households located in the valley have eight sheep, a pair of oxen, sometimes a cow, a horse or a donkey, one or two pigs, poultry, and guinea pigs. On the mountains the average number of sheep per household is fifty with a variable, but usually smaller, number of oxen, cows, horses, donkeys, and pigs.

The problem of land fragmentation is partially offset by the avail-

TABLE 1. Distribution of Land in Cantón Tiraque, 1984.

Size of Landholding in Hectares	Number of Households	
	N	Percent
0	19	20.2[a]
0.1–0.5	14	14.9
0.5–1.0	9	9.6
1.1–1.9	6	6.4
2.0–2.9	11	11.7
3.0–3.9	28	29.8
4.0–>30[b]	7	7.5
Total	94[c]	100.0

Source: Author's survey.

[a] This figure includes landless households of young couples who have not yet inherited land from their parents, but who receive a parcel of land on loan from them and work it as if it were their own.
[b] The largest landholding captured in my survey had 30 hectares; however, there are larger holdings in the region. A few households have 50 or 100 hectares of land, and one former hacendado retained all of his hacienda lands, which amount to 180 hectares.
[c] Data from two interviews could not be used because of incomplete information.

ability of irrigation and the quality of the soil. Irrigation allows for diversification and further intensification of production. Households with access to irrigation can produce three potato harvests in one agricultural year and diversify production by planting peas, maize, and tarwi. Yet, only 5 percent of the land in Tiraque is irrigated; the vast majority of households have to depend on seasonal rains. Land, however, is not equally distributed among households (see Table 1).

The current unequal distribution of land in Tiraque stems from the pre-1952 reform land-tenure structure and land distribution, and from processes of division and consolidation of land that have taken place since the agrarian reform. In a situation where the population-to-land ratio is about 0.5 hectares of land per individual, many households, in particular poor households, have been forced to split, with some members leaving their homes permanently. The remaining household members either migrate seasonally or engage in non-agricultural activities, or both, to complement household income. These activities include wage labor in the fields and handicrafts such as metalwork, masonry, weaving, and knitting. Some seasonal migrants are employed as daily laborers in the cities of Cochabamba, Santa Cruz, and Punata, although most of them work as menial laborers in the illegal cocaine trade. About sixty townswomen make chicha on a regular basis, which they sell in their chicherías. These bars fill up on Fridays and Sundays when many people come to town for market day and for Mass. Members of rich households, sometimes the entire household, have also migrated permanently from Tiraque in search of better economic opportunities. Among those who have remained, some own land in the neighboring province of Chapare, where they produce coca and, often, cocaine.

Every household in Tiraque, to a greater or lesser extent, engages in commercial and/or barter exchange as producers, consumers, petty traders, or merchants. A number of agricultural goods are sold in the marketplace. The most important of these is potatoes, followed by broad beans, barley, maize, and peas. Campesinos also take pigs, sheep, and cattle to sell in the market. The remaining agricultural products such as oats, oca, papalisa, quinoa, *ch'uño* (freeze-dried potatoes), eggs, dried broad beans, cheese, and very small potatoes, which bring a low price in the market, are reserved for consumption and occasional barter.

Goods and animals are exchanged in the villages, in town, or in local and regional markets, depending upon the distance from the market place, the available means of transport, and the volume of goods. Some people walk to the closest market carrying not more than a sack of potatoes on a horse or donkey, but the majority of people take trucks from their own villages, towns, or other market towns to travel to more distant markets. Tiraqueños have several rotating marketplaces to choose from: Aguirre, Cañacota, Cochabamba, Colomi, El Puente, Punata, and Tiraque (see Map 2). These are held on different days of the week on a rotating basis. Almost everyone who goes to market at all goes to Punata on Tuesdays, leaving the town of Tiraque practically deserted and few campesinos in their villages. Besides Punata, people tend to go to markets located close to their villages; only rich townsfolk and campesinos take their products to the Cochabamba market.

Local markets have certain general characteristics of their own, distinguishing them from the regional market of Punata and the market in the city of Cochabamba. First, they take place on days of the week which do not coincide with the days of the Cochabamba market (Wednesday and Saturday). For instance, Monday is the day for the El Puente market, Tuesday for Punata, Thursday for Cañacota, Friday for Tiraque, and Sunday for Colomi. Second, both commercial and barter exchanges take place in these markets, especially in Cañacota and Aguirre, where barter is the predominant mode of exchange.

Third, local markets are smaller, with less variety of products sold. All attract large-scale rural merchants, petty-traders, campesinos, and truckers alike.

Other differences exist among these markets as well. Punata is the largest regional commercial center. On Tuesdays, the town is a bustling, crowded place where regional differences in dress and speech may easily be noticed. It attracts campesinos, truckers, and merchants from the immediate vicinity, as well as those coming from faraway villages, towns, and the city of Cochabamba. People arrive in crowded trucks and buses, carrying agricultural products and livestock with them. After unloading the passengers and the cargo, the vehicles—hundreds of them—can be seen parked everywhere in town. The market spreads over the entire town but there are various *playas* (marketplaces) where different products are offered for sale: grains, livestock, potatoes, coca. All kinds of fabricated and manufactured goods are also sold in stalls located alongside the streets.

The El Puente market is the second largest in the region. It is located close to the Santa Cruz highway in an area that only comes to life on Monday, market day. The market site is an open space bounded by adobe houses where merchants sell food, chicha, and sugar-cane alcohol. Stalls are set up on the market grounds by a large number of merchants who sell many different products. Potatoes and barley are the main goods sold at this market. Tiraque and Colomi range third in size among the markets of the region. Both have important potato markets. The Tiraque market stands in an open space on the outskirts of the town. It has three rectangular, roofed platforms surrounded by an open space, lined on two sides by adobe rooms where Tiraqueñas sell chicha and food on market days. One of the platforms is used for the sale of potatoes, broad beans, and peas; another for the sale of vegetables and fruits; and a third for clothing.

The small markets of Aguirre and Cañacota are in a category of their own. They are located on the side of two main highways, and in both barter is the principal mode of exchange. They attract a small number of merchants and truckers who come from as far away as Cochabamba and other towns in the Valle Alto, as well as campesinos from the immediate vicinity.

With the exception of Punata, an active market throughout the year, the size of the other markets varies according to the agricultural cycle. In Tiraque, for instance, the market is almost empty between July and December. Beginning in January, when the potato harvest starts, more and more people come to the market every Friday, until it reaches a peak during May and June. During these months, approximately 50 trucks, 250 traders, and 30 wholesale potato and barley buyers leave the region every week with about 500 sacks of potatoes (at 100 kilos each).

Since Tiraqueños actively engage in commodity markets, commerce and transport are two closely related, lucrative activities in the region, engaging, however, a minority of the total population (7 percent of the households owned vehicles). Trucks are not only the most important means of transportation in the region but truckers are organized in an exclusive union to check competition from other regions and to control local transport. Furthermore, most truckers engage in commercial transactions, establish sharecropping agreements with producers, own shops and chicherías in town, and lend money. Their wives and daughters play an important role in these activities, taking care of the shop or chichería in town and buying and selling agricultural products while traveling with their husbands, fathers, or brothers. This family-run enterprise, involving both transport and commerce, has made these families the new dominant class of Tiraque. Many of them rose from amidst the town's poor families and others from the peasantry; they thus share many values and "traditions" with the rest of the population. To understand the processes leading to the formation of this new dominant class and their sociocultural relations with subordinate groups, it is necessary to look at a much larger social context as well as the long-term and more recent historical processes that transformed Tiraque.

Chapter 2
The Emergence of a Merchant Class and Landowning Peasants

> Coca is, among Indians and plebeians, such a valuable herb that they need it more than bread and meat; without it, they will not work at all because they think coca is a magical source of strength. . . . The decree (1, Title 14, Book 6) which deals with the idolatry, ceremonies, and fetishisms which the Indians are led to by coca and by illusions from the devil, as well as by the much suffering they experience in the hot and feverous environment where coca is grown, allows its use, nevertheless, in order not to take away this one respite from them, although this respite is only in their imagination. The very next decree asserts that it is this herb that most enriches the provinces in the kingdom of Peru because of the great quantities of silver that it makes possible for the Indians to take out of the mines.
> (Viedma 1793/1969:161–62)

The importance of coca[1] in Andean culture led Governor Viedma to suggest that the promotion of coca cultivation in the newly opened yungas of Yuracarees (present-day Chapare and Vandiola) would be greatly beneficial to Cochabamba: it would save the money Cochabamba expended in the import of 168,000 pounds of coca from La Paz; it would reduce its cost and thus benefit mine owners who could then reduce salaries; and it would provide a source of employment to a majority of idle mestizos in Cochabamba. He also suggested that rather than going through Santa Cruz, a new road should be built to connect Cochabamba with the recently founded Indian missions in the yungas (ibid., 162). Viedma's predictions were correct, although the opening of the yungas for colonization had to wait until the mid-nineteenth century, when the market demand for coca increased with the recovery of the mines.[2] This brought significant changes and transformations to Tiraque: the opening of Vandiola, from which coca, wood, and hot peppers were exported to the mines, provided new opportunities for advancement to people of diverse origins. The most successful were able, in the early 1900s, to accumulate wealth and replace an early aristocratic oligarchy of hacendados.

This chapter presents the central social actors in Tiraque from 1900 to 1952 and traces the formation of a new, regionally based merchant class and the emergence of piqueros, or landowning peasants. Merchants had existed, of course, since the early colony, and the origin of landowning peasants dates back to at least the eighteenth century. The purpose here is to reconstruct the careers of those families whose presence was felt or remembered in Tiraque during the period of field research. Furthermore, the lives of our characters were dramatically influenced by transformations taking place in Bolivia since its integration into the capitalist world market in the late nineteenth century and by the revolution and agrarian reform of 1952–53.

The colonization of Vandiola took place at a time when Bolivia was undergoing major economic, political, and legal transformations. Bolivia's defeat in the Pacific War in 1879 coincided with the consolidation of the nation-state and the recovery of the mining economy. The new liberal state, which served the interests of the mining industry, promoted private capital investment in the mines and in the construction of railroads to link the mines to the Pacific Coast. British and Chilean capital was heavily invested in the rehabilitation of the silver mines (Mitre 1981), and soon afterward the mining industry experienced a spectacular growth with the transition from silver to tin and the consolidation of tin mining in the hands of three tin barons: Simón Patiño, Mauricio Hochschild, and the Aramayo family. In the 1880s, legal reforms were introduced to "modernize" the nation and its "traditional" agrarian structure. The most important of these reforms was the abolition of Indian communal lands; the abolition of Indian tribute—until then the most important source of government revenue (Klein 1982); and the replacement of church tithes by the *Contribución Personal* (a head tax paid by landed property owners) and a cadastral tax (*El Heraldo* 1882; Sánchez-Albornóz 1978). These measures were the culmination of a number of reforms enacted after independence (1825) to abolish Indian communal ownership of land.[3] State policies militated not only against the interests of indigenous communities but also against even the more prosperous hacendados of Cochabamba, who were no longer able to speculate with church tithes (Larson 1988).

In 1840, the Bolivian government began to grant land, free or at a very low cost (for instance, ten cents of a Boliviano per hectare), ranging from about 250 to 1,000 hectares, to those qualified to petition for the land and willing to mark the boundaries of the property and work the land. Smaller portions of these generous land concessions were later sold to small colonizers by their original purchasers. Clearings in the forest did not begin until 1849, but by 1900, the yungas of Vandiola were described as a region "thriving in agricultural production" (Blanco 1901). Mule trails were opened up from the central valleys to the long stretch of yungas valleys in the north, and one of these connected the town of Tiraque with the yungas settlements of Santa Rosa and Vandiola. The yungas of Vandiola attracted not only large plantation owners, colonizers, and laborers, but also a large number of traders, merchants, muleteers, and maintenance workers along the mule trails, coca customs house employees, and entrepreneurs who provided accommodation, food, and animal feed to the many travelers in the region. To some extent, all these individuals were involved in the commercialization of coca. They thus contributed to the circulation of money in the region as a whole, except in Vandiola, where barter remained the chief mode of exchange. Only when coca from Vandiola reached Tiraque or other towns in the Valle Alto, such as Arani, Cliza, and Punata, was it sold in the market. With the money made from these transactions, valley products needed for subsistence in the yungas were purchased for consumption in Vandiola or to exchange for coca, thus restarting the exchange circuit, that was only partly monetarized and which combined commodities and non-commodities.

The renewed expansion of trade in the region, involving both barter and commercial exchange, accelerated processes of rural differentiation and class formation that were not new in Tiraque: the emergence of new merchant and hacendado families and the formation of piqueros. This chapter analyzes the process of class formation and examines each set of characters separately. Although there were divergent outcomes from this process, the lives of these people intertwined in various ways. Thus, another concern is to examine the manifold relationships within and between these two main emergent classes. The narrative begins in 1900, a time when merchants and landowning peasants were interstitial in an agrarian society dominated by hacendados who extracted rent from a majority of landless peasants and controlled regional markets. I focus also on the emergence of merchants and landowning peasants in this period, however, in order to provide the necessary background for understanding later events and transformations in Tiraque.

Tiraque in 1900

In 1900 the town of Tiraque, then part of the province of Punata, was upgraded to capital of the *Tercera Sección* Punata,[4] consisting of the cantones Tiraque, Vandiola, and Vacas.[5] The town was thereby entitled to establish both a *Concejo Municipal* (Municipal Council),[6] made up of a president and twelve councilmen, and a local courthouse. These changes were made in response to an increase in population and to the economic growth the town and its region were experiencing. Tiraque's new prosperity was due to its proximity to the recently opened yungas of Vandiola and to the influx of many immigrants from the rural towns of the Valle Alto and the city of Cochabamba. Located at the crossroads where the Vandiola mule trail met the road leading to the central valleys, Tiraque grew into a busy town. Revenues increased with an internal customs house that was set up in Santa Rosa to charge an export tax on the coca leaving the yungas, and the numerous pack mule trains passing through the town had to pay a road toll. In the 1900s, the town had three hotels, restaurants, well-stocked shops, resident lawyers, and several barber shops (AAT: Rol de Patentes e Impuestos, 1914). These establishments no longer exist in the town today.

In 1900 the total population of Tiraque amounted to 13,995 inhabitants, 51.20 percent of whom were men, and 48.80 percent women (see Table 2). The larger proportion of males contrasts with sex ratio figures for the entire department, indicating that Tiraque offered new possibilities to land-hungry men from other regions. Cantón Tiraque received the bulk of the immigrants. From 1880, when the total population of this cantón was 3,621 inhabitants (*El Heraldo*, June 16, 1881), to 1900, the number of Tiraqueños had almost doubled.

Another characteristic of Tiraque's population was that, according to the 1900 census, the majority of men and women were classified as mestizo (see Table 3). The census recognized four categories: Indian, mestizo, white, and black. Blacks were not a numerically significant category; whites comprised 13 percent of the population of Bolivia and approximately 17 percent of Tiraque. Table 3 shows that Indians were the most numerous census category in Bolivia (50.80 percent), and in the department of Cochabamba, mestizos were slightly more numerous (51.55 percent). But in Tiraque the percentage of mestizos was unusually high (58.91 percent). The only cantón within the jurisdiction of Tiraque with a substantial number of Indians was Vacas (35.91 percent) where, until the 1880s, there had been Indian corporate communities. Indians in the rest of Tiraque were few even prior

TABLE 2. Population Distribution by Sex, 1900.

Location	Total	Male		Female		Not Censused	
		N	%	N	%	N	%
Department Cochabamba	328,163	159,223	48.52	166,940	50.87	2,000	0.61
Tercera Sección Tiraque	13,995	7,166	51.20	6,829	48.80	0	0.00
Cantón Tiraque	7,132	3,704	51.93	3,428	48.07	0	0.00
Cantón Vacas	6,422	3,200	49.83	3,222	50.17	0	0.00
Cantón Vandiola	411	262	59.41	179	40.59	0	0.00

Source: República de Bolivia, 1900/1973.

TABLE 3. Population Distribution by Ethnic Category, 1900.

Location	Total	Indian		Mestizo		White		Black		Undetermined	
		N	%	N	%	N	%	N	%	N	%
Bolivia	1,812,851	920,864	50.80	486,018	26.81	231,088	12.75	3,945	.22	170,936	9.42
Department Cochabamba	328,163	75,514	23.01	169,161	51.55	60,605	18.47	161	.05	22,722	6.92
Tercera Sección Tiraque	13,995	2,464	17.61	8,244	58.91	2,348	16.78	0	0.00	939	6.70
Cantón Tiraque	7,132	145	2.03	4,869	68.27	1,662	23.30	0	0.00	456	6.39
Cantón Vacas	6,422	2,306	35.91	3,192	49.70	513	7.99	0	0.00	411	6.40
Cantón Vandiola	411	13	2.95	183	41.50	173	39.23	0	0.00	72	16.32

Source: República de Bolivia, 1900/1973.

to this decade. One of the last Indian censuses (PC: Padrón General de Indígenas, 1867) classified only 643 individuals as landless Indians who were settled in eight haciendas in cantón Tiraque, only 51 of whom paid tribute.

Agriculture, commerce, and crafts of various kinds were the main activities engaging Tiraqueños by 1900. Among those making a livelihood out of agriculture in the Tercera Sección Tiraque were 85 *propietarios*[7] or hacendados, 3,871 agriculturalists (owners of small landed properties), 3,223 landless peasants, 100 shepherds, 90 servants, and 488 traders and merchants. There were also five priests. The rest of the population were muleteers, butchers, and artisans, including masons, carpenters, cigarette makers, seamstresses, tailors, bakers, hat makers, and weavers (República de Bolivia 1900/1973).

Hacendados, Colonos, and Sharecroppers

As in the rest of the central valleys, haciendas developed in Tiraque early in the colonial period when Indian land was appropriated in the irrigated, fertile valley and the mountains. Originally few in number, haciendas expanded, fragmented, and sometimes reconsolidated. In the eighteenth century, haciendas were stagnating due to economic decline in the mining sector, the ensuing lack of demand for agricultural products, the burden of accumulating debts, and competition in the market with petty commodity producers (Larson 1988). After the onset of their decline, most haciendas never recuperated. They shared one common characteristic: most of their land was parceled out among a landless mestizo and Indian population of colonos who had to pay rent in labor and in kind for usufruct rights to parcels of land and pasture for their animals on the hacienda. Besides colonos, sharecroppers and occasional day laborers also worked on the hacienda. Labor relations were complex and varied, and differed from one hacienda to the next, but ground rent was the main form of surplus extraction.

The amount of land each colono household held in usufruct varied according to the size of the household, the size of the hacienda, and the total number of colonos residing on it. These factors, in turn, determined the number of days colonos had to work for the hacendado. The number of days demanded for cultivating the land reserved for hacienda production might range from one or two days to three or four days per week. For this work, each household was obliged to provide labor, tools, manure, oxen and plows, horses for threshing, and mules or donkeys for transporting hacienda products to the market towns in the Valle Alto or to the city of Cochabamba.

Colonos were also required to provide domestic service[8] in the hacienda house or in the hacendado's house in the city. This work obligation was executed by both colono men and women, generally for a whole week, when two members of the household moved to the hacendado's house to carry out such tasks as taking care of the hacienda's animals, making *muko* (maize flour chewed for chicha), spinning wool, cooking, and cleaning the house. Households rotated among themselves to serve as *pongos*, which meant that on the haciendas where colonos were few, this type of labor service came around more frequently than on haciendas where there was a large colono population. Usufruct rights on land did not include pasture rights, which required payment of one of every ten pasturing sheep for grazing rights. Colonos also had to contribute to the cadastral tax, either in money or in extra work obligations. It was also customary for the colono to give occasional "presents" such as eggs, wool, and hens to the hacendado in "gratitude" for his usufruct rights.

On many haciendas, colonos and other individuals not settled on the hacienda produced in *compañía* (sharecropping) with the hacendado. In such agreements the landowner provided land and seed, while the sharecropper contributed labor, manure, traction animals, and the plow. The harvest was either divided in two parts between the partners, or the crop was divided according to the number of furrows planted, the hacendado receiving the harvest of one furrow in three. In addition, hacendados often hired seasonal, non-resident laborers to carry out tasks during peak agricultural work periods or to do other types of work that needed a large labor force. This labor was paid for with the harvested produce or with a minimal wage.

The organization of work in the haciendas in the Valle Alto and Tiraque was not transformed even after the recovery of the mines in the late nineteenth century and the increased demand for agricultural products in the mining camps. Hacendados simply could not compete with Chilean food imports and few hacendados could arrest the process of hacienda fragmentation.[9] Many haciendas were burdened with mortgages, often forcing landowners to sell or lease parcels of land or the entire property.[10] Partible inheritance worsened the situation of indebted haciendas. Together with land, houses, water mills, and water rights, each family member inherited the obligation to pay a proportional part of the interest on all outstanding debts. Only the unmortgaged haciendas, such as the hacienda Toralapa in Tiraque, remained large in spite of the inheritance rules. In this case, soon after partition the estate was reconsolidated by one member of the family through the purchase of land from the other heirs.[11] But this strategy was more the exception than the rule, leaving the countryside dotted with miniscule properties and small- and medium-sized haciendas which, in many cases, were parceled out in noncontiguous plots of land often situated in different localities. Unlike the large haciendas, these smaller properties did not have a large colono population settled on the land. At most, there were usually two or three colono households and/or four or five sharecropper households holding land in usufruct and paying rent in labor and in kind to the hacendado.

Like the haciendas, the households of colonos and sharecroppers exhibited certain similarities, but they also differed in some basic ways. These households produced mainly for their own subsistence, although in good years they might have had a surplus to barter or exchange. Work relations within these productive units were based on family labor and *ayni* (reciprocal labor exchange between households). But within each hacienda, these households were internally differentiated according to the amount of land each controlled in usufruct, as well as by the size of its labor force. The developmental cycle regulated, to an extent, the size of the household and its labor force, but some households also benefited from the presence of *arrimantes* (landless men and women) attached to them. In many instances, these were the married sons of colonos who had not been given land by the hacendado; others were more distant kin, or were not related to the family. If there was land available for distribution, the head of a large household could conceivably bargain with the hacendado to hold more land in usufruct or plant occassionally in unused portions of land.[12] Under certain conditions, a large labor force had its advantages, since it enabled the household to fulfill labor rent obligations while, at the same time, other members were free to produce a surplus above subsistence needs that could be exchanged in barter or commercial transactions. A minority of these households were able to buy small parcels of land while they remained working in the haciendas as colonos. Others were able to free themselves from the hacendados to become landowning peasants. Often, however, members of a large household with access to a small parcel of land had to leave the household, either moving from hacienda to hacienda in search of land or attaching themselves to the households of other colonos. Some moved to escape from a particularly exploitative hacendado. Members of colono households also moved to the mines or to cities in search of work. Thus, although colonos were leased and sold with the hacienda, they were not, in the strict sense, a "fixed" population. The "wandering" lives of these people are recorded both in the accounts about their lives that the elderly shared with me and in the agrarian reform records, which show that few colonos had been born on the hacienda where the agrarian reform judges found them after 1953.

Landowning Peasants

The formation of piqueros in Tiraque was a slow and hesitant process that was intimately related to the fragmentation and expansion of the hacienda.[13] Once formed, some households were able to endure as piqueros; in others, some members returned to the hacienda as colonos. In yet other instances, piqueros were able to accumulate wealth.

Two historically distinct developments led to the formation of piqueros in the Valle Alto and Tiraque. The first was related to the processes leading to hacienda fragmentation and the participation of rural artisans, colonos, and sharecroppers in the market. The second took place after 1880, when Indian communal lands were transformed into individual private properties by governmental decree. Historical evidence for the first appearance of piqueros in the central valleys has been provided by Brooke Larson (1988). They originated from those mestizo town artisans who purchased small portions of land (around a third of a hectare) in the mid-eighteenth century. It was not only through the purchase of land that landowning peasants came into being, however. In one instance, the owner of the once large hacienda Punata extended perpetual ownership of the plots of land held in usufruct by some of his colonos in gratitude for their defense of the hacienda during the Indian rebellions of the 1780s (AHM: Leg. 571, 1820). Whether his example was followed by other hacendados is impossible to tell, but by 1900 there were in Tiraque some twenty-four *piquerías*, or localities, of landowning peasants.

The second distinct process leading to the formation of landowning peasants involved the governmental decrees of the late nineteenth century. By the time the last Revisitas were undertaken in the 1880s, there were only three regions with Indian communities in Cochabamba: Tapacarí, Arque, and the cantón Vacas in Tiraque. Although Indian communal lands had been under constant pressure since early colonial times, these laws were probably the most efficient in opening the way for the appropriation of a large part of the remaining Indian land (Grieshaber 1980; Platt 1982).[14] Yet in other parts of Bolivia, Indian communities have persisted until the present. This was not the case in Vacas, where soon after the granting of individual land titles, Indians were to be found selling their land to hacendados and to rural town mestizos.[15] By 1940, for instance, much of the land owned by Indians formed part of the large hacienda Vacas, which was owned by the Municipal Council of Cochabamba.[16] This meant that the majority of former village Indians—turned peasants by the decree that abolished communal land-holding—soon became colonos on their own lands.

The autonomy that piqueros might have had when they bought their parcels of land was often illusory, since few were completely independent of hacendados or merchants. As their holdings were generally small, they had to rely on the hacienda lands for grazing their sheep, a right they acquired by either relinquishing part of their flocks or by sharecropping on hacienda lands. Piqueros also provided the labor pool for the hacienda when seasonal laborers were employed for agricultural production, the construction of defenses against floods, and other tasks, receiving a minimal wage for their labor. They also fell prey to merchants and moneylenders, risking the loss of their land if they could not pay their debts on time. Landowning peasants also had to contribute a land tax to the state, and piqueros as well as colonos owed additional taxes and personal services to the state. Both were obliged, for instance, to pay market taxes every time they participated in market exchange, to pay taxes on the coca they consumed, and to provide rotating labor service for the construction of roads (*prestación vial*).

The situation of piqueros was thus precarious, and few households were able to accumulate wealth. Their small holdings, often fragmented by partible inheritance, precluded this possibility, leading to the migration of some members of the household back to the haciendas, where they settled once again as colonos. Others searched for work in other regions. The case of the Vía family illustrates this movement. Conrado Vía, a former colono, was a piquero in the locality of Curuzani, but he did not own enough land to distribute parcels among his married sons. One of them, Ezequiel, moved to the hacienda Urmachea in Tiraque, where he settled as a colono. Some piqueros, however, were able to buy additional land and to remain piqueros until the agrarian reform of 1953.

Large Plantation Owners, Colonizers, and Plantation Colonos

The large plantation was a tropical adaptation of the hacienda.[17] Labor relations were based on ground rent, but differed considerably from hacienda labor relations. In the yungas, colonos were not subjected to domestic service obligations and they had to work for the plantation only during weeding and harvest seasons, when they were also paid a *cesto* of coca (the equivalent of 12 pounds) each working day. These labor obligations, and the fact that coca does not have a strict a schedule for harvesting, left more time for the colonos to produce coca on land they held in usufruct. Furthermore, since coca is not a subsistence crop, colonos were forced to exchange it for goods necessary for subsistence. The yungas colonos were thus much more closely integrated into the market economy than their counterparts on the hacienda; some of them were able to accumulate wealth. Small- and medium-sized plantations, ranging from 10 to 100 hectares, were obtained by colonizers who resided in Vandiola most of the year, cultivating the land themselves and hiring seasonal laborers who were paid a wage in kind: a cesto of coca for a day's work.

Coca was the principal product cultivated on all these plantations, although other products such as bananas, avocados, oranges, hot peppers, and coffee were also grown. Several factors contributed to this preference: first, coca enjoyed a high market demand throughout Bolivia; second, the characteristics of the coca plant itself made the production of coca virtually risk-free and quite profitable. The plant takes about three years to develop and ready for harvest, and it lasts for ten or more years. As only the leaves are removed, the plant may be harvested four times a year. Furthermore, except for times of harvesting and weeding, which is done immediately after harvest, the coca plantation may be left virtually unattended. Third, the coca leaf is a light product that can be transported in large quantities. The *tambor* or bundle of dried leaves wrapped with tree bark weighs sixty pounds; two of these, which are called a *carga*, could be carried by a mule on the two-day trip from Vandiola to Tiraque. This gave coca a comparative advantage over the transport of the heavier and bulkier tropical fruits. In sum, coca was of such importance in the yungas that the coca plants valorized the land, because without them land had little or no value. Often the trees, rather than the land, were bought and sold.

The Town and Its Townsfolk

Although still connected to agricultural production in various ways, the remainder of the population was urban. Most lived permanently or temporarily in the small town of Tiraque, although a few of the wealthiest or "aristocratic" owners of large haciendas resided in Cochabamba or Punata. Some *vecinos*, as those living in town are called, owned medium-sized haciendas, others were yungas colonizers (also called *yungueños* or *cocaleros*) and agriculturalists, a category used to designate small and medium-sized landowners who did not consider themselves piqueros or hacendados. They distinguished themselves from piqueros by virtue of their residence in the town rather than on the land, and from the hacendados because they actually worked their land. The size of their holdings ranged from one to sixty hectares of land. There were also several artisans. Although their principal source of income was derived from their craftsmanship, most were also involved in agricultural production, either on small plots of land or on the land of others in sharecropping arrangements or as daily laborers. Finally, there was a mobile group of male and female merchants and muleteers who lived in the town and traveled between the yungas and the valley market towns. Some were in transit from other towns or the city of Cochabamba. The only person generally not associated with agriculture was the town priest, since the church did not hold any landed property in Tiraque, although the priest might own land himself.

Boundaries between the activities performed by all these individuals were not well-defined, since both the rural poor and the rich were involved in many activities at the same time or sequentially throughout their lives. Hacendados, agriculturalists, and yungueños were involved not only in agriculture but also in commerce and transport. Colonos, sharecroppers, piqueros, muleteers, and artisans operated in barter and small-scale commercial activities, competing from the mid-eighteenth century on with hacendados in the regional markets (Larson 1988). Their participation in the market depended not only on its vagaries, on the climate, on the size of the labor force at their disposal and the land they controlled, but also on their relations with landowners and the state. In any case, their participation was felt by the number rather than the volume of their transactions. In this, they were unlike the hacendados, who had larger volumes of agricultural products to sell in the markets of Cochabamba and Punata. Thus, while hacendados controlled, to a large extent, the circulation of agricultural goods in Cochabamba, almost every group in the region was involved to a lesser or greater extent in exchange in Tiraque, in other markets in the Valle Alto such as the towns of Punata, Arani, and Cliza, and in the city of Cochabamba.

Merchants and Piqueros in an Expanding Frontier

The colonization of Vandiola in the late nineteenth century started a bonanza of new economic opportunities for Tiraqueños and vallunos in general, but particularly for those who became yungueños. Some were able to accumulate wealth through coca production, commercialization, and transport. Although they did not control as much land, labor, and capital as the large hacendados and large plantation owners, they became a powerful elite in Tiraque. Chief among them were the Siles, Terrazas, Arandia, Terceros, Covarrubias, Montaño, Quiroga, Casanovas, Ferrufino, Ochoa, and Muñoz families.

The historical reconstruction of the activities and careers of individuals and families such as these sheds light on processes of rural differentiation and class formation in the area. It also illuminates the fluidity and subjectivity of local constructions of class and identity. Most of these families came from a common background, and their members followed similar careers.[18] Their origins varied: some of the male heads of households were recent immigrants to the region who had come from the town of Tarata (an important economic and political center during the colonial period); others came from other valley market towns and the city of Cochabamba. Among the immigrants, a few were Syrian. Most were from the town and environs of Tiraque. Although it was possible to determine their main occupations while they resided in Tiraque, it was not possible to determine what their occupations had been in their places of origin or before they achieved dominant status.

The parish records refer to such men as cocaleros or yungueños, terms variously used to describe a population which derived its livelihood from the yungas. In fact, all these families owned land in the yungas, the size of their properties ranging from 200 to 750 hectares.[19] There they produced coca with colonos and, at times, with seasonal laborers who also transported it out of the yungas to sell in the valleys. They reinvested the capital obtained from coca production and exchange in diverse economic activities, such as acquiring land and enlarging their plantations in the yungas, commerce, transport, municipal tax collecting,[20] moneylending, and, ultimately, in land accumulation in the valley and mountains of Tiraque itself.

Naturally, all these activities were complementary, but the last two, moneylending and land accumulation, were interrelated. Coca was the main source of capital for moneylending, but some of the lenders also borrowed from banks or private individuals, using their land as collateral, at low interest rates (12 percent per year). This they later lent in Tiraque at higher rates ranging from 24 to 96 percent annually.[21] Yet others lent agricultural or manufactured goods that had to be repaid in coca or labor at double their cost. The high and usurious interest rates were legally recognized, since the moneylenders had to register with the Municipal Council and pay an annual tax, which varied according to the interest rate they charged.

Money and products were lent to piqueros, small agriculturalists, yungas colonos, and colonizers. Often debtors, unable to repay the loan, lost portions of their land or other belongings in public auction.

In such cases, the moneylender had the first option to buy the property at 75 percent of its value. It was principally through this mechanism that the upwardly mobile were able to buy parcels of land often located at a distance and spaced far apart, but sometimes collectively larger even than some haciendas. Some were able to consolidate contiguous parcels of land into one large property, and others bought entire haciendas settled with colonos. Thus developed a new group of families who became hacendados, in some instances replacing old and "aristocratic" hacendado families. Unlike the earlier hacendados, this new regional elite did not move to Cochabamba but continued to live in Tiraque for long periods of time.

The process of land accumulation led to a changed configuration of the agrarian structure in the valley and mountains of Tiraque. In several localities, such as Millumayo, Canalmayo, Parrarancho, Rodeo, Cotani, Pukawasi, Palca, Chapapani, Qolqeqhoya, and Sacabambilla, where previously the land was parceled out among small agriculturalists and piqueros, small- and medium-sized haciendas were consolidated at their expense. Some of the small property owners lost not only their lands but also their fragile autonomy, becoming colonos or sharecroppers on the new haciendas. Unfortunately, the process of land accumulation cannot be substantiated with quantitative data, but there is sufficient indirect evidence to indicate that such changes were taking place in Tiraque. Yet, at the same time that piqueros were losing their land, other artisans and colonos were able to buy small parcels. The historical record reveals, then, a continuing process of hacienda fragmentation and reaccumulation of land, and a flow of emergent and dispossessed piqueros, by which upcoming families replaced old ones. Whereas in 1900 there had been 303 landed properties (Blanco 1901), by 1910 there were 404. This latter figure, however, included a total of 1,087 landholdings, because it was common for some families to own several properties, sometimes contiguous but often situated in different localities (see Table 4).

Small and medium haciendas continued to fragment after partible inheritance, but some families were able to consolidate more land through marriage alliances. The nouveau riche were few in numbers and tended to marry among themselves, which contributed to the consolidation of their power. Furthermore, since they lived in the town of Tiraque, they controlled all the political offices. From 1900 to 1952, only two "aristocratic" hacendados became president of the Municipal Council, one for a year, and the other for six months. For the rest of the period, every position in the Council (president, vice president, and councilmen) was occupied by a member of one of the newly wealthy families, among whom the officers rotated. All of these men

TABLE 4. Size of Landholdings in Tiraque, 1910.

Size in Hectares	Number of Landholdings	
	N	%
>1	514	47.29
1–4	354	32.57
5–9	85	7.82
10–14	16	1.47
15–19	14	1.29
20–30	31	2.85
31–50	15	1.38
51–100	24	2.20
101–200	15	1.37
201–300	4	.37
301–400	5	.46
401–500	4	.37
501–600	2	.18
<600[a]	4	.37
TOTAL	1,087	100.00

Source: Catastro Rústico, PC.

[a] Range of 807–8,830 hectares.
[b] This material consists of an unnumbered, bound collection of cadastral records from every province in the department of Cochabamba. It records all rural properties, tax rolls, number of colonos working on each property, and other economic information. The collection is not dated but the document can be placed between 1910 and 1914, according to the names of landowners. Reyeros (1963:167), however, dates these cadastral lists to 1947, and one employee at the Tesoro de Hacienda corroborated his view. But very few of the landowners listed in Tiraque were alive in 1947, their properties having been bought by others long before; further, the names of more recent hacendados *do not* show on the list. On the basis of this and my detailed knowledge of the lives of prominent Tiraqueños, I estimate that the cadastral list for Tiraque was prepared between 1910 and 1914.

were also members of the Junta de Propietarios Industriales de los Yungas de Vandiola, several of them being on its board of directors (AAT: Correspondencia, 1921–30). The membership of the Junta de Propietarios, organized in the 1920s, consisted of Tiraqueños and small and large plantation owners from other places such as the city of Cochabamba, Punata, and Cliza. Although the junta encompassed people of different backgrounds, they shared a common interest in Vandiola. The coca customs house at Santa Rosa provided the revenues for the junta to maintain the mule trails in Vandiola.

The upward movement of these families to gain power and wealth was not devoid of cunning, excesses, and conflict. This contrasts with the idyllic portrayal of rural life presented by Cajka (1979). In trying to advance, members of these families took advantage of almost everybody and every situation. Some of them illegally harvested coca and other products from the land of others; some altered the boundaries of their property to include adjacent properties; some stole water and animals, and even broke into stores in the town; some charged excessive taxes; and others were involved in fights with their relatives over the partition of inherited land and goods. Almost all were involved in countless lawsuits, some filed against them and some filed by them against others for unpaid debts and libels. An accusation voiced by Isaac de la Rocha charged that these ambitious townsfolk, "councilmen, *carajos*,[22] troops of ignoramuses, cholos, tailors, carpenters, blacksmiths, thieves, bandits, are stealing all my belongings" (JT: Criminal Cases, 1926).

The paths followed by these social climbers to acquire wealth and prestige was by no means linear.[23] Rather, family fortunes rose and fell as they engaged in risky and often speculative enterprises, overextending themselves and losing within one or two generations the properties and wealth they had acquired so rapidly and easily. The Montaño-Sandoval family was one such case. By all accounts, the sisters, Asencia and Candelaria, and their brother, Benjamín Montaño, were probably the richest family in Tiraque. They were the biggest moneylenders in terms of volume and high interest rates (60 to 96 percent). The three owned land in Vandiola, Candelaria's holdings amounting to 750 hectares that the government had granted her in 1914. In addition, they bought land in the valley and mountains of Tiraque, principally from their creditors. In 1885, Asencia had married Adolfo Sandoval, with whom she had two sons. One son became a priest, and the other, a sickly youth, never married but had a son, Walter, by his maidservant. In 1920, Asencia moved to Cochabamba, where she died; her illegitimate grandson inherited her possessions. Walter, however, was an extravagant spender who lived well and was not too preocupied with maintaining or increasing his wealth. In 1928 he broke into the store of Manuel Abujiara, stealing currency in pounds sterling, jewelry, and expensive cloth, an action that sent him to jail. After his release, he sold most of his properties to pay off accumulated debts.

Other families and their descendants were successful throughout their lifetimes. For instance, Facundo Terrazas, an immigrant from Tarata, in 1881 married Gavina Siles, the daughter of Domingo Siles, owner of a medium-sized hacienda and yungueño. Both husband and wife lent money, accumulated portions of land in several places in Tiraque, and finally bought the large hacienda K'aspikancha. They were socially recognized in Tiraque as "lady" and "gentleman," forms of address that symbolized wealth and power. Between 1900 and 1914, the year of his death, Facundo served as president of the Municipal Council six times. A few years later, in 1922, Gavina ordered a new statue for the church's pantheon, the Virgen de las Angustias, who thereafter was adopted as the virgin of the successful vecinos. Gavina's brothers were also active members of the Muncipal Council. Gavina and Facundo did not have any children, but their nephews and nieces inherited their properties, most of which remained in the family until the agrarian reform of 1953.

At first, middle yungueños did not control as much land and power in the region as the nouveau riche. Nevertheless, they shared many of the characteristics of the very rich, some occupying positions in the Municipal Council and intermarrying with the elite. These included the Pacheco, Gutiérrez, López, Estrada, Marín, and Velarde families, some of whom, like the Pacheco and Gutiérrez, became hacendados in the 1930s. Because they were just beginning to emerge as wealthy families, it is easier to establish their origins. Most were the sons and daughters of artisans and merchants, and at least one, Herbas, had been a colono on the hacienda Iluri. Manuel Gutiérrez, a tailor's son from the town of Arani, was able to buy two medium-sized haciendas in Tiraque and was once elected president of the Municipal Council.

Beneath these families was another cluster of poor mestizo artisan-yungueños or yungas' colonos, the majority of whom remained poor all their lives even though they engaged in numerous activities in order to subsist and to maintain a certain degree of autonomy. But their autonomy was so marginal and precarious that they remained vulnerable and dependent on the rich. In this they were not unlike piqueros, whose lives were also tightly bound with the lives of the social climbers. For instance, when Roberto Moya reached seventy-six years of age in 1982, he had taken up one activity after another until he was not able to work any more and was dependent on his veteran's pension to scrape together a living. He had been born in Tiraque, the son of a hatmaker. As a teenager, he had himself been a hatmaker's apprentice. He then worked as a muleteer until he was drafted to fight in the Chaco War (1932–35). On his return, he settled in Vandiola as a colono, later moving back to Tiraque, where he made his living as a weaver. He was poor all his life, but others of poor origin, such as the Torrico, Flores, Torres, and Rodríguez families, were more successful at least in providing an inheritance for their children to give them a "start in life" (Thompson 1976:359)[24] and were able to move up both economically and socially. Hilarión Torrico, for instance, a colono on the land of Benjamín Montaño, bought some five hectares of land in

Qolqeqhoya in 1917. He thus became a piquero. Much later, in the 1950s, his son Juan acquired more land and became a medium-sized hacendado.[25] The Rodríguez family exemplifies another success story. Sandalio was a tailor in the town of Arani when he married Florinda, the daughter of a chicha maker in Punata. Since Sandalio made very little money sewing clothes, the two decided to try their luck in the yungas of Vandiola. They traveled through the region bartering valley products for coca and did so well that they decided to sell their plot of land in Arani and settle as colonos on the yungas plantation of Timoteo Ferrel. They held a large piece of land in usufruct and, together with hired labor, were able to produce thirty cargas of coca a year. In the 1940s, they sold the coca plants to another colono and bought thirty-five hectares of land on the mountains of Tiraque.

To summarize, the reconstruction of the formation of a regional merchant class of medium and, sometimes, large hacendados reveals a common pattern among successful families. Without doubt, coca production in the yungas was the most important resource tapped by members of these families. At first, they cultivated coca themselves, sometimes with the help of seasonal laborers and colonos. They invested part of their profits in diversified and often speculative activities such as usury, commerce, transport, and tax collection. They then invested capital in the purchase of land outside of the yungas, which they worked with colonos and sharecroppers. Their mode of operation reveals a characteristic pattern in the circulation of money and capital. Agrarian capital, originating in coca production, was converted into commercial and usury capital that was then reinvested in the purchase of haciendas, the means to extract surplus in the form of ground rent. The purchase of an hacienda, however, did not entail leaving behind the yungas plantations and the speculative activities. On the contrary, it seems that the most successful families were those that were able to maintain and even diversify such activities. Ownership of land in the mountains and valley of Tiraque was often viewed as an asset that could be used as a guarantee to obtain low-interest credit from banks and as a guarantee to engage in other speculative enterprises such as municipal tax collection.[26] In the final analysis, the practices of these entrepreneurs did not transform Tiraque; like their predecessors—the aristocratic hacendados—they remained speculative *rentiers* without transforming agriculture and without divorcing direct producers from the means of production. Although in their accumulation of land and merchant capital they did dispossess landowning peasants and artisans, and many of these worked as wage laborers in the mines and cities, many also returned to the land as piqueros, sharecroppers, or colonos.

In spite of the social and spatial mobility portrayed above, ethnic distinctions, based on a no longer existing colonial system of evaluation, divided Cochabamba society. By 1900, Cochabamba was the most predominantly mestizo of all departments in Bolivia, and in Tiraque the proportion was even higher. Yet Tiraqueños were, and still are, keenly aware of "racial" distinctions. Ethnic classifications of self and others were made independently of phenotypic traits; rather, distinctions loosely corresponded to social categories or occupations. Ownership of land, for instance, was an important criterion for including an individual in the "white" or "Spanish" category. Most hacendados, but also some piqueros, filled this category in the local parish records of births and marriages, whereas all others were classified as mestizo and very few as Indian. Other criteria were also important, such as language (Quechua was spoken by both vecinos and the rural poor, but Spanish was spoken almost exclusively by town and city folk), wealth, place of residence, dress, manners, and family background. The ambiguity and subjectivity permeating "racial" classifications meant that individuals could "pass" from one category into another, as indeed happened among Tiraqueños as family fortunes rose and fell. By 1910, all the emergent merchant-hacendado families were classified in official and parish records as "Spaniards" or "white," indicating that by that time they had achieved a socioeconomic status above that of mestizo. And the loss of land by some "white" piqueros, agriculturalists, and artisans meant their loss of white status: they became mestizos. This, of course, did not mean that others agreed with the way in which some families "passed" from one ethnic category into another. Don Roberto, who is old enough to remember the wealthy families, told me: "They were indeed rich but they were not 'señores,' they were 'cholos.'" In Don Roberto's eyes, many hacendados were nouveau riche mestizos who lacked the proper family background and cultural accouterments associated with "white" status, such as dress and manners. Many people classified by others as "mestizos" defined themselves as "white" and, in the eyes of most vecinos, the rural poor remained "indios," regardless of their own or official classifications.[27]

Economic Decline, Stagnation, and the Advent of Truckers

The period of bonanza and economic opportunity did not last long. The Depression had devastating effects on Bolivia. The drop in the international price of tin not only led to the drastic decline of the mining sector, but also affected the entire economy. Laid-off miners returned to the countryside. The demand for agricultural products was drastically reduced, and political discontent and conflict set in. Confronted with a situation of economic stagnation and political unrest, President Salamanca led the country into a "corrupt, bloody and bottomless defeat and disaster" by declaring war against Paraguay in 1932 (Klein 1982:190). The war lasted until 1935, and the defeat of Bolivia meant the loss, by death or desertion, of 65,000 Bolivians and the loss of extensive territory to Paraguay.

The end of the war began a twenty-year period which is crucial for the understanding of the Bolivian National Revolution. In the midst of increasing economic deterioration,[28] the traditional political parties that had been in control of national politics since 1880 were challenged by the middle class, factory workers and miners, young officers, and the rural poor. Reformist movements and a radical left emerged. Issues that previously had never been addressed came to the fore. These involved the land question, the Indian problem, the organization of labor, and the fact that the most important source of foreign exchange was in the hands of the so-called tin barons. New parties, encompassing a wide political spectrum, emerged during these decades: parties of the radical left, such as the Partido Obrero Revolucionario (POR) and the Partido de la Izquierda Revolucionaria (PIR); right-wing parties, such as the Falange Socialista Boliviana (FSB); and right-of-center parties, such as the Movimiento Nacionalista Revolucionario (MNR). Reformist military governments, attempting to implement minimal welfare and pro-syndicalist reforms,[29] alternated with governments led by political coalitions in which conservative forces tried to regain political control (Klein 1969). The whole situation was transformed with the National Revolution of 1952.

In Tiraque these events and their consequences affected people in very different ways. During the war, men were drafted into the army or volunteered to join the military forces. Veterans, mainly townsfolk who were low-ranking officers and are proud of having participated in and survived the war, tell of this episode in a simple language by which they talk neither about great victories nor about great defeats. Instead of referring to their heroic behavior in battle, their accounts refer mainly to their daily lives as soldiers in a frontier region that was felt to be even more threatening than the enemy. As one veteran put it, "In the Chaco, we fought against the insects, especially against the mosquitoes, the many sicknesses we contracted, the lack of water, and often the lack of food which was never adequate and . . . against the *pilas* [Paraguayan soldiers]." For the rural poor used as cannon fodder in the battle front the experience was even worse. For those who survived, the experience brought them into contact with other Bolivians and acquainted them with miners, urban workers, the middle sectors, and young reformist officers. No doubt these contacts served to shape the political consciousness of all, since these sectors of the population later played such an important role in Bolivian politics. Miners and rural schoolteachers were active in the countryside, working side by side with peasant leaders to organize the Indian Congress held in La Paz in 1942 and to mobilize colonos in the haciendas (Dandler and Torrico 1984; Harris and Albó 1976).

The most successful of these efforts was that of the colonos in the hacienda Cliza in the Valle Alto, which belonged to the Monastery Santa Clara. In 1935, colonos organized to establish a rural school on the hacienda, for which they received the support of schoolteachers and state institutions. While similar experiments had also been carried out in other parts of Bolivia, what made this experience different was that the colonos also organized the first peasant union in Bolivia, which later became the well-known Ucureña. Through the union, officially recognized in 1937 by a pro-syndicalist military regime, colonos rented the hacienda from the monastery. Even though the union was challenged by hacendados and departmental authorities, and later by conservative governments, its strength rested on its close association with the school, which no one actually opposed. In opening and running the school, the colonos gained the experience that would thrust them to the vanguard of the peasant movement in 1952.[30]

Peasant leaders in Tiraque were also actively organizing colonos in the haciendas and they, too, encountered strong opposition and violence from the hacendados. Martín Salazar, the son of a colono who died in the Chaco war and himself a piquero, was beaten up several times by thugs paid by hacendados and was twice imprisoned for his political activity. As he told me,

We have walked with people from the countryside. Some hacienda foremen always wanted to beat us until the death of President Villarroel. [Once] the authorities from Tiraque wanted to kill me, but I was in Palca [in his mother's home]. My wife came to let me know. My granny and my mother cried, saying: "Why do you get involved in those things, child?" I escaped to Korani to work where they were making the road.

In the twenty years following the war, the region experienced generalized unrest and violence. Hacendados reacted to the general decline in agricultural demand by increasing their exploitation of labor, while some colonos challenged hacendados by attempting to organize and by filing lawsuits against them, and others attacked or robbed hacendados on the roads or in their homes. On the hacienda Toralapa, for instance, colonos filed a lawsuit against the hacendado, Mateo Hinojosa, arguing that he was "treating them inhumanly by increasing their labor obligations," which were more burdensome than the ones imposed by the previous hacendado. Not surprisingly, Hinojosa won the case, arguing that colonos were not really treated as colonos in his hacienda but as "partners" since

[the] harvest is divided in three parts, one for the hacienda, one for seed, and one for the laborers. . . . The time they have to work for the hacienda is not more than five or six hours a day . . . and it is not true that domestic obligations are more burdensome now than before, since each household only has to serve once every two months because of the large number of colonos in the hacienda. . . . Although colonos are not wealthy, they still have a substantial income as they have a large number of animals. . . . In sum, the people in Toralapa enjoy a very good standard of living. (JT: 1932)

Most of the attacks on hacendados and robberies by small groups of armed men were attributed to "unknown men, artisans, that is, town residents" from Cliza, Punata, and other valley towns. In some cases, however, colonos attacked hacienda houses and hacendados. On the hacienda Juntutuyo in Vacas, for instance, Napoleón Calvi, who leased the hacienda from the Municipal Council of Cochabamba, reported that

armed *originario*[31] Indians from Juntutuyo, forgetting their obligations toward the hacendado . . . have attacked me and they would have killed me if I had not miraculously escaped from their hands. I was forced to abandon the crops. . . . This has been a real insurrection with the purpose of making me leave the hacienda. (JT: 1930)

Colonos were also accused of robbing the hacienda house of money, agricultural products, and animals. Occasionally, hacendados were charged by colonos with stealing their animals, and neighboring hacendados fought among themselves over the boundaries of their properties.

Plantation owners and colonizers in Vandiola suffered the effects of economic decline more acutely than did the hacendados. During the Chaco War the departmental authorities had decided to build a motor road from Cochabamba to the nearer yungas of Chapare, using for this the labor of Paraguayan prisoners of war. The construction of the road and the appearance of trucks led to the expansion and development of Chapare at the expense of the other yungas in the department, including Vandiola. This created two immediate problems for plantation owners in Vandiola. One was a shortage of labor, since many former colonos and laborers moved to Chapare where they were able to acquire their own land. This problem affected mainly the small plantations that relied more on a small, permanent labor force and seasonal laborers. On the large plantations, colonos were more settled, because they held larger amounts of land in usufruct, yet they also felt the shortage of seasonal labor. Plantation owners resorted to debt peonage to solve the problem. They lent money with interest that had to be repaid with work on the plantation for a stated number of years. The number of lawsuits filed by plantation owners against their debtors indicates, however, that debt peonage was not a very efficient solution for the labor shortage.

The second problem plantation owners and colonos experienced was competition with Chapare colonizers, for whom the truck was a more efficient means of transport than the mule. The truck was not only a faster means of transportation, but it also allowed for the production and export of other tropical crops such as fruit which, until then, had been left to rot in the yungas. Confronted with this situation, Vandiola landowners made several attempts to build a road from Tiraque to Vandiola. Eduardo Vergara, a Punateño owner of a plantation in Santa Rosa and a wood and lumber company in Punata, made the first attempt in 1944. After investing one-and-a-half million bolivianos on the rehabilitation of fifteen kilometers of road, Vergara requested the collaboration of the Junta de Propietarios de Vandiola. Not until 1950, however, did the junta embark on the road construction with finances obtained from the Banco Agrícola de Bolivia (BAB). Even then, the road did not extend beyond the eastern mountains, and the route was never completed [32] (AAT: Correspondencia, 1950–52).

The decline of Vandiola affected in particular those families who were beginning to accumulate wealth but who had not yet bought a small- or medium-sized hacienda. Since Vandiola could not offer the same opportunities as before, some of them obtained land in Chapare instead; others remained in Tiraque, some of them buying trucks. Emilio Estrada, a Syrian Moslem who converted to Catholicism a year after his arrival in Bolivia in 1914, bought the first truck in 1927. Estrada had settled in Tiraque as a merchant and soon became a yungueño. He married María Castillo, daughter of a vecino. They owned a hotel in town, collected taxes, and lent money. Shortly afterward, five hacendados (Benjamín Montaño, Mateo Hinojosa, Severo Camacho, Juan Pacheco, and Juan de Dios Quiroga) bought trucks. Prior to the construction of the road to Chapare, Pacheco had a large plantation in Vandiola. This he sold in 1937 to buy a 4,600-hectare plantation in Chapare, located near the new road. He exported up to 120 tambores of coca after every harvest. A few years later, he bought the hacienda Urmachea in Tiraque.

In the 1940s, two more hacendados (Lidia Terrazas and Paulino Flores) and nine "middle" yungueños (Juan Torrico, Luis Sandoval, Flaviano Ochoa, Crisólogo Sandoval, Demetrio Torrico, Félix Irigoyen, Jaime Ferrufino, Nicasio Navia, and Flavio Estrada) bought trucks. Among yungueños, there were three moneylenders, two muleteers, and one cattle dealer and butcher from Punata who had settled in Tiraque. Although all of them had some land in Tiraque, their trucks provided them with an unexpected means by which to accumulate wealth. Unlike the large hacendados who used trucks for the transport of hacienda products and hired chauffeurs to do the driving, most of the yungueños did their own driving (except old truck owners who hired chauffeurs but still traveled in their trucks), hired out their services to others, and spent a considerable amount of time on the road. They traveled to the towns in the Valle Alto and to Chapare, Santa Cruz, Cochabamba, Sucre, Oruro, and La Paz. Since the roads were narrow in mountainous terrain and unpaved, they traveled in caravans of ten or twelve trucks so that they could help each other if something went wrong. The road to Chapare was so narrow that they designated specific days for one-way trips from Cochabamba to Chapare and other days to make the return trip. The trip to Santa Cruz (some 400 km.) took two weeks during the rainy season, when the road was so muddy that they often had to wait several days for the surface to dry out.

These men specialized in a new activity which slowly transformed them into *transportistas* (transporters). In the early stages of their careers, they engaged mainly in the long-distance transport of goods and passengers and in regional exchange with Chapare colonizers, Tiraque agriculturalists, and piqueros. Very few, if any, of these transactions were carried out with colonos in the haciendas. Most hacendados would not permit traders or merchants on their properties, and colonos still relied on their own animals for the transport of their surplus products to markets.

Not all pioneer truckers became successful as transportistas, however. For some the purchase of a truck brought economic ruin. This was so in the case of Nicasio Navia. In 1947, he bought a second-hand truck on credit from the large hacendado, Ireneo Hinojosa. But Nicasio lacked experience with motor vehicles and did not know how to repair the truck. As he put it, "I had to work simply to pay for the repairs on the truck and could not repay the debt." Finally, he was forced to sell part of his land and the truck to pay the outstanding debt.

Involvement in transport did not distract truck owners from other economic activities. On the contrary, they continued to cultivate in Vandiola and Tiraque, keep their mules to transport coca from Vandiola, lend money, and engage in tax collection and commerce. Just like the wealthy families, they reinvested their capital in the purchase of land in Tiraque. With the exception of Juan Torrico, however, none was able to consolidate large land-holdings or occupy political office in Tiraque. Only one, Flaviano Ochoa, who married the daughter of Manuel Ochoa, was elected president of the Municipal Council (1940–41). It was not until the revolution and the outmigration of hacendados that the middle yungueño-transportistas became the dominant families in the region.

Chapter 3
Revolution, Agrarian Reform, and the State

Ahí llegó la reforma [Then came the reform]. My *compañeros* [comrades] put me in as leader of Chapapani, saying, "You are experienced, you know." During the reform we attacked hacienda houses. Since the *patrones* [landowners] used to take away our sheep and oxen, we returned them to their owners. During that time, one could hear *pututus* [horns] here and there. Because of that, the patrones got scared and fled to the cities.

(Martín Salazar)

Indeed, the "violent and treacherous" actions of generally "passive and lazy," but now "awakened Indians," who took over hacienda lands and arrested, mistreated, and in some regions even killed hacendados, was a cause of deep concern for hacendados and townsfolk alike. Through these actions, colonos, sharecroppers, piqueros, and artisans, organized in armed *sindicatos agrarios* (agrarian unions), were able to bring about dramatic immediate and long-term transformations to Tiraque. Former colonos and sharecroppers became de facto or legal owners of the lands they worked. Hacendados left the area, and ground rent obligations and sharecropping agreements were abolished. Since then, too, former colonos and sharecroppers were referred to as, and called themselves, campesinos. For a short while—the first years following the revolution—campesinos thus enjoyed unprecedented power and autonomy. Slowly but steadily, however, these gains began to erode. Indeed, by the early sixties, when the government insisted that they return the arms previously given to them, campesinos had already lost much of their political leverage and some of their autonomy as "independent" producers. The reasons for this should be sought first in the special yet ambiguous relationship that developed between the state and the peasantry, and second and relatedly, in local processes of rural differentiation and class formation.

This chapter discusses the manner in which colonos and sharecroppers became landowning campesinos; how, together with piqueros, they organized in powerful unions; and how they lost much of this power and became dependent in new ways. I examine the intended and unintended consequences of rural mobilization, agrarian reform, and state policies, practices which both ruptured and restructured social relations, leading to new forms of rural domination and exploitation, and to the further erosion of peasant autonomy. The discussion centers on the peasant union, since it was around it that campesino "communities" were structured in Tiraque, becoming the nucleus of the villages' political organization and the locus of peasant mobilization. The union was also instrumental in the actual implementation of agrarian reform. It is thus an excellent entry point for discussing the distribution of land in Tiraque, which preserved inequalities in land tenure among former colonos. Through the union and higher levels of peasant organization, too, the state was able to control the peasant movement. By defusing and dividing the movement, favoring corrupt leaders and repressing others, the state has often relied on the peasantry for political support while at the same time controlling campesinos politically. The state thus played a crucial role in influencing the course of structural transformations and political change in Bolivia.

Revolution and Rural Mobilization

It only took three days of fighting in April 1952 by armed civilian forces, the national police, and a few army units, led by the Movimiento Nacionalista Revolucionario party (MNR), to defeat the armed forces and overturn the old order of domination (Dunkerley 1984; Klein 1982; Malloy 1971). Although the rural poor did not directly participate in the armed uprising, soon after, colonos from Ucureña reorganized their union under the leadership of José Rojas and took the vanguard of the peasant movement, especially in the Valle Alto and surrounding highlands (Dandler 1984; Huizer 1972; Iriarte 1980; Pearse 1975). Following the example of Ucureña and often promoted by the MNR, sindicatos agrarios organized in every piquería, hacienda, and rural village in Bolivia, and many of these unions were given arms to support the revolution in lieu of the disbanded army.[1]

Under the direct influence of Ucureña, the first peasant unions in Tiraque were organized as early as 1952. Two years later all local unions were grouped into the Tiraque subcentral campesina, which was upgraded to the level of central campesina in 1964.[2] While former colonos led the unions established in the haciendas, it was mainly the piqueros and sharecroppers, who had been politically involved in previous years, that occupied positions of leadership at the central level of organization. They tended to maintain those positions well into the 1970s. Martín Salazar, for instance, was elected first secretary general of the Central Campesina and remained in that position for eight years.

As armed militias, campesinos mobilized to defend the land they had seized from the haciendas, guarding the haciendas with groups of armed men and filling the countryside with the sounds of their pututus, calling for urgent meetings and actions to be taken against all those considered enemies of the revolution. In June 1953 a large number of campesinos, headed by leaders from Ucureña, marched into the town of Tiraque, where they took over all the arms owned by vecinos. According to the horrified mayor, they also "committed all sorts of abuses against vecinos besides stealing money and agricultural tools" (AAT: Correspondencia). Mobilized campesinos also sounded their pututus to take actions against hacendados and members of the opposition party, Falange Socialista Boliviana (FSB). The fear these actions produced among vecinos was of such magnitude that personal enmities among them were resolved with accusations made to the Central Campesina. It sufficed to accuse someone as an FSB sympathizer to have that person arrested and beaten up. Nemecio Torres, a trucker and FSB party member, was forced into hiding for two months before going to Argentina, where he stayed for three years, returning only when the campesinos had been "pacified." Punitive actions were also taken against those hacendados or wealthy merchants who had been brave enough to stay in Tiraque. But the majority left soon after the revolution. These included the Covarrubias, Quiroga, Gutiérrez, Ferrufino, Arandia, Casanovas, Terceros, Siles, and Terrazas families.

Plantation owners, too, slowly began to abandon their properties in Vandiola, leaving behind their personal belongings. They were afraid to remain on isolated plantations in the midst of "unruly" and "aggressive" colonos and laborers, particularly after they learned about the fate of many hacendados in the valleys. When they left, the campesino unions of Vandiola requested that the Tiraque authorities construct a road to this "forgotten frontier." They were not successful, and their situation worsened after a paved road to Chapare was built in 1965, until finally they, too, abandoned the yungas. Eventually, the lands reverted to the state in the 1960s.

With the final abandonment of Vandiola, the small town of Tiraque lost the status it once enjoyed as one of the gateways to the yungas. The townsfolk long for the lost paradise with nostalgia, magnifying in their memories the fertility and the richness of the land. The yungas had provided the means for a better life which they had lost. As the mayor put it in 1983, "We have lost the body; now we have only the head of the cantón and we cannot do much with it. We must recover the yungas if we want development." There is a grain of truth in this perception of the importance of Vandiola, but the mobilization of campesinos and the distribution of lands to their former colonos was, in fact, more devastating to hacendados than the loss of Vandiola.

Agrarian Reform and Land Distribution

Once in power, the MNR, supported and even pressured by armed militias of workers, miners, urban civilians, and campesinos, instituted the most revolutionary reforms ever passed in Bolivia. Among the most important of these were the nationalization of the mines owned by the tin barons, the elimination of a literacy requirement in the franchise (which increased the electorate from 200,000 to one million), and agrarian reform.

Enacted on August 2, 1953, on the Day of the Indian in Ucureña, the agrarian reform was, above all, a political measure instituted in response to pressures from colonos, piqueros, and other social groups seeking to transform the wider society. And the agrarian reform was an important step in that direction, since 92 percent of total arable land in Bolivia, involving properties larger than 1,000 hectares, was in the hands of 6 percent of the landowners (República de Bolivia 1950). The reform was also a political compromise conciliating different demands for change within the MNR, since the party consisted of a heterogeneous coalition of forces with divergent interests that were reflected in contradictions in the agrarian law itself and in opposing provisions between the law and state policies for economic development. The law, for instance, legalized the de facto occupation of hacienda lands, but the state simultaneously reserved ultimate patrimony over the land, granting it to campesinos as long as they worked it. Failure to do so meant that the land could be reverted to the state.

As we shall see, this provision has often been used by the state as a threat against the peasantry. The reform law also abolished unpaid labor and sharecropping contracts, but in 1954 the Ministry of Agriculture and Peasant Affairs allowed sharecropping for one year (AAT: Correspondencia, 1954). Other provisions of the reform were similarly contradictory. It recognized various types of rural property: the small- and medium-sized family farm, the communal property, the cooperative, and the agricultural enterprise. It did not recognize the *latifundio*, which it defined as "the large, rural holding which is minimally exploited by antiquated labor-intensive methods, and which perpetuates a system of feudal oppression" (Heath et al. 1969). The maximum amount for each property was determined according to type and geographic zone, ranging from one-half hectare in Cochabamba to 2,000 hectares for agricultural enterprises in the eastern lowlands. Thus, in abolishing the latifundio, the law provided for the agricultural enterprise, which it distinguished from the latifundio by its large capital investment, modern technology, and salaried labor. Such a distinction is, at best, ambiguous, allowing for the formation or persistence of the large property and leading to the conditions that have been central to the model of accumulation pursued by a dominant faction of the MNR and later governments. This model, seeking to diversify the export economy, has sought the development of agricultural enterprises in the Oriente at the expense of peasant farms. Other objectives of the reform were the promotion of Indian communities, the stimulation of agriculture, the preservation of natural resources, and the promotion of internal migration to the eastern lowlands and Chapare.

The sindicatos agrarios were instrumental for the enactment and implementation of agrarian reform, first, by seizing land and pressing the government to decree a reform law, and second, because it was through the union that legal procedures for the distribution of land could be initiated. These began in Tiraque in 1954, but the actual implementation of reform was a drawn-out process not devoid of manipulation and, occasionally, struggle, with some of the procedures taking from three to eleven years. In some former haciendas it has not yet concluded. Over the course of these years, the state agency in charge of implementing agrarian reform, the Servicio Nacional de Reforma Agraria (SNRA), reviewed sixty-four cases in Tiraque involving mainly large- and medium-sized haciendas. Table 5 shows the distribution of land in the sixty-four properties. The number of documented cases does not, however, represent all the landholdings at the time of reform, because very few vecinos and piqueros

TABLE 5. Distribution of Land before Agrarian Reform in
Tiraque, 1953.

Size of Property in hectares	Number of Properties	
	N	%
<10	8^a	12.5
11–20	3	4.7
21–50	12	18.8
51–100	8	12.5
101–200	7	10.9
201–300	2	3.1
301–500	5	7.8
501–1,000	11	17.2
1001–2,000	3	4.7
2001–3,000	0	0.0
3001–4,000	4	6.3
4001–5,000	0	0.0
>5,000	1	1.6
Total	64	100.0

Source: Servicio Nacional de Reforma Agraria, Exp. 6675, 7005, 6614, 7662, 6166, 8625A, 7375, 7272, 11784, 12237, 10179, 15409, 13426, 15859B, 11800, 16796, 16347A, 41178, 38588, 37370, 23060, 5976, 6313B, 8731, 9285, 9969, 732, 3577, 2930, 3436, 3542, 3438, 2706, 4103, 4932, 4712, 4970, 5324, 5519, 5825, 5566, 4930, 5133, 2573, 2381, 1979, 2460, 4076, 4074, 4098, 4096, 3828, 4075, 3829, 4100, 3920, 4579, 4525, 4128, 4101, 4121, 28569, 11010.

^{a}One of these, listed as one property, actually consists of the holdings of 146 piqueros. Since all of these holdings are in the same locality, their owners decided to have their lands individually recognized in one legal procedure to minimize expenses.

with small landholdings bothered to take their cases to the SNRA. The main reason for this was that legal procedures were not only long and complicated but also costly. A legal claim had to be filed with the SNRA by the secretary-general of the peasant union, or by the landowner of small- and medium-sized properties for recognition of property rights. A topographer was then sent to the property to undertake an inspection and to collect all the necessary information regarding the area, colono population, and labor relations. This information was included in a technical report that, together with the statements made in court by colonos and landowners, formed the basis for the agrarian judge to pass judgment based on the previous classification of the property. A court assessment and judgment was then made. The judge's sentence was subse-

TABLE 6. Hacienda-Owned Land Cultivated Directly by the Hacienda and Hacienda Land Allocated to Colonos and Sharecroppers, Cantón Tiraque, 1953 (in hectares).

Type of Property	Arable Land	Cultivated by Hacienda		Cultivated by Colonos		Sharecropped	
		N	%	N	%	N	%
Latifundia	10,437	2,215	21.22%	7,809	74.83%	412	3.95%
Medium	1,875	802	42.77	775	41.33	298	15.90
Small[a]	494	409	82.79	4	0.81	81	16.40

Source: Servicio Nacional de Reforma Agraria, Exp. 6675, 7005, 6614, 7662, 6166, 8625A, 7375, 7272, 11784, 12237, 10179, 15409, 13426, 15859B, 11800, 16796, 16347A, 41178, 38588, 37370, 23060, 5976, 6313B, 8731, 9285, 9969, 732, 3577, 2930, 3436, 3542, 3438, 2706, 4103, 4932, 4712, 4970, 5324, 5519, 5825, 5566, 4930, 5133, 2573, 2381, 1979, 2460, 4076, 4074, 4098, 4096, 3828, 4075, 3829, 4100, 3920, 4579, 4525, 4128, 4101, 4121, 28569, 11010.

[a] Includes one piquería.

quently reviewed by the Consejo Nacional de Reforma Agraria, which might uphold or reverse his judgment. The president of the Republic made the final decision in a *Resolución Suprema*, which could not be appealed.

Taking into account only the size of cultivable land rather than the size of the entire property, as well as the amount of capital invested and the nature of labor relations in the landholding, the SNRA classified twenty-seven properties as latifundia or large estates, seventeen as medium-sized haciendas, and twenty as small properties.[3] Table 6 shows the total amount of arable land these properties entailed and the size of land cultivated directly by the hacienda and by colonos or sharecroppers. On the latifundia, only 21 percent of the land was cultivated by the hacendado, the remainder being distributed among colonos and sharecroppers.

All the lands of those haciendas classified as latifundia by agrarian judges were distributed among former colonos. Medium-sized haciendas were partially affected. Hacendados maintained a portion of cultivable land, and former colonos received individual parcels of land. Both the hacendado and the colonos had communal access to grazing and noncultivable lands. Properties considered agricultural enterprises when the hacendado had invested capital and paid wages were not affected. Finally, properties worked by the landowner himself and without resident colonos were categorized as small properties and were recognized as belonging to the owner.

The outcome of land distribution was unequal for all groups affected by the reform (see Table 7). For hacendados the final verdict could result in the loss of the entire property or the recognition of a substantial amount of land; some large haciendas of about 250 hectares were categorized as medium-sized estates and their owners were able to keep over 100 hectares, while smaller haciendas (of about forty hectares) were declared latifundia and all the lands were distributed among colonos.

But it was not only the size of cultivable land and the type of estate that was responsible for this outcome. It often depended on the hacendado's political connections and party affiliation, and on the organization and militancy of colonos on the hacienda. The hacienda Urmachea, for instance, totaled 248 hectares, 138 of which were under cultivation, and it had 16 colono households settled on the land. Yet, in 1960, it was declared a medium-sized property, and 115 hectares of cultivable land were granted to the hacendado and his son, Juan and Rodolfo Pacheco. In spite of their party affiliation and personal friendship with members of the MNR, the Pachecos were not able to cultivate their land because former colonos challenged their doing so. Only in 1964 was Rodolfo able to return to what had been his hacienda after reaching an agreement with the campesino union. He was forced to sell them a large portion of the land and keep for himself only forty hectares. Although Rodolfo wants to move to the city, he is forced to live in Urmachea and work the land; otherwise, he might risk another lawsuit for not working the land and have it revert to the state. In 1984, when he tried to sell portions of the land, campesinos of Urmachea forced him to sell it to them.

Juan Torrico's case illustrates a situation in which the hacendado was doubly successful: he kept his land and was not opposed by militant campesinos. After his father bought five hectares of land in Qolqeqhoya in 1917, Juan bought up small- and medium-sized parcels of land in the locality until he accumulated 144 hectares. Yet, he was building his hacienda—Qolqeqhoya/Churu—from 1951 to 1954, during the implementation of agrarian reform. He was, however, a member of the regional MNR party cell and had personal relations with the MNR departmental leadership. In 1958 he filed a claim to have his property legally recognized. Both the rural judge and SNRA declared the property small in size and recognized it as belonging in its entirety to Torrico. The president of Bolivia reversed this judgment, however, declaring the property medium-sized and therefore to be distributed between the seven sharecroppers settled on the land and the hacendado. Of the hacienda's forty-four cultivable hectares, some nineteen hectares were to be retained by the hacendado and thirty-one hectares to be distributed among the sharecroppers, an

TABLE 7. Mean Size of Cultivable Land[a] Distributed to Colonos by Agrarian Reform, Cantón Tiraque, 1954–66 (in hectares).

		Allocated to			
Hacienda[b]	Hacen-dados	Colonos	Share-croppers	Other[c]	Total
Boquerón Khasa	0.00	5.66	0.0	0.0	82
Boquerón Khasa	0.00	7.50	0.0	0.0	158
Boquerón Khasa	0.00	6.88	1.7	1.1	209
Cebada Jichana	46.75	5.90	0.0	0.0	114
Chapapani	180.00	1.66	0.0	0.0	259
Chawpi Koari	0.00	4.05	0.0	3.4	167
Ch'aqo	0.00	16.88	0.0	0.0	72
Chullpamoqo	18.89	3.23	0.0	0.0	13
Cochimita	8.38	8.90	0.0	0.0	26
Cotani Bajo	52.00	10.60	0.0	0.0	288
Cotani/Churu	0.00	5.90	0.0	5.0	68
Dami Rancho	0.00	6.33	0.0	1.8	73
Huaylla Qhochi	63.77	6.66	0.0	0.0	84
Iluri Grande	0.00	4.06	0.0	1.4	144
Iluri Grande	0.00	3.56	0.0	0.0	66
Iluri Grande	68.37	5.00	1.5	3.0	233
K'aspikancha	0.00	26.59	0.0	0.0	582
Kayarani	22.20	3.94	0.0	0.0	308
Koari Grande	0.00	7.17	0.0	4.1	258
Millumayo	n.a.	6.00	0.0	0.0	176
Minas Pampa	0.00	4.54	2.0	0.9	48
Parrarancho	0.00	6.79	0.0	1.5	157
Pucara Grande	17.38	5.79	0.0	0.0	342
Qolqeqhoya	0.00	8.37	0.0	0.0	219
Qolqeqhoya	3.53	0.00	5.2	0.0	19
Qolqeqhoya/Churu	18.68	0.00	2.5	0.0	43
Rodeo	0.00	2.47	0.0	0.0	38
Rodeo	12.00	2.42	0.0	0.0	25
Rodeo	20.51	1.06	2.0	0.0	33
Rodeo	0.00	4.43	0.0	0.0	23
Rodeo/Pukawasi	46.91	1.87	0.5	1.0	69
Sacabambilla Alta	0.00	4.83	0.0	3.0	257
Sacabambilla Alta	0.00	5.59	0.0	4.3	346
Sacabambilla Baja	0.00	2.56	0.0	0.0	226
Sank'ayani	0.00	17.45	0.0	0.0	16.99
Tholapampa	0.00	5.43	0.0	0.0	232
Toqorancho	0.00	4.84	0.0	3.0	83
Toralapa	0.00	13.22	0.0	0.0	2,239
Tuturuyo Alto	45.24	12.14	0.0	0.0	197
Tuturuyo Bajo	0.00	6.65	0.0	2.8	274
Urmachea	115.02	2.00	0.0	0.0	137
Virbini	0.00	7.87	2.0	0.0	142
Wakawasi	0.00	5.07	0.0	3.4	220
Zapata Rancho	0.00	6.03	0.0	0.0	168

TABLE 7 *continued*

Source: Servicio Nacional de Reforma Agraria, Exp. 4076, 4074, 4075, 2930, 2917B, 1978B, 4101, 4930, 4579, 3436, 8626A, 16796, 4525, 10179, 4121, 2573, 4712, 7005, 5133, 3920, 9285, 6675, 6166, 5976, 5566, 4932, 3829, 3828, 9969, 6614, 37370, 4100, 5519, 2706, 4096, 4128, 6213B, 2460, 3542, 3577, 4098, 8731, 4103, 3438.

ᵃBesides the land distributed to individual households, other portions of land were singled out for collective and/or cooperative production and communal grazing.
ᵇA few haciendas shared the same name although they belonged to different hacendados. This is further evidence of land fragmentation in Tiraque.
ᶜThese include arrimantes.

average of four hectares each. The remaining uncultivable hectares and the grazing lands were to be for the communal use of both parties. In practice, however, Torrico remained in full control of the entire property and the sharecroppers continued to cultivate with him until 1983, when he began to sell portions of the land, about fifty hectares, to rich campesinos. Meanwhile, the sharecroppers, who are old, illiterate, and very poor, fear the hacendado, mainly because they depend on him for having access to their own land and do not have the means and the connections to get involved in a long legal process.⁴

The amount of land colonos received under the terms of the reform varied according to the size of the hacienda on which they lived and the number of colono households settled on it. It also depended on whether the hacienda was distributed in its entirety to colonos or whether the hacendado kept some portion of the land. In most cases, the land granted to former colonos was about the same as they had held in usufruct on the hacienda, and these varied in size. The exceptions were the few instances in which the hacienda was so small that there was not enough land to distribute among the young men over eighteen years old who had worked, until then, on their parents' plots. They were granted lands on nearby large haciendas. Piqueros retained ownership of their land, but they were not granted additional parcels, even if their property was very small. Besides those hacendados who had part of their hacienda lands recognized, those most favored by the agrarian reform laws were those colonos who were, at the same time, piqueros. They retained their piquerías and received lands from the haciendas where they were settled.

Table 7 serves to illustrate the distribution and fragmentation of land within localities and in the region in general, but fails to show the unequal amounts of land that different households owned after reform. An examination of how land was distributed within one hacienda illustrates this inequality. The hacienda Sank'ayani of Lidia Terrazas, for instance, had a total area of 3,084 hectares, 736 of which

TABLE 8. Distribution of Land Prior to and after Agrarian Reform among Colonos, Sharecroppers, and Piqueros in Former Hacienda Sank'ayani, 1961 (in hectares).

Name	Age	Land in Usufruct	Land Distributed	Land Owned in Other Areas Prior to Reform
Colonos				
Trinidad Solís	60	5.79	26.57	5.43
Sabino Hidalgo	30	8.69	25.72	0.00
Asencio Coca	40	8.69	18.79	10.13
Valentín Coca	34	5.79	20.16	1.81
Manuel Montaño	34	8.69	13.23	1.81
José Ocampo	27	5.79	23.95	0.00
Valentín Rios	50	8.69	15.12	1.44
Victor Coca	28	8.69	14.36	0.00
Santusa Coca	50	5.79	13.21	0.00
Manuel Durán	42	5.79	25.23	2.17
Juan Solís	46	5.79	18.67	0.00
Benedicto Segarra	34	5.79	22.42	2.89
Luis Montaño	50	2.89	11.40	3.62
Manuel Rojas	38	1.44	17.23	2.89
Rigoberto Terrazas	29	1.44	12.00	0.00
Emigdio Nina	32	0.36	14.80	0.00
Prudencio Nina	20	2.17	0.00	0.00
Pablo Hidalgo	43	0.00	24.26	5.43
Delfín Coca	46	0.00	8.57	2.89
Hilarión Coca	102	0.00	11.11	6.51
Rufino Hidalgo	26	2.89	11.52	0.00
Arrimantes[a]				
Cirilo Nina	21	0.0	12.41	0.0
Cornelio Solís	20	0.0	16.46	0.0
Prudencio Solís	18	0.0	49.20	0.0
Sixto Durán	18	0.0	12.00	0.0
Herder				
Silverio Segarra	24	5.79	21.10	0.0
Independent[b]				
Pedro Terrazas	50	0.0	15.21	0.0
Martín Durán	27	0.0	11.62	0.0
Mariano Durán	25	0.0	15.21	0.0
Nicanor Solís	30	0.0	14.72	2.8
Juan Jaimes	35	0.0	10.82	0.0
Added by SNRA[c]				
Andrés Coca	46	0.0	29.58	n. a.
Ricardo Coca	18	0.0	11.81	0.0
Leocadio Montaño	70	0.0	16.82	0.0
Julio Rojas	n. a.	0.0	22.50	0.0

N = 35

TABLE 8 *continued*

Source: Servicio Nacional de Reforma Agraria, Exp. 4096.

[a] Landless, single, and married sons of colonos.
[b] Although these were not colonos, they were nonetheless related to the hacienda. They provided two days of work per week. Some were piqueros.
[c] SNRA added four names to the list presented by colonos, but excluded eleven individuals who had also petitioned land in Sank'ayani.

were cultivable before the reform. Former colonos received a total of about 608 hectares of land distributed in unequal amounts, ranging from 8.5 to 49 hectares (see Table 8), although colonos had requested that the land be distributed in equal amounts, "since all had been subject to the same obligations and services" (SNRA: Exp. 4096).[5] For this hacienda, the legal processs took seven years, from 1954 to 1961, because there was a dispute over the number of colonos settled on the property.

According to the owner, there were only thirteen households, but colonos presented a list of twenty-one to the SNRA. In the lawsuit, the hacendada disputed this number, claiming that many had moved into the hacienda "by force of arms" after the promulgation of reform, that some had worked in the hacienda but had moved out years before the reform, and that others were piqueros unrelated to the hacienda. These arguments were used by the hacendada in order to have her property classified as a medium-sized hacienda. The final verdict designated the hacienda a latifundio and recognized the right of thirty-five households for land distribution. These included twenty-one colonos, four arrimantes, one herder who used to pasture his animals on the hacienda, and nine piquero households (SNRA: ibid.). Of the remaining land, 103 hectares were designated for collective work, 11 hectares for a school, and 2,182 hectares as common pasture land. Since 1961, the campesino union has distributed portions of this land to young couples and to men who have not yet inherited land. Table 8 also shows that, prior to reform, twelve of the twenty-one colonos owned land in other localities which they retained at the same time they received lands from the hacienda.

Although most haciendas were partially or totally affected by the reform, many campesinos still did not have legal titles to their lands at the time of field research in 1982–85. Gaining title entails another long bureaucratic process requiring frequent trips to Punata, Cochabamba and, eventually, to La Paz, as well as the hiring of lawyers and topographers who usually ask for *t'inkas* ("gifts" such as agricultural products, animals, or money) in addition to their fees. Many peasants lack the means and the time to engage in this frustrating procedure, so their property rights are based solely on the reform's final judgments and on the fact that they work their land.

By legalizing the seizure of land, the agrarian reform decree transformed former colonos, sharecroppers, and the landless into landowning campesinos, erasing previous categorical distinctions among them. But what shaped their "campesino" consciousness, "conceived as a deep, horizontal comradeship" (Anderson 1983:16), was their mobilization against their common enemy, the merchant hacendado. Both this political awareness of "community" and their organization into militant unions were instrumental for the re-creation of communities in Tiraque and the central valleys of Cochabamba. Only then did a wandering population settle, albeit often temporarily, in specific localities or villages.

In most instances, the newly formed community has the same boundaries as the former hacienda or piquería, but where the hacienda had been large, as in the case of Toralapa, five different unions were organized, dividing the former colonos among five distinct communities. Where the haciendas were small, or where they had few colonos, the union often combined former colonos of one hacienda, nearby piqueros, and former sharecroppers. In most cases, communities took the name of the hacienda. The only exceptions are two unions formed on the outskirts of town that affiliate former sharecroppers and landed townsfolk; their lands, which are located in different villages or near the town of Tiraque, however, do not form a "community."

The campesino union also became the only political institution regulating those matters affecting the entire village such as the construction and cleaning of irrigation canals, communal work to build a schoolhouse or dispensary, and cultivation of communal land. It is, however, at the level of the Central Campesina or higher levels of organization that communities become "active" (Williams 1973), enabling campesinos to articulate their political demands and mobilize to carry them out. As we have seen above, their actions were most militant during the early postrevolutionary years, but by the time peasants received legal possession of their land, they had lost much of their political power and autonomy. To understand this, it is necessary to examine the manner in which the state related to this newly created peasantry.

The State and the Peasantry

From the beginning, the MNR tried to control the social forces unleashed by the revolution in the countryside. It was nevertheless difficult both to stop the mobilization of colonos, sharecroppers, and piqueros in the Valle Alto and regions near La Paz, and to counter the pressure from leftist factions within the government that had already succeeded in forcing the government to decree an agrarian reform law. Yet, the twelve years of MNR rule (1952–64) continued to be characterized by shifting alignments and conflict among those in power and powerful regional campesino leaders. A lack of consensus on the part of the government as to what action to take regarding the peasantry divided the campesino movement from early on.[6] In 1956, when rampant inflation eroded some of the massive popular support the MNR had previously enjoyed, Bolivia received the largest amount of United States aid to Latin America to implement the Plan de Estabilización Económica. To put into effect this stabilization plan, the Bolivian government was pressured by the International Monetary Fund to end state intervention in the economy and promote foreign investment. This led to the realignment of forces. The MNR turned against the left and labor, began to reorganize the army, and relied on peasant militias to control the forces challenging the government. The peasant-labor alliance was thus broken up.[7] To consolidate its alliance with campesinos, the MNR appointed José Rojas (the leader of the Ucureña union) to the Ministerio de Asuntos Campesinos. Thus, militias from the Valle Alto, including Tiraque, were among those sent to the mining camps to "pacify" the miners. Twice they were sent to put an end to armed revolts staged by the Falange Socialista Boliviana in the departments of Santa Cruz and Beni (Martín Salazar, personal communication).

In 1959, the conflict within the MNR leadership became even more acute when different party candidates put themselves forward for the presidency and sought the support of different regional campesino leaders. This, together with the long-standing rivalry between leaders in the central valleys of Cochabamba, led to the *ch'ampa guerra* (1959–64), an armed conflict between two campesino factions in the Valle Alto that erupted over the control of the campesino movement. One faction, led by Rojas, operated out of Ucureña; the other, led by Miguel Veizaga, had its headquarters in the town of Cliza (Dandler 1984). The conflict extended throughout the whole region. Tiraqueños were called in to join Rojas, but Martín Salazar, leader of the Tiraque subcentral campesina, refused to fight, as he put it, "in a war in which they did not even know what they were fighting for." For this he was persecuted by Rojas's supporters, forced underground, and finally replaced by a protégé of Rojas. The conflict ended with the intervention of an air force general, René Barrientos, who in 1964 overthrew the MNR government. He was a member of the MNR's newly organized army which, since then, has become a central actor in Bolivian politics. Barrientos claimed to be the only leader able to pursue both the nationalist and development strategies of revolution that had been abandoned by the MNR factions in the course of their power struggle. Unlike the MNR, he sought to accomplish these goals with the backing of the army, which was called in to repress the miners and other sectors of the population,[8] and by relying less and less on popular armed militias, which were asked to return the arms given to them by the MNR. Although not everyone did so, the militias, in practice, ceased to exist. Yet, Barrientos's leadership style was populist. He appealed to the campesinos by making use of his reputation as the person who had ended the ch'ampa guerra and championed the formalization of the state-campesino alliance known as the *Pacto Militar Campesino*.

Barrientos was and still is very popular in Cochabamba. He was born in the valley market town of Tarata, was of humble origins, and was a fluent speaker of Quechua. He was, in fact, the only president in recent Bolivian history who spoke a native language. He traveled extensively within the country, flying to every small town and village, where he was received by large crowds of campesinos and vecinos, especially in Cochabamba. The Alcaldía of Tiraque, for instance, opened a landing strip in the outskirts of the town so that Barrientos's plane could land in his frequent visits to this region.[9] He often participated in the celebration of the patron of Tiraque, the Virgen de las Angustias, and he played an important role in promoting and financing the building of an irrigation system in Tiraque, the control of which is today an important issue in regional politicking. Barrientos died on one of his trips when his plane crashed near the town of Arque, Cochabamba.

After Barrientos's death and the two short-lived governments of General Alfredo Ovando and General Juan José Torres, General Hugo Banzer took over the reins of government. He quickly moved to suppress "communist" infiltrators, purge the labor and campesino movement of those elements considered dangerous (many of whose members went underground or into exile), and replace them with individuals loyal to the government. These were the infamous "coordinators" appointed by the government to occupy union leadership positions in lieu of elected officials. In an effort to exercise control over another strategically important sector of the population, Banzer decreed in 1973 the mandatory unionization of transportistas (truck, bus, and taxi owners and drivers). In the meantime, Banzer continued the policy of campesino patronage, but did not hesitate to send in the army in 1974 to crush a road blockade staged by campesinos in several locations in Cochabamba to protest the inflationary effects of the devaluation of the Bolivian peso. When the army marched against the campesinos, the latter thought that, following Barrientos's style, there was going to be a dialogue between them and the army. Instead, many unarmed campesinos were massacred by soldiers in the Cochabamba blockades in Epizana, Totora, Tolata, and Melga. The exact number of men, women, and children killed has never been known.[10]

Manuel Solís, a campesino from Tiraque who witnessed the massacre and wrote an account of what he saw in Totora, expresses his feelings about the violence of the state in no uncertain terms:

As a member of the Tiraque Central, I went to observe what had happened in that place, but I had such sorrow and such tremendous suffering to see my brother campesinos, who were like in a corral, surprised like slaves, the poor peasants of Totora. . . . I think their bodies had blown in all directions, and the heads of some had remained stuck on the walls like plaster. . . . The soldiers and the *comandantes*, I imagine, have killed the campesinos as if they were street dogs. They did not treat them like human beings or as parts of God, but we are all made by God in Bolivia. In the year 1974, they treated us campesinos like slaves, not like human beings. This can be remembered one day when the government will be on our side. This history should never be forgoten in Bolivia, and so much of this history remains engraved in the heads of campesinos.

Several years later, after I read Manuel's account, he told me that witnessing the direct intervention of the state was the event that changed the course of his life, his interpretation of the present, and his vision of the future. He is now one of the most militant leaders in the region.

The massacre was also a turning point in the state-campesino alliance, since it divided the peasantry into two broad factions. One faction, defining itself as "nationalist," remained in the Confederación Sindical de Trabajadores Campesinos de Bolivia (CSTCB), which still supports the Pacto Militar-Campesino. The other dissident faction organized the Confederación Sindical Unica de Trabajadores Campesinos de Bolivia (CSUTCB) as a parallel confederation in 1974. This faction opposes the military-campesino alliance and instead supports the campesino-worker-student alliance, and is a member of the Central Obrera Boliviana (the Bolivian central organization of labor).[11] The campesino-state alliance was thus broken up, but after the "pacification" of labor and the government control of all unions, General Banzer did not have to rely on the peasantry for political support.

It was in this context of newly consolidated state power that the state was able to put new forms of economic pressure on campesinos and carry out successfully the development strategy begun by the

MNR. The principal aim of this strategy was rapid economic growth. The expectations of liberal MNR ideologues were that agrarian reform would transform campesinos into agricultural entrepreneurs and that agricultural production would increase. To the dismay of the government, however, the opposite occurred. Immediately after the reform, agricultural production declined in Bolivia.[12] The government's reaction to this "crisis" was prompt: in a memorandum to the campesino federations, it informed them that it was their "patriotic duty" to intensify production in "defense of the agrarian reform, the government, and the National Revolution."[13] The memorandum suggested that agricultural production had declined because some campesinos were lazy and were thus responsible for the economic crisis and the rampant inflation Bolivia was experiencing at the time. This myth of the lazy but "free" campesino still pervades the perception of bureaucrats who implicitly or explicitly blame campesino "traditionality" for Bolivia's underdevelopment.

In 1956, the mayor of Tiraque received the following telegram:

For the last time please inform campesinos in your jurisdiction to initiate immediate cultivation of all available land. If they need seed, the Ministerio de Asuntos Campesinos will provide it, payable in easy installments. Parcels of land not cropped will REVERT TO THE STATE and be distributed among those interested in cultivating the land. This notification should be transmitted to provincial authorities and sindicatos agrarios. FOR THE NATIONAL REVOLUTION. (AAT: November 17, 1956) (emphasis in the original)

The state wanted campesinos to increase both production and the amount of goods brought to the market. Threats were accompanied by the promotion of marketplaces exempted from municipal taxes to encourage campesinos to participate more in the market. To this effect, the government issued Decree No. 03501 on August 8, 1953, authorizing the establishment of these tax-free markets (or *ferias francas*), "where campesinos will sell, freely and directly, the goods they produce at prices set by supply and demand" (AAT: Correspondencia). This was hardly necessary, however, because most campesino households in Bolivia, principally those in the areas near the cities of La Paz and Cochabamba, increased market participation and contributed to opening new marketplaces and to building access roads to the markets and their villages.[14] Since the late 1960s, too, campesinos in Cochabamba responded positively to state and private promotional campaigns for chemical fertilizer which were carried out through on-site demonstrations and distribution of free fertilizer.[15] Although few campesinos turned entrepreneurs, almost all of them have become more dependent on commodity markets, yet in an increasingly asymmetric and subordinate position. At the center of this intensification of petty commodity production, the state focused its small capital investment on agriculture not in the campesino regions, but in the lowlands.

Since the revolution, the state has sought to achieve economic growth through the reactivation of the mining sector, "modernization" of agriculture, and development of the Oriente, or eastern lowlands, with the production of export crops and import-substituting crops and livestock. Most of the public investment in agriculture (on average only 3.2 percent of total expenditure) has been directed toward the Oriente "in the form of roads [two all-weather roads, one to Santa Cruz and the other to Chapare, completed in 1956 and 1965, respectively], credit, price support programs, colonization projects, and the promotion of mechanized, modern agriculture" (Wennergren and Whitaker 1975:40). The allocation of credit best exemplifies the state's priorities for rural development. From 1964 to 1979, the Banco Agrícola de Bolivia (BAB)[16] granted about half of its total loan volume (49.9 percent) to medium- and large-size farmers, most of whom were in the department of Santa Cruz; 41.5 percent to associations, groups and societies; and about 8.6 percent to campesinos.[17] The distribution of credit changed somewhat in the mid-1970s when USAID financed the Second Agricultural Refinancing Fund (FRA-2) and other similar lines of credit designed to provide credit to small farmers and cooperatives. Since then, more credit has been directed to campesino households. In 1982, for example, campesinos received about 32 percent of the total loan volume. Nevertheless these new credit lines involve long and complicated bureaucratic procedures that raise the borrower's transaction costs and often result in the untimely delivery of credit (Ladman et al. 1979). Few private banks have made loans to small producers because few campesinos have land titles to deposit in the banks to guarantee the loans. As Ladman et al. (1979: 8) indicate, it is fairly obvious that the state has used credit "As a political instrument or in response to political pressures brought on the government by individuals and groups, typically medium-sized and large-sized farmers in the Oriente. Often loans made on this basis have become delinquent. In some cases, political considerations would not permit banking institutions to press for repayment."[18] Many of these state-financed loans were diverted to speculative enterprises and to the illegal processing of cocaine paste (cf. Gill 1987). Thus, by allocating resources unevenly to different classes and regions, the state contributed to establishing new conditions for the accumulation of wealth in Bolivia. The agricultural enterprises and the cocaine industry rely on campesino households for the supply of a cheap, seasonal labor force, even though most campesinos in Bolivia have intensified production and increased their participation in the market as producers and consumers.[19]

There is no question that campesinos in Tiraque also have intensified both production and their engagement in commodity markets since the agrarian reform. But to understand this process, we should move beyond the market because, as Eric Wolf (1983:48–49) points out,

The modern neo-orthodox economics, which takes its departure not from classes and relationships among classes, but from 'firms' (including households), variously endowed with factors and services. This initial endowment is taken as given. Interest focuses not on classes of "firms" and possible conflict among such classes, but on their encounter in the market place where they exchange the factors and services in their possession against economic inducement sufficient to initiate such exchange, . . . rent appears not as a transfer of labour, product, or money to holders of economic or political power by virtue of existing relations of production, but as an inducement to firms holding the scarce factors of real estate or housing to release them for exchange. Such usage can illuminate consumer behavior and consumer satisfaction in price-setting markets. It cannot, of itself, lead to an adequate anatomy of society.

In the first two decades following the revolution in Tiraque, few campesinos took their crops and animals to the improvised market that operated in the town square on Sundays. Instead, they sold or bartered their products in their villages, at the houses of merchants in town, or in the market of Punata, where they obtained better prices. On several occasions, to capture revenues from these exchanges and to "protect" peasant interests, the mayor of Tiraque issued ordinances instructing peasants to take their crops and animals to Tiraque, forbidding them to sell to merchants or traders in places other than in the local marketplace. Fines or "heavy" export taxes were to be imposed if they did not comply with these new regulations (AAT: Ordenanzas Municipales, January 15, 1955, February 5 1956, August 9, 1956). These threats and pleas were to no avail, because involvement with traders and merchants meant more to campesinos than the exchange of goods. Simmons (1974) shows that a considerable number of households in hacienda Palca had spent all their savings and become indebted in lawsuits against the former hacendado after the agrarian reform. They, as well as many others in Tiraque, needed "help" when they lacked seed or manure to initiate production in their recently acquired land, or to cover unexpected expenditures, and they obtained this help from those who were economically more powerful than themselves: itinerant rural traders and merchants who traveled on foot or in trucks to the villages to engage in barter or commercial exchange, or from merchants in town. Venustiano Villarroel and his wife, powerful merchants of Punata, for instance, "helped" campesinos in a village in Tiraque by taking their crops on their truck, without charge, to Punata, driving them directly to their own house where they purchased the crops themselves, at prices lower than in the marketplace. They also helped villagers by, without charge, transporting sand and rocks to build a school. This couple also established sharecropping agreements with campesino households and purchased cash crops in the village (ibid., 82). Both Villarroel and his wife were still operating in cantón Tiraque at the time of my fieldwork, and I was able to hear many stories about this couple. These ties of dependence, which developed immediately after the rural poor became landowning campesinos, I argue, have underwritten processes of social differentiation among campesinos and simultaneously led to intensified campesino participation in markets (cf. Warman 1978).

Indeed, since the reform campesinos have brought more land under the plow and, since the early 1970s, some 70 percent of the households have also adopted the use of chemical fertilizer and pesticides for potato cropping. This has inevitably forced campesinos into more intense participation in markets and a heightened dependency on credit. Not only have campesinos increased the volume of products they sell, but new products have also been brought into the market in recent years. Apart from potatoes, the most important crops are fava beans and barley, both of which used to be produced mainly for household consumption. Campesinos also purchase more products now than they did formerly. Notably, they buy chemical inputs and agro-industrial commodities such as flour, sugar, animal fat, cooking oil, macaroni, sugar cane alcohol, and rice. They also buy heating alcohol, propane gas, kerosene, soap, bread, salt, matches, chicha, vegetables, and fruit that they do not grow themselves. They also spend money on clothing, school equipment, and medicine.[20] The number of rural markets that have sprung up in the countryside is yet another indication of the increased participation of campesinos in the market (Barnes de Marschall and Torrico 1971). This participation, however, has taken place in a situation of continuous undervaluation of campesino-produced goods vis-à-vis industrial commodities that household members purchase in the market. Between 1973 and 1977, for instance, the price of agricultural products increased by 300 percent, while the price of industrial goods increased by 500 percent (Cipca 1979). From 1979 to 1984 the price of potatoes increased by 186 percent and the price of agricultural inputs by 431 percent.[21]

Confronted with this situation in which they see the purchasing power of their cash crops decrease, campesinos need more money in order to produce, to buy the necessities of daily life and, ultimately, to reproduce their social relations and themselves.

This process of commoditization or "simple reproduction squeeze," which Bernstein (1979:427) summarizes as increasing costs of production and decreasing returns to labor brought about by intensification of land and labor, use of expensive means of production, and deteriorating terms of exchange, has, of course, been uneven in Bolivia, affecting diverse regions in different ways. In the central valleys and potato-producing highlands of Cochabamba, the commodization of campesino households has been particularly pronounced since the 1970s. Yet, rather than explaining this outcome by the impending penetration of capitalism, I argue that the main force for the setting of these conditions is to be sought in the emergence of new forms of domination of the peasantry. In order to understand this social process, it is necessary to examine both the relations of work and production and the ways in which culture intertwines with the labor process.

Chapter 4
Production, Sharecropping, and Class

> In the case of small landed property the illusion is fostered still more that land itself possesses value and thus enters as capital into the price of production of the product. . . . The expenditure of money-capital for the purchase of land, then, is not an investment of agricultural capital. It is a decrease *pro tanto* in the capital which small peasants can employ in their own sphere of production. It reduces *pro tanto* the size of their means of production and thereby narrows the economic basis of reproduction. It subjects the small peasant to the money-lender, since credit proper occurs but rarely in this sphere in general.
>
> (Marx 1894/1977:810)

Campesinos perceive the revolution and agrarian reform as events that have given them basic freedoms and autonomy. To preserve this autonomy and to insure the reproduction of the household as a viable economic unit, campesinos maintain, as much as possible, direct production outside the influence of the market. In order to do this, most households rely on non-monetarized household and extra-household labor to undertake direct production and, if needed, borrow land, animals, manure, and chemical fertilizer rather than hiring or purchasing these factors of production. Like the pathways campesinos built instead of roads after the revolution, these strategies serve to preserve a relative and delicate autonomy. Marginal as this possibility may be, it is "important not only for their produce, but for their direct and immediate satisfactions and for the felt reality of an area of control over one's own immediate labour" (Williams 1973:103). These strategies, however, may also be traversed in both directions—away and into roads and markets—thus revealing a central paradox: to preserve their autonomy, campesinos must intensify production, sell a larger share of their produce in the market, sell their labor, and engage in other nonfarm activities, intensifying, at the same time, their dependence on a new merchant class.

It is precisely because campesinos participate in commodity markets that most households exchange and borrow resources from each other, and this, of course, leads to an increased dependence between households. On this widespread basis, more elaborate and dependent forms of borrowing develop, such as usury and compañía (a particular sharecropping relation which I will describe below), which is the most common form for borrowing seed, manure, chemical fertilizer, and insecticides to produce cash crops. By engaging in this form of productive arrangement, outlawed in 1953 by an agrarian reform decree (but still continuing), some households relinquish part of their cash crop while averting money indebtedness. At the same time, however, they underwrite the new terms of their own subordination by entering into alliances with an emergent merchant class.

This chapter examines the manner in which households have access to and exchange resources and instruments of labor in production; these exchanges form the material and social-relational basis of these alliances in production. This perspective will serve to analyze ongoing processes of internal differentiation and class formation within the peasantry in a context where the ideology of equality and reciprocity permeates most social relations, and where the ambiguities of domination, resistance, and accommodation become most salient. Much of the following discussion pertains to the entire cantón Tiraque, but I will use case material from the sindicato agrario Sank'ayani to illustrate the argument in more detail.

The union Sank'ayani is formed by households from three adjacent localities: Sank'ayani, Huaylla Qhochi, and Qolqeqhoya/Churu.[1] Prior to agrarian reform, Sank'ayani was a large hacienda, Huaylla Qhochi and Qolqeqhoya/Churu were small haciendas, and Huaylla Qhochi was also a piquería. After reform, the union coalesced these three localities into the "community" Sank'ayani. The community, in the Cochabamba mountains at altitudes ranging from 3,500 to 4,000 meters above sea level, lies about fifteen kilometers from the town of Tiraque. The settlement is dispersed with houses standing at about half a kilometer from each other, except for clusters of houses belonging to married sons and daughters who live near their parents. The houses are built of stone and adobe with thatched roofs. Pathways built by campesinos connect every house with the road to Tiraque, which was built in the 1950s by the Junta de Propietarios de Vandiola in its effort to reach the yungas by truck. Sank'ayani also has an elementary school and an unfinished dispensary.

Several reasons contributed to my selection of this sindicato: its good agricultural yields, relatively large number of animals (principally sheep), and marked differentiation between households which originates in the differential control of labor, land, and animals. This control allows some households to produce and sell a larger volume of agricultural products in the market than the average household. At the time of my research, there were eight truck owners in Sank'ayani, the largest number in any one village in Tiraque.

My understanding of the processes of rural differentiation and class formation within villages is rooted in an analysis of the organization of work and the social relations of subsistence and petty commodity production.[2]

Household Composition and Labor

Sank'ayani has seventy households and a total population of 419 inhabitants, 52.7 percent males and 47.3 females. Household size ranges from one to eighteen members, with a mean size of 7.4 members per household and a median of five members. The composition of households and family forms are quite varied, as can be appreciated in Table 9. There are two one-member or non-nuclear/conjugal households, one a bachelor and the other a single woman who, nevertheless, has a married daughter who lives elsewhere. These two households do not have any land, and its members are very poor. Nuclear families are the most numerous (44); two of these are formed by husband and wife and adopted children. There are eight extended families that have been divided into two groups: one group has at least one married child living with his spouse and her children in his parents' household; in the other group, all the children are single except one or more daughters who have their own illegitimate children (often adopted by their husbands should the women marry). A similar distinction has been made for stem families. This family form, encompassing a total of sixteen households, includes single and widowed parents living with their children, and in seven cases, with their grandchildren, too; grandparents with young grandchildren; grandparents with a married grandson, his wife, and child; and widowed grandparents living with one grandchild. Six of these households are headed by women.

Most young couples and some of the old live in *concubinato* or common law marriage and perform the civil wedding after several years of cohabitation. Only those couples that have attained a comfortable

TABLE 9. Family Forms and Household Composition, Sank'ayani, 1984.

Family Form	Headed by Women	Household Composition
One Member		
1		Bachelor
1	1	Single woman
Nuclear		
1		Husband and wife
41		Husband/wife and children
2		Husband/wife and adopted children
Extended		
4		Husband/wife/married children and grandchildren
4		Husband/wife/single children and grandchildren
Stem		
2	2	Mother and children
1		Widowed father and son
5	2	Widowed parent/married children and grandchildren
2	1	Widowed parent/single children and grandchildren
1		Grandparents/married grandchild and great-grandchildren
2		Grandparents with grandchildren
3	1	Widowed grandparent with one grandchild

Source: Author's census.

enough economic situation to allow them to celebrate their marriage have a religious wedding ceremony. Some couples wait from seven to fifteen years before they can afford their wedding celebration, and others never go through with the religious ceremony. Men and women from Sank'ayani find marriage partners within the locality, in neighboring villages, and for a few, from more distant villages and regions. Out of fifty-five couples, sixteen only involved men and women from Sank'ayani; thirteen men and seven women were married to people from neighboring villages; and four men and seven women found their partners in more distant places. There were also eight families, most of them old former colonos, in which both men and women were born in other villages, since there were few colonos who had been born on the haciendas where they were settled at the time of reform.

The preferred residence pattern is neolocal, although it is often the case that the woman moves to the household or village of her partner, where they generally live with his parents until they can establish their own household. There are a few instances of men moving into the village of their wives. The choice of place of residence ultimately depends on the availability of land. When land is scarce and all children have married, parents either provide them with parcels of land on which to build their own homes, while they work on the parents' land and share the harvest, or they might give them a pre-mortem inheritance. Some land is kept by the parents until they die, when it is generally inherited by the heirs who remained in the household taking care of the old couple, or the surviving member of the couple. Since grandchildren often move into their grandparents' homes, or remain there to help with household chores and agricultural production when their mothers marry, they are the ones to inherit movable and inmovable property not distributed previously. This practice is common among both poor and rich households, because the immediate concern of the grandparents is to have a young grandchild who can provide the labor necessary to carry out basic household chores.

The centrality of household labor for the viability of the campesino farm has been widely documented, but the manner in which shortages of labor are solved varies between households.[3] As we have seen, in Tiraque, grandchildren move into their grandparents' homes, childless couples adopt children of relatives or nonrelatives, and female heads of household with young children rely on male siblings or fictive kin for some tasks. All available labor is mobilized: children who have reached the age of five and the elderly also participate in productive activities.

The division of labor within the household is set along gender lines for certain activities that are mutually interdependent. Men are more directly involved in agriculture and the care of draft and traction animals, while women and children take care of the sheep and small animals. But the entire household participates in every step in the labor process. The rhythm of men's work is marked by the agricultural cycle. Work is intense at times, but there are also periods of free time. In contrast, the work of women never ends. They are the first to get up in the morning to prepare food for household members. Besides this and other household chores, women and children take the sheep to the grazing land, skirting through planted fields and taking care that the animals do not eat the crops. Every time a woman's hands might be unoccupied, she spins wool. This she later washes and dyes for men or older women to weave into *bayeta*, or rough cloth, which is used to make skirts and trousers or woven into ponchos, blankets, or sacks. Besides these everyday activities, women also participate in agricultural work. Except for plowing, which very few women do, they carry out any other activity related to planting and harvesting and prepare the food for the people working on the land. But the workloads of women both in and out of agriculture usually increase with the seasonal migration of men and younger members of the household, as well as when men pursue political careers, from which women are usually excluded, such as positions of leadership in local unions and other political institutions. From our perspective, drudgery characterizes the daily life of the women; few distractions break up their monotonous lives. The occasional ritual festivities celebrated in the village or household lead them to work even harder in the preparation of food. They make few visits to the marketplace and only occasionally exchange gossip during the church-sponsored meetings for mothers of infants or while they wash clothes in the rivers. On the other hand, most men attend union meetings twice a month, go to the marketplace more often than women, and play soccer every Sunday.

Except for eight households, which undertake all the steps in agricultural production by themselves because their plots of land are too small or because the work force of the household is sufficiently large, most households depend on extra-household labor to undertake agricultural activities requiring a large labor force. For this, they use a combination of different forms of labor exchange: *ayni*, or reciprocal labor exchange; payment in kind (the worker receiving a portion of the crop being harvested); occasional wages; and compañía or sharecropping (all these forms will be discussed below in more detail). *Minka*, or communal work, is another method of mobilizing labor to carry out tasks that benefit the entire village, such as the cleaning of irrigation canals, the upkeep and construction of roads and paths, and the building of the school and dispensary.

Land and Animals

Sank'ayani includes approximately 483 hectares of arable land, about half of it (272 hectares) fallow in 1984. Table 10 shows the distribution of land per household. Inequalities in land ownership originate from differences in the amount of land colonos, sharecroppers, and piqueros held in usufruct or owned prior to agrarian reform, from the unequal distribution of land by reform, and from land sales and purchases after reform.

The campesino union Sank'ayani affiliates members from three localities (Sank'ayani, Huaylla Qhochi, and Qolqeqhoya/Churu). In the union, there are then former colonos from the large hacienda

TABLE 10. Distribution of Land by Household in
Sank'ayani, 1984.[a]

Size of Landholding	Frequency Distribution	
	N	%
0	15	22.7
0.1–1	4	6.1
1.1–3	12	18.2
3.1–5	6	9.1
5.1–10	10	15.2
10.1–15	8	12.1
15.1–50	11	16.6
TOTAL	66	100.0

Source: Author's census.
Mean = 7.5 hectares
Median = 3.5 hectares

[a]Information on the amount of land held by four households was incomplete and could not be included in the table.

Sank'ayani, former sharecroppers from the small hacienda Huaylla Qhochi, sharecroppers from the hacienda Qolqeqhoya/Churu, and piqueros from Huaylla Qhochi. Before the reform, the size of landholdings of piqueros from Huaylla Qhochi ranged from eight to twelve hectares, ownership of which was recognized as theirs by the agrarian reform judges. These piquerías bordered the haciendas of Huaylla Qhochi, Qolqeqhoya/Churu, and Sank'ayani, which were all affected by reform. Huaylla Qhochi was declared a medium-sized hacienda; the hacendado had sixty-four hectares recognized, which he later sold to campesinos, and about twenty hectares were distributed among three sharecroppers, each one receiving on average 6.6 hectares of land. Qolqeqhoya/Churu was also declared a medium-sized hacienda, and the seven sharecroppers settled on it were granted an average of 2.5 hectares each, although the hacendado remained in control of the entire property until 1984, when he sold most of the land to rich campesinos (see Chapter 3). The hacienda Sank'ayani, the largest of the three, was declared a latifundium and all the land was distributed among thirty-five households, each receiving on average seventeen hectares (see Table 8, Chapter 3); furthermore, fourteen of these colonos also owned lands in other localities prior to reform. Thus, former colonos of Sank'ayani, on the whole, have larger amounts of land than former sharecroppers and piqueros.

Although there are considerable differences in the amount of land each household controls today, all have access to land and, with one exception, all cultivate the land. Access to land is possible through loans from parents or grandparents or through various sharecropping agreements. Of the fifteen landless households, four were settled on the former hacienda Qolqeqhoya/Churu as sharecroppers, providing half of the harvest as ground rent, and one old woman, together with her granddaughter, took care of the former hacendado's sheep, for which they received food and a minimal monthly "wage." Members of two other households sharecropped on the land of a rich campesino who provided them with only land in exchange for a third of the harvest. A bachelor received land in usufruct from a rich household in exchange for labor, and, finally, seven households worked on land received on loan from parents. All were young couples and single women with children who had not yet inherited land. Landed households acquired land through the agrarian reform (27.3 percent), inheritance (18.2 percent), purchase (16.4 percent), *dotación* involving the granting of non-distributed land from the former hacienda Sank'ayani by the sindicato agrario to households (3.6 percent), and by a combination of all of the above (34.5 percent). All the farms consist of noncontiguous small or medium-sized parcels of land, only some of which are irrigated. Only three households do not have access to irrigation; forty-one have both irrigated and nonirrigated land; and twenty-five have all of their land under irrigation. In addition to this land, thirty-one households have land in nearby localities. The land was acquired by purchase or inheritance, or it had belonged before marriage to one member of the household.

Ownership of animals also varies among households (see Table 11). Sheep comprise the largest number of animals, and most households have them, since they are an important source of protein and wool. They provide the manure needed for cultivation, are not so costly to maintain as traction and draft animals, and may be sold easily in times of need. Thirty-two households (46 percent) do not own oxen, and seven of these households do not have any of the other animals listed on the table; but even households without any large animals (such as oxen and horses, which are essential for cropping, threshing, and transport) still have access to them through reciprocal exchanges or various forms of share systems. The most common for oxen and pigs is *al partir*, an agreement whereby the owner of young oxen gives them to somebody else to raise until the animals reach the age when they can be harnessed to the plow. After the ox reaches maturity, its owner generally sells it, recovering the original capital invested in the purchase and dividing the rest of the money with the person who took care of the animal. Twenty-one households have one or two oxen belonging to others in partnership, and the remaining eleven borrow

TABLE 11. Distribution of Animals by Household in Sank'ayani, 1984.

	Number of Households With or Without Animals			
Number of Animals	Sheep	Oxen	Cow	Horse/ Donkey
0	7	32	7	7
1–4	0	32	27	35
5–9	1	5	3	1
10–14	11	1	0	1
15–19	4	0	0	0
20–29	15	0	0	0
30–49	16	0	0	0
50–99	13	0	0	0
100–149	0	0	0	
<150	3	0	0	0
Total Number of Animals[a]	2,551	121	56	76

Source: Author's census.

[a] In addition to these animals, there were 99 pigs, 280 hens, 84 guinea pigs, 9 llamas, and 30 other animals (ducks, pigeons, rabbits).

oxen from others when they need the animals for plowing. Some of the oxen given out in share belong to households outside Sank'ayani.

Share systems for sheep are somewhat different. One, called *con precio* (with price), involves caring for and grazing someone else's sheep to receive in exchange half of the animal's wool, half of the lambs born to ewes, and all the manure. Another form of sheep-share agreement involves caring for the animals as a favor to a relative or friend. In all forms of animal share systems, the partnership always involves a rich campesino or townsperson and a poor household unable to buy oxen, sheep, or pigs. At a basic level, the relationship is unequal, because the owner of the animals does not spend any money or labor in their care, but at the same time, poor campesinos have access to expensive draft animals which they cannot buy or, as is the case with sheep, it enables them to increase slowly their own flock of sheep. In both cases, the poor also have access to wool and manure. Through share agreements, then, most households have their own or somebody else's animals in a share system: one or two oxen and a horse or donkey, as well as a variable number of sheep, cows, pigs, guinea pigs, poultry, and the ever-present guard dogs.

These agreements are not devoid of tensions, however. Sheep owners often complain about their partners taking advantage of them, because they often sell the sheep but claim that the animals died;

others doubt whether the money they receive from the sale of oxen or pigs really represents half of their share.

Production and Rural Differentiation

The differential access to labor, land, and animals by households and the manner in which households exchange, lend, and borrow these resources from each other in production will serve to unravel the logic of borrowing and the process of social differentiation within the locality.

The main crops cultivated in Sank'ayani are, in order of importance according to the volume cultivated and the number of households that cultivate them, potatoes, broad beans, oats, barley, oca (*Oxalis tuberosa*), papalisa (*Ullucus tuberosus*), peas, tarwi (*Lupinus tauri*), quinoa (*Chenopodium quinoa*), and wheat. Only potatoes and beans are sold in the market; oats are produced for animal fodder and the rest are grown for household consumption and barter exchange. Potatoes are the most important crop and the one that marks the beginning of the crop rotation cycle. Three potato harvests are possible in a year when irrigation is available: *mishka* (early harvest), *chawpi mishka* (middle harvest), and *jatun tarpuy* (large harvest). These, of course, have different planting seasons, beginning in June and ending in December, and after a six-month cycle the plant is ready for harvest from December to June. The following year, broad beans are planted in the parcel of land where potatoes were planted the year before. The third year, barley, oats, tarwi, papalisa, oca, or a combination of these crops are planted in the same parcel of land. The fourth year, the plot of land is left fallow for a number of years, if the farm has sufficient cultivable land to allow this. The planting season for grains extends from August to December, and the cutting, threshing, and winnowing takes place between March and July. Leguminous crops are planted between May and August and harvested between January and June. The agricultural cycle thus extends throughout the year with periods of more intensive work. The busiest months are April and May, when everybody is harvesting jatun tarpuy potatoes. June and July are also busy months, with the threshing and winnowing of grains, preparation of land for the next planting season, and the making of *ch'uño* (freeze-dried potatoes) that can be preserved for many years.[4] By November, potatoes begin to flower, but this is the hungry season (after planting and six months before the harvest), and the time when there is less work in the fields.

Domestic units fully utilize all available household labor to undertake agricultural production. Households such as those headed by females with young children or those requiring additional labor for some activities, such as the potato harvest or the threshing of grain, depend on extra-family labor. Although various forms of labor exchange are used, ayni, the reciprocal lending of labor from one household to another, is the most important for planting, whereas *paga*, or payment in kind, is used more for harvesting potatoes and threshing grain. A paga of potatoes amounts to a fourth of a sack (a sack weighs between 100 and 120 kilograms) for each day's work. Only a few households pay wages. In money terms, the paga earns the laborer more money than the daily wage although, in both instances, laborers receive food, cigarettes, coca, chicha, and occasionally lodging. Yet, not everybody can be hired as a paga laborer, because this type of relation is based on long-term friendship and *compadrazgo* (fictive kin tie) relations established between members of two households. Paga laborers come from the locality, nearby villages, or from the Valle Alto. Those from the locality generally work for others for a paga when their own production does not satisfy their household consumption or cash needs. Many also work for a paga to obtain the seed to plant in the following planting season, because they are too poor to reserve seed from that allotted for consumption or because their harvest has not been good. Yet others exchange paga as a reciprocal form of labor relation. Campesinos from the Valle Alto, on the other hand, harvest potatoes in Tiraque[5] in order to supplement their own smaller harvest and to obtain better seed for planting[6] or for sale. Very few households in Sank'ayani pay wages, although in other villages this is more common.

The importance of potatoes in the household economy cannot be overemphasized. Campesinos take particular interest and care when farming potatoes, since it requires the largest investment of labor and inputs. Potatoes are their main staple as well as their principal means of market and barter exchange. To minimize risk of frost, disease, and drought, campesinos plant more than one potato variety in each plot of land, since each variety responds differently to these hazards.[7] All households add manure to the land. Most households (73 percent) use chemical fertilizer, and all apply insecticides to the plants. Chemical inputs or manure are not used for any of the other crops except oca and papalisa. These are generally planted together with potatoes; if they are planted separately, few households add manure or fertilizer.

Cipca (1983) estimated the amount of labor expended in a year for the production of potatoes. Potato mishka, which is produced with irrigation, requires the largest amount of labor per cropped hectare of land, namely, 218 days; jatun tarpuy, or non-irrigated potato, takes

197 days of labor.[8] This work is carried out with a rudimentary technology, agricultural tools consisting of steel-tipped, ox-drawn, wooden plows and shovels, picks, and hoes. There are only three tractors in Tiraque, one of which is in Sank'ayani. But only those households with large, leveled plots of land can make use of tractors if they are willing, or able, to spend money to hire them.

To illustrate the above account, the different activities in which campesinos engage, as well as the amount of inputs and labor they invest to produce potato mishka in one hectare of land, will be described in more detail. Campesinos use from ten to twelve sacks of potato seed of 100 kilograms each for one hectare of land, incorporate some 250 kilograms of chemical fertilizer in the soil and two truckloads, of 4,200 kilograms each, of manure and from 1.0 to 1.5 liters of insecticide. Ideally, six months before the planting of potatoes, the land is prepared by clearing stones from the land—an arduous and back-breaking task. Then the land is opened with the plow several times in a criss-cross fashion. For a hectare of land, this work, carried out by one man using one plow, takes about fifteen days. In practice, however, the time is generally shortened with the use of two men and two plows.

The planting of potatoes is generally completed in one or two days by at least ten people and two plows. One *yunta* (a plow with oxen) begins the planting by opening the land in a straight furrow. It is followed by a man or boy in charge of the chemical fertilizer, which is dropped into the furrow. Immediately after comes the *mujiri*, generally a woman, who carries the potato seed in a cloth tied around her neck and drops it into the furrow at an even pace and distance. Next comes the *guaniri*, the person in charge of dropping manure into the furrow, on top of the seed. Finally, the other plowteam closes the furrow. Except for the plowmen, each of the individuals working in the field has an assistant (generally a young boy) who refills the sacks used to place the fertilizer or the cloth in which the women carry the seed. Besides the laborers participating directly in the planting, there are also one or two women preparing food, which everybody shares twice a day at mid-morning and at about two in the afternoon. Food, chiefly potatoes and broad beans, is provided and served by the owner of the land along with coca, chicha, and cigarettes.

Between September and January, the following activities must be carried out: *aporque*, or the loosening of the soil around the plants; weeding; irrigation; spraying of plants with insecticides; and foliage cutting (a few weeks before the harvest).[9] The loosening of the soil can be carried out in one day if three plowteams and eight men work at it. Weeding requires six persons for a day of work if the weeds are not abundant. The plants are sprayed three or four times during this period; each treatment requires the work of one person for a whole day. The number of times the land is irrigated depends on the rains, but fields generally require five days of irrigation, a task that can be carried out by one person each day.

The harvest requires the largest number of workers, about fifty, if the work is carried out in one day, which is seldom the case. This is probably the most strenuous activity, involving men, adolescent and younger boys, and sometimes women, all of whom dig potatoes with picks or hoes, picking potatoes up and throwing them onto a pile nearby. Potatoes are left on the field for sorting and then placed into sacks. Campesinos separate out those potatoes that will be used for seed the following year; then the remaining potatoes are selected according to size.[10] Sacks of potatoes are then carried on horses or by truck to the house or, in the case of some households, directly to markets. Table 12 summarizes the above description and provides an estimate of inputs and costs of production for one hectare of potato mishka.

Harvest yields on the farm are low, and it is difficult, or next to impossible, to provide average yields because of variability from year to year. Potato yields range from $1:5$ to $1:8$ and, in exceptional years, $1:10$.[11]

TABLE 12. Labor and Inputs Expended in One Hectare of Potatoes[a] in Sank'ayani, 1983.

Inputs	Costs
Seed 10 sacks (100 kilograms at $b28,600 each)	$b286,000
Fertilizer (250 kilograms at $b11,500/kg. each)	57,500
Manure (2 truckloads of 4,200 kg. each at $b25,000 each)	50,000
Insecticide (1.5 liters at $b7,550 per liter)	11,325
Transport of manure from valley to village	50,000
Labor[b]	
Preparation of land, 15 workers	
Planting, 2 teams oxen, 10 workers	
Aporque, 3 teams oxen, 8 workers	
Weeding, 6 workers	
Disinfection, 3 workers	
Irrigation, 5 workers	
Harvest, selection and transport (on own horses), 50 workers	

Sources: Author's census and interviews.

[a]Other expenses not included in the table are the food, coca, cigarettes, and chicha consumed by workers while they work.

[b]Labor is not accounted for in money terms by campesinos.

To estimate income and wealth differences among households, development institutions and researchers often estimate the cost of production of crops.[12] There are, however, many problems involved in the calculation of costs in an economy that makes extensive use of the non-monetarized labor of men, women, and children. To solve this problem, researchers assign a wage value to the labor expended by the household in production and a market value to inputs not bought in the market, such as manure, and estimate income according to the market price of the entire harvest. But nothing could be more distant from reality, because campesinos do not compute labor, and often, instead of working the estimated eight hours, they work either for many more hours in fewer days, or for fewer hours per day over a much longer time. Nor do campesinos sell their entire crops, but rather consume a large proportion of it, often harvesting just enough potatoes to put inside the pot so that the actual yield is lower than the one usually reported. Campesinos use part of the harvest for barter and gifts, too.

To add to the problem, calculations of inputs and costs vary according to the criteria used by the researcher. In other words, the costs of production estimated by agronomists are often based on inputs and quantities that they suggest will yield better results, but these are generally not used at all by campesinos or, if they are, they are used only in smaller amounts unless they are cultivating "demonstration plots" under the immediate direction of agronomists. The problem becomes even more acute when one attempts to estimate the cost of production of animals, because the labor expended in raising animals consists mainly of the labor of women and children, which is considered even less of an expenditure than the work of men. Yet the raising of cattle and sheep involves a considerable daily expenditure of labor, since the animals are taken to distant grazing lands and care is taken that they do not trample the planted fields and eat the crops. Cattle are tied and left unattended until early evening, but during the dry season, when grasses are scarce, the cattle feed on oats, which need to be especially cultivated as fodder. Sheep need constant surveillance from the women or children in whose charge they are placed. The labor invested in these activities is not reflected at all in the price of the animal when it is sold at the market. Thus, attempts to calculate precise costs of production and income are nearly impossible, since it involves imputing monetary values to noncommoditized factors of production.

A further complication is that factors of production themselves often do not belong to the household that is making use of them but are borrowed from other households, and these loans entail a claim on the labor of those borrowing them. We have already seen that fifteen landless households farmed land loaned by their parents or owned by others and sharecropped. Campesinos also borrow animals for plowing and obtain sheep and pigs in share systems. These animals provide part of the manure to fertilize the soil, but manure requirements are generally larger and campesinos need to complement their own supply with manure they acquire from campesino households in the Valle Alto. Manure is cheaper if purchased, but most households prefer to exchange four sacks of potatoes, delivered after the harvest, for a truckload of manure.

Labor, too, is widely borrowed or exchanged between households. Although all households make use of reciprocal and paga work relations at some stage in the production process, differences exist in the manner in which households participate in these relations. Rich campesinos, for instance, employ laborers in paga work relations, but they never work as paga laborers themselves. They also establish a network of reciprocal work relations with several households, but while poor campesinos provide their own labor, the rich do not reciprocate with labor, providing instead oxen for plowing or horses for threshing. On the whole, rich households own more animals than the average household. As many of the animals are given to poor campesinos in partnership, the rich do not invest any labor in the breeding of these animals. Thus the ownership of more than one pair of oxen indirectly translates into the potential for access to a larger labor force without incurring any labor, production, or money expenses. Even though the idiom of reciprocity persists in the community, it does not entail the exchange of the same service. This pattern of unequal exchanges and inequality is quite widespread in the Andes, as noted by several scholars (cf. Alberti and Mayer 1974; Orlove 1977; Painter 1991).

While inequality exists at the level of noncommoditized factors of production and exchanges, differences among households are exacerbated, or become more pronounced, once commodities are introduced in production and money is needed to obtain them. It will be recalled that in Sank'ayani, as in the entire cantón Tiraque, most campesinos add chemical fertilizer to the soil and insecticides to the plant when they produce cash crops, mainly potatoes. Rich campesinos purchase these imported chemical inputs in the market, while poor campesinos, who are generally short of money, obtain them by borrowing money, or through the more ubiquitous compañía or sharecropping agreements. Compañía contracts vary in each specific case, since they are established between two or, occasionally, three parties.[13] Broadly, there are two forms of sharecropping agreements. One which was widely used before agrarian reform involved an agreement between a hacendado or landowner who provided a parcel of land, as well as seed, to a landless household which, in turn, provided labor, manure, traction animals, and the plow. The harvest was then divided in two parts. This form of agreement continues to be used by landed townsfolk and three former hacendados who were able to maintain portions of their land. In this "modern" form, the landowner might provide, besides the land, all inputs except labor, or none at all, and then decide how the harvest will be divided. For the landless, this form of compañía is a way to have access to land and produce; for the landowner, compañía generates ground rent.

On the surface, the second and more ubiquitous compañía agreement is similar to the one just described, except that the terms are inverted. In this case, the landowner is a poor campesino who seeks a partner to overcome his or her lack of money to buy the necessary inputs for potato cropping. The campesino landowner provides all inputs available to the household, namely, land, labor, traction animals, and often manure or seed. The "capitalist" partner, in turn, provides chemical fertilizer, insecticides, and often seed. The harvest is divided according to the share of inputs each partner provides in the agreement, although the share received by the landowning campesino often depends on his degree of dependence or bargaining power. If the "capitalist" partner provides seed, the harvest is divided only after he recovers the seed advanced. Occasionally, sharecropping agreements are established among equals as a way of sharing costs and minimizing risk.[14]

The importance of compañía as the main means of producing cash crops may be illustrated with material from Sank'ayani. In the agricultural year 1982–83, for instance, thirty-four households undertook their own planting, thirty-two worked in compañía, and four households did not plant. The following year, after a drought, the proportion changed slightly: thirty-two households produced alone, and thirty-six in compañía. Most of these contracts were established to plant potatoes. Few households—mostly very dependent, landless households or households headed by women without working-age men—enter into these agreements to produce other crops destined for household consumption or as use values. In Sank'ayani only three households planted all their crops in compañía; women heads of household sharecropped potatoes and other crops, and few households sharecropped fava beans, oats, and barley on the irrigated land of others. In that year, however, the number of households producing in compañía in Sank'ayani was actually lower than in other villages, since two groups of about fifteen households each worked with a development agency, receiving low-interest credit from it to purchase fertilizer and insecticides.

All compañía agreements reduce risk, since the owner of the land is not usually required to repay the cost of the inputs supplied by the capitalist partner if the harvest is lost. In some few cases, however, the partners who advanced inputs might seek to get their share back by demanding that their partners provide their share from whatever sources they might find. Another advantage for the landowning campesinos is that as owners of the parcels of land and other means of production, they may choose their partners and lay a claim on a share of the harvest. In fact, campesinos generally seek a rich partner who is willing to establish a sharecropping agreement with them. After the drought, for instance, several households asked Trinidad, the richest man in Sank'ayani, to become their partner in potato cropping, and he, indeed, planted thirty-one sacks of potatoes in compañía, for which he also provided eleven truckloads of manure and 1,000 kilograms of fertilizer. The year before, he had only sharecropped one sack of potatoes. Whether Trinidad did this to take advantage of an increase in potato prices due to lower market supply or because he was "forced" to help other households in his and other villages that had lost most of their harvests and did not have enough money or seed to undertake the following season's planting, is difficult to determine. But this case shows that compañía does, indeed, shelter poor campesinos from collapse.

In most instances, however, compañía involves a relation of inequality: land and labor enter into this relation as noncommoditized factors of production, while chemical inputs are commodities, resulting in an unequal distribution of the harvest. Further, the campesinos temporarily yield control over *their* sharecropped parcels of land, since the decisions on how to plant as well as the quality of inputs used for cropping are generally made by the partner providing fertilizer, manure, and seed,[15] even though the landowners invest their labor, as well as the labor of other household members, with no compensation other than their share of the harvest.

Sharecropping turns out to be a two-faceted system. On the one hand, it enables poor households to produce cash crops with minimal risk, since they do not have to repay the cost of fertilizers and insecticides if the crop fails. On the other hand, rich campesinos produce in compañía to expand their access to arable land, labor, and produce, especially after economic downturns. Compañía means that the rich can ultimately regulate cash crop production and exchange, because compañía also opens up the possibility for the rich to buy the other half of the sharecropped harvest, thus enabling them to profit from the unequal exchange. Local differences in measurement also come into play here because merchants buy potatoes in the villages by volume rather than by weight.[16]

The logic of compañía as a relation of domination and accommodation becomes explicit when we examine in more detail household participation in the market. Naturally, the manner and the outcome of this encounter varies for each household. Some are able to profit, whereas for others a shortage of money remains a chronic problem, and it is in the light of this need for money and the attempt to minimize the risk of indebtedness that compañía makes sense. In the event of a failure of the harvest, or a sharp decline in market prices, at least poor households would not lose their land.

Market Participation and Nonfarm Activities

Apart from three very poor households that do not sell their harvest, the rest of the productive units in Sank'ayani sell or barter part of their crops and animals in the market.[17] In an agricultural year when the harvest has not been affected by drought, frost, insects, or diseases, campesinos sell on average about 40 percent of their cash crops, keep 40 percent for consumption and direct exchange, and set aside 20 percent as seed to be used in the next planting season. When the harvest is not good, as happened after the drought of 1982–83, most households sell very few or no agricultural products. At this time, campesinos have to eat even the seed they would have set aside for initiating the following year's productive cycle and sell animals to provide some of the necessary cash. Sheep and pigs are, in fact, the "savings account" of the household and, indeed, are called *qolqe cajitas* (little money boxes); their raising is thus viewed as an investment and a saving. But the drought had a negative effect on the price of animals. Too many households sold them not simply to obtain cash but because they could not feed them. Supply and, particularly, the timing of when these animals were sold—the "hungry season," after planting and six months before the harvest—drastically reduced the amount of money campesinos could obtain from their sales. Although market conditions had worsened for campesinos in 1982–83, we should recall that they always participate in the market in ever-increasing negative terms of exchange (see Chapter 3).

For most campesinos the principal means of earning additional money is through the sale of their labor. There are, however, as we have seen, few money-earning opportunities in Tiraque. This has obliged members of many poor households to leave their homes and settle elsewhere. The exact number of permanent migrants from Sank'ayani cannot be reported, since this topic was, unfortunately, not included in my census questionnaire. Family life histories indicate, however, that at least fifteen individuals migrated from Sank'ayani in the last fifteen years.[18] As is the case for the entire region, the poor migrated to Santa Cruz and Cochabamba to settle as colonizers or to work as wage laborers or maidservants. Members of rich households moved to Punata or the city to get a better education or to engage in transport, commerce, or other profitable enterprises. Most of the migrants maintain their ties with their village by keeping and cultivating their land, making frequent visits, and maintaining membership in the campesino union. Seasonal migration is much more common. About 63 percent of the households in Tiraque indicated that at least one member had migrated to Punata, Santa Cruz, Cochabamba, Chapare, or other rural regions in the department. Chapare attracts the bulk of the migrants, as more money can be made there in cocaine processing.

Until 1982, when a relatively more efficient control of coca marketing in Chapare was introduced to restrict the amount of coca that could be taken out of the area, many Tiraqueños went to Chapare to transport coca leaves on their backs, walking through the uninhabited yungas of Vandiola until they reached the Cochabamba-Santa Cruz road, where trucks were waiting to transport the leaves to the department of Santa Cruz. This illicit work took three to four days and paid about $b2,000 in 1982. At that time, the daily wage was $b100. After 1982, when the government lifted controls on the extraction of coca from Chapare, cocaine paste began to be produced in Chapare. Tiraqueños, along with people from other regions of Bolivia, worked for periods of from a few days to a month stamping on the coca leaves, the first phase in the processing of cocaine. Laborers were paid for an *entrada* (entry), that began around six in the evening and ended the next morning around four A.M., or when they had finished one tambor of coca.[19] Wages for this type of work increased with inflation, but they were always much higher than the daily wage. The payment for an entrada was raised considerably after July 1984, when army troops entered the yungas, supposedly to stamp out the production and commercialization of cocaine. The measure was, however, announced weeks in advance, so that when the troops reached Chapare, they were unable to find one drug dealer or a trace of the drug. All had moved to the Valle Alto, where almost every household was involved in cocaine production. After the troops left Chapare, cocaine production continued in the Valle Alto and in Chapare. Both places competed for laborers. In the Valle Alto, entradas earned $b150,000, while in Chapare they were paid $b400,000. This is a considerable sum, given the fact that the daily wage ran from $b8,000 to $b20,000.

Yet not everybody involved in cocaine production gets rich. A substantial amount of capital is necessary for the purchase of coca leaves, the price of which skyrocketed as demand increased and wages rose. The rural poor can only participate in cocaine production as menial laborers. They often take their working-age children and womenfolk with them, working for ten hours in the tropical heat, contracting diseases,[20] abandoning or neglecting their fields, which they plant or harvest late in the season, and overextending themselves to earn badly needed money. For many, Chapare was the only solution to starvation when they lost their crops and animals in the drought of 1982–83. But everything costs about ten times more in Chapare than in the rest of the department, and so the high wage they earned was drastically reduced by transport and food costs while they lived there. When the entrada paid $b7 million in January 1985, for instance, a bowl of soup cost $b1 million and a bottle of beer $b2 million.

Sources of Credit

Should the need for cash be immediate to cover, for instance, unexpected expenses related to sickness and death or other life-cycle rituals or, simply, if the household cannot release young men and women for seasonal wage labor, campesinos are often obliged to become indebted by borrowing money and goods from banks, moneylenders, and merchants.

Credit markets are well developed in Bolivia, but for several reasons, they are not available to most households.

1. A money loan always entails a land mortgage, and many campesinos still do not have land titles.
2. A mortgage involves risks which only the rich are willing to take.
3. Loans granted by banks have to be repaid within six months.
4. Since agrarian reform, the Bolivian state has virtually neglected small producers and channeled very few resources to this sector of the population (see Chapter 3), perpetuating the continuing need for other forms of credit among potato growers.

In Tiraque, Banco Agrícola de Bolivia provided a total of twenty-five loans from 1953 to 1980[21] and eighteen loans in the agricultural year 1984–85,[22] representing some 0.5 percent of the population. Partly filling the vacuum left by the state and private banks, several private institutions provide credit to Tiraqueños. The most important among these is the Cooperativa Integral de Servicios (CIS), located in the town of Punata, from which it operates throughout the Valle Alto and surrounding highlands. It functions as a credit union, extending credit for agricultural and livestock production, commerce, capital goods, and emergency loans. In 1984, 375 Tiraqueños, or some 10.6 percent of the total population, were members of the cooperative. The percentage of members who borrowed money in 1984 was even smaller, at 4.8 percent. The Cooperativa de Ahorro y Crédito San José, also located in the town of Punata, operates along similar lines to the Cooperativa Integral. Only recently established, it has few Tiraqueño members.

Four private development agencies, funded by European and North American agencies, also work in Tiraque. Although their stated goal is to promote association or communal work within entire villages to overcome the "limitations" of small-scale production, in practice they work only with small groups of campesinos willing to produce in association with others in a few villages. Once the groups are organized, initial credit, in the form of money with minimal interest rates or inputs, is extended to the group so that it may begin production. Although I lack information on the number of households reached by these institutions in 1984, an educated guess would set it at approximately 5 percent. Even more significant, most of the loan recipients belong to rich and middle-income households.

Credit may also be obtained from a wide variety of informal sources, including friends, relatives, merchants, truckers, and moneylenders. Small money loans from friends and relatives do not generally require the payment of interest. Campesinos refer to these loans, too, as ayni, stressing a reciprocal relationship in which the lender may become the borrower at another time. Sometimes, though, these loans are considered a favor for which free services, such as labor, a free ride, or free delivery of manure, are provided in exchange. Large money loans require the payment of interest. The legal monthly interest rate was 4 percent in July 1984 and 12 percent in December 1984. But the monthly rate charged by moneylenders in Tiraque ranged from 12 to 50 percent.[23] There is no good measure available to quantify the volume of informal credit, since most of these contracts are based on verbal agreements. Nevertheless, quantitative information on informal credit may be partially reconstructed from estimates provided by two Jueces de Mínima Cuantía.[24] According to their estimates, some 130 money loans with interest were extended in 1984—a figure that is probably not indicative of the actual volume of credit, since many of these loans are extended without a contract.[25]

Usury was, however, not as prevalent as I had expected. The main reason for its small incidence is the existence of other hidden forms of credit, such as *arriendo* (land lease), *anticresis* (property given in usufruct against a money loan), and *seña* (advanced harvest sale that also involves the mortgage of land or crops). In 1984, some forty individuals leased parcels of their land in regular leases and 360 in anticresis. This latter arrangement is a contract between two parties in which the owner of the land gives it in usufruct to another person for a specified amount of money and for a minimum of three years, so that the person who is farming the land may make use of the residual effects of the fertilizer placed on the soil at the beginning of the agricultural cycle. At the termination of the contract, the owner of the land returns in full the money advanced to him by the other party who, in turn, gives up the usufruct right to the land. It is often the case, however, that the landowner works on his own land given in anticresis as a laborer or sharecropper in lieu of interest. Seña is a cash advance or crop mortgage, entitling the lender to purchase agricultural products before they are even planted or harvested, and at a price agreed upon at the time the money is advanced.

Table 13 summarizes data on these forms of credit and shows the estimated number and percentage of these transactions. Advance sales are not shown, since these contracts are never registered. The table illustrates that of all the forms of credit listed, anticresis is preferred, because it is an interest-free loan. Yet anticresis also has its

TABLE 13. Estimated Volume of Formal and Informal Loans[a] in Tiraque, 1984.

Type of Loan	N	Percentage
Formal Loans		
BAB	18	0.5
CIS	170	4.8
Development agencies	171	5.0
Informal Loans[b]		
Anticresis	360	10.0
Money loans	130	3.7
Land lease	40	1.1
Total Loans	895	25.1

Sources: Interviews with BAB's and CIS's regional representatives, Punata, and with development agencies' personnel; Records Jueces de Mínima Cuantía in Tiraque.

[a] It was impossible to obtain information on the amount of money lent in most of these loans.

[b] Records Jueces de Mínima Cuantía.

drawbacks. If the debtor defaults, having spent the money on other things, he is often obliged to "sell" or give away the parcel of land held in anticresis to the other party in the contract, who always reserves the right to buy it if repayment is not made. In one village where a large number of households were indebted to rural merchants, an alcoholic had accumulated such a large drinking debt that he was obliged to give his land in anticresis to his creditor. When the contract expired and the man was not able to return the money, he had to give the parcel of land to the merchant in order to cancel his outstanding debt. These involuntary sales account for the wide variability in the price of land of similar fertility and location observed in Tiraque.

Even after taking into account both formal and hidden forms of credit, the number of debtors (25 percent) is still relatively low, especially if we consider that few campesinos had money due to the drought of 1982–83 and that some individuals received loans from different sources. Actually, campesinos avoid entering into these relations as much as their conditions permit because the risk of losing portions of their land by default is high. Furthermore, as Eric Wolf (1983:54) suggests, when the peasant mortgages land to obtain money, he is indeed selling his "imaginary capital" and its rent, and thus becomes "a tenant paying rent for occupance or possession of his 'own' land." Thus to avert such risk and preserve a certain measure of autonomy, poor peasants engage in sharecropping agreements. Unlike the other alternative available to poor peasants—borrowing money and becoming tenants on their own land—compañía is the best strategy they can choose, since it reduces the risk of initiating a cycle of indebtedness, even though they have to surrender half of the crop and increase their dependence on the rich.

This dependence originates in the differential control of labor, land, and animals which, in turn, allows some households to produce and sell a larger volume of agricultural products in the market than the average household. Taken by themselves, however, these differences are not necessarily transformed into class differences, since the amount of labor, land, and animals each household controls could very well vary with phases in the developmental cycle of the household (Chayanov 1966; Shanin 1973; C. Smith 1984). Similarly, the generalized borrowing of resources between households could serve as a way to ensure access to resources by all households within and outside the village (cf. Glavanis 1984; O. Harris 1982b; G. Smith 1989; Warman 1980).

The question I have sought to answer here is: What kind of relations congeal these basic differences in resources and differential exchanges into more permanent relations of inequality? In Tiraque, these are credit relations involving, by imposed necessity, money, but more importantly, seed, manure, and/or chemical fertilizers and insecticides. In both cases, these credit relations stem from the peasants' needs for money. Both translate into the indirect control of peasant land, labor, and harvest when they are obliged to produce cash crops with the rich regulating, as it were, the labor process of poor peasants.[26] Through these relations some households have been able to accumulate wealth. This is then invested in the further extension of generalized, yet unequal, lending and borrowing relations, and in the purchase of land and trucks. Most of these relations are based on mutual trust. No papers are signed, hence the importance of the partners' knowing each other before land, animals, money, or inputs are advanced. If they are not relatives already, such partners usually become ritual kin.

To summarize this discussion, I will review the criteria used to define each category of campesino. The rich cultivate more than twenty hectares of land in Sank'ayani and in other villages. Besides planting in compañía with other households, they have a variable number of animals, but generally own more than two oxen. They pay paga but do not work for others except in reciprocal labor exchanges that usually involve the lending of draft animals. They are moneylenders, merchants, and/or truck owners (and, in one case, a tractor owner), and own houses in Tiraque, Punata, and Cochabamba. There are eleven households (or about 16 percent of the total number of households) in Sank'ayani that fit these criteria.

Middle peasants form the largest group, forty-two households or 60 percent of the total. They have from three to ten hectares of land in Sank'ayani and/or other places which they cultivate alone and/or in compañía. Most of them have at least one or two oxen that they own or hold in a share system and a variable number of sheep. Among this group, horizontal reciprocal relations are ubiquitous. They engage in reciprocal ayni and paga labor exchanges and in reciprocal credit. They tend not to be involved in other economic activities unless they are "moving up." Members of households like these frequently move to other regions, such as Chapare, for short periods of time.

Finally, there are seventeen households (24 percent) that may be categorized as poor. These households do not own land, or if they do, have less than three hectares. They have no or few animals and none has oxen. The majority of them cultivate several of their crops in compañía, using the household labor force or ayni. In addition, they work as paga or wage laborers for others. Except for seasonal migration to Chapare or permanent migration to the cities, where they work as maidservants or wage laborers, they do not engage in money-making activities in Tiraque.

This brings us to the point where we may productively examine ongoing processes of class formation and discuss how these relate to ideologies of "community."

Rural Differentiation and the Ideology of Community

Most analysts regard the introduction of wage relations as the crucial breaking point in the transformation of agrarian social relations, but this mistakes a symptom for a cause and also emphasizes external relations. This analysis seeks to determine the point at which differentiation becomes crystallized into class distinctions that do not necessarily entail the "proletarianization" of the poor. Although peasant needs for money and credit are at the center of this process, poor peasants remain poor rather than becoming "proletarianized" because land can still be borrowed from their parents or from those more wealthy than they.[27]

It is the wealthy who develop new opportunities for joining the ranks of an emergent merchant class while they continue to rely on these noncapitalist forms of labor mobilization and other resources of production. In becoming a merchant class, they increasingly tie their "traditional," poorer covillagers into a developing world capitalist system. This is the essence of their strength and also their limitation. Their strength is that they can capture both labor and "surplus" products in the village through "traditional" forms and traditional loyalties; their limitation is that they cannot really break the ties that bind them with poor households, and so remain subservient to larger capitalist forces and the state. Nothing more clearly illustrates the paradoxes of their strengths and limitations than their newfound Protestant religion, as we shall see in the last section of this chapter.

The processes leading to the making of a village "elite" occupied a surprisingly short time—the thirty years following the implementation of agrarian reform. It is important to underscore the fact that some differentiation among households was already present prior to the reform, but the speed of their transformation was based on two factors: (1) the agrarian reform and the collapse of the hacienda, and (2) the effectiveness with which wealthier households made use of traditional practices and relations for their own benefit.

The manner in which the Coca and Solís families, which owned the eight trucks present in Sank'ayani at the time of my research, were transformed into a merchant-trucker "elite" is not very different from the paths followed by other upwardly mobile vecino families in

Tiraque. Already in 1956, the Servicio Nacional de Reforma Agraria records classified the Solís and the Coca families as "very rich" (SNRA: Exp. 4096). Several factors contributed to placing these families in an advantageous position vis-à-vis the rest of Sank'ayani. Both before and after the reform, they controlled more land than most families, and when they bought piquerías, their households were in the maximal phase of extended family development. Trinidad Solís and Hilario Coca were then well over forty years old, married, with grown sons and daughters who provided the labor force necessary to cultivate several plots of land. At that very time, labor rent could be provided for the hacienda. Household size was essential for colonos if they wanted to expand the amount of land under cultivation to produce a surplus to sell in the market, to own and take care of more sheep, and, possibly, to engage in other economic activities such as commerce and barter and the purchase of small parcels of land.[28]

The eldest sons of these men also received land with the reform. Two sons of Trinidad, Cornelio and Prudencio, received 16.46 and 49.20 hectares, respectively, which, together with Trinidad's land, amounted to a family total of 92.23 hectares. The reasons for the relatively large parcel of land granted to Prudencio are not clear. Yet the fact that he was the eldest son of Trinidad, who was one of the leaders of the sindicato Sank'ayani at the time of the implementation of agrarian reform, may be one explanation.[29] Altogether the Cocas (Hilario, his four sons, and two grandsons) received a total of 127.77 hectares. After the reform, these families, holding relatively large amounts of land, maintained the extended family as the unit of production and consumption. This was the case with the Solís family also, since Prudencio remained single and Cornelio died shortly after the final decree of reform. Even after all of Trinidad's sons and daughters married and established their own households, their houses remain clustered around his house, and they still pool some of their resources. They lend money to each other, for instance, and help each other with transport and labor. The life histories of these two families illustrate how they establish cultural alliances in production with other households within and outside their village.

The Solís Family

In 1956, Trinidad bought the first truck in the village for his son Cornelio. The family used it to transport their own harvest and manure for cultivation as well as that of other village members. The truck was an old, second-hand vehicle that broke down frequently but still allowed them to engage in transport and commercial activities.

Trinidad replaced the truck several times with other second-hand trucks until, finally, he could afford a new one. In 1966, Trinidad bought eighty hectares of land in a neighboring village, five hectares of which he sold in the 1970s to one of his sons and one son-in-law. Discounting this sale, the estimated amount of land Trinidad had in 1984 outside Sank'ayani was 106 hectares. Trinidad has sufficient capital to produce in compañía with other households. We might recall that in 1984 he planted thirty-one cargas of potato in compañía, for which he provided fertilizer and manure. He also lends money to campesinos in his village as well as in other villages, and even to townspeople. He also buys potatoes in Sank'ayani. Yet, in spite of his wealth and age, Trinidad still works the land with the help of a grandson (who lives with him and drives his grandfather's truck), ayni, and hired paga laborers.

In the late 1970s and early 1980s, Trinidad lent money to his three sons and two of his sons-in-law for them to buy trucks. They have also bought land in the locality and in other villages, and like their father or father-in-law, they are very successful economically. Some bought houses in Tiraque and some are building houses in Cochabamba, but they still live in Sank'ayani. Only the youngest son, who married a *rescatista* (rural merchant) from Punata, has moved to the city of Cochabamba. Nevertheless, he still cultivates his land in compañía, travels often to Sank'ayani and to the Tiraque market, and remains a member of the sindicato agrario Sank'ayani. Another son used to plant in compañía with the hacendado of Qolqeqhoya-Churu. As both partners stand on very similar ground in terms of wealth, the contract was considerably different from the sharecropping agreements that the hacendado has with the campesinos settled on his land. While that relationship is based on ground rent, the hacendado's sharecropping relation with Trinidad's son is completely different. They share equally in the provision of inputs, planting in alternate years on the land of one or the other. Both pay wages or paga to laborers and divide the harvest in half. Like Trinidad, his sons, daughters, and sons-in-law engage in commerce, plant in compañía with poor households, distribute sheep in partnership, lend oxen in exchange for labor, employ paga laborers, and are moneylenders.

The Coca Family

The family history of the Coca family is similar to that of the Solís family. But Hilario Coca was over 100 years old at the time of the reform, and his four sons already had independent households. Andrés had eight children; one of his daughters was married to Damián

Solís who, after his wife's death, married her younger sister, Valentina. Through the years, Andrés bought several second-hand trucks until finally he was able to buy a new one in the early 1980s. His youngest son, Julián, drives the truck. Julián is married to a rural merchant from Punata and has moved there, taking his father with him. They still cultivate the land in Sank'ayani with the help of Andrés's grandchildren and in compañía. Before they moved to Punata, Julián used to engage in commerce and transport in Sank'ayani, but he does not go there so often since the Solís family has bought so many trucks. Julián remains an active member of the Tiraque transporters' union and the Sank'ayani campesino union.

Valentín also had eight children. He lives together with his son, Simón, with whom he and his other son, Emilio, bought a small truck in 1981. They then sold this truck in order to buy a larger one just before a devaluation of the Bolivian peso made their money worthless. Simón is a merchant. The other two Coca brothers, Asencio and Delfín, have died, but their families are rich, although they do not have trucks and do not engage in commerce. Delfín's son, Gregorio, who is married to Trinidad's daughter, Marta, owns a truck, buys locally produced agricultural goods, and is a moneylender. His brother, Víctor, is also a moneylender. Most of the Coca family members also have land in other localities and houses in Tiraque.

Kinship, Marriage, and Class

In addition to the economic relations established between rich and poor households, affinal relations among the wealthy themselves, and fictive kin relations between them and the poor are also very important. Rich campesinos tend to marry rich campesinos; marriages between the Solís and Coca families are frequent. Froilán Solís, who did not marry a woman from Sank'ayani, nevertheless married the daughter of a rich campesino who lives in Tiraque.

Poor campesinos tend to select their fictive kin among the rich mainly because they expect to receive more from them than from their equals. From the rich, they can borrow money to cover unexpected emergencies requiring large cash expenditures, animals, and advances of money or inputs for production. The Solís and the Coca families are the most sought-after candidates for fictive godparents or coparents. The establishment of a network of kin relations is as important for the wealthy as for the poor. From a network of fictive kinsmen and kinswomen, they can tap a labor resource pool. Fictive kin are there to help in times of need, helping in production and in the preparation of food for ceremonial festivities such as weddings and burials. The fact that poor campesinos also use kinship to tie themselves to the wealthy makes kinship all the more powerful as a form of domination.

Unlike the Coca and Solís families, the Ríos family lacks such established networks. The Ríos provide the clearest proof of the importance of mobilizing traditionalist ties in the accumulation of wealth, having moved out of Sank'ayani into Santa Cruz, where Valentín Ríos did not have already pre-established social networks. Valentín is younger than Trinidad and Hilarión, but he also bought land when he was a colono. Before the revolution of 1952, he was very active in colono organization. He led underground meetings to organize and demand better working conditions on the hacienda. Because of his political activity, he was considered a "dangerous element" by the hacendada, who had him arrested. After the revolution and the formation of sindicatos agrarios, Valentín, along with Trinidad Solís, became the first secretary general of the Sank'ayani union.

In 1965, Valentín bought a truck that he used to transport agricultural goods as well as animals. In 1970, however, he decided to move to Santa Cruz. The decision was made because one of his sons was very sick and he thought the milder climate of Santa Cruz would be better for his health. They moved to Chané, a recently established colony in the lowlands of Bolivia, leaving behind the eldest son. Valentín took his second-hand truck with him but sold it in 1969 to his son-in-law, Hilarión. Settling in Santa Cruz was difficult, since it entailed learning to cultivate new crops in a completely different environment and among strangers. As with many colonizers, his experience in the lowlands was not very successful.[30] In 1978, one of Valentín's daughters, Eva, and her husband, Hilarión, returned to Sank'ayani. A few years later, in 1983, Valentín decided to return, too, with most of his family. Two sons stayed in Santa Cruz. By then, most of his sons and daughters were married, so Valentín decided to partition his land among them, keeping for himself only two hectares. Apart from Eva and the eldest son, all live in the same house, although each family maintains a different kitchen.

Returning to Sank'ayani, the Ríos family did not even have seed for planting, and so they cultivated very little during the agricultural year 1983–84. They also have very few sheep but are slowly trying to increase the size of their flock. Besides these two activities, the Ríos family has a watermill for grinding their own and other campesinos' grain, an activity that provides them with additional income. Although the Ríos are not poor when compared with other families in Sank'ayani, they are not as wealthy as the Solís and Coca families. Two important factors truncated Valentín's economic career. He left

Sank'ayani just at the time that he was improving his standing, and in Santa Cruz he could not mobilize traditionalist loyalties.

Marriage and fictive kin relations may also be used as springboards to social mobility by poor campesinos. The cases of Toribio Zamora and Casto Terrazas show how these men make use of these relations and were beginning to thrive, although they were initially poor. Toribio is the son of Ezequiel Zamora, a sharecropper in the former hacienda Qolqeqhoya/Churu where he received 3.84 hectares of land after the reform. Toribio married the daughter of Rufino Hildago in 1976. For this marriage, they chose Prudencio Solís and his wife as godparents. Both his father-in-law and his godparents helped him with money to buy three hectares of land in 1975 and half a hectare in 1980. He also planted in compañía with Juan Torrico. Toribio began to engage in small-scale commerce, buying potatoes from other campesinos in the area and transporting agricultural products on his godfather's truck to the Tiraque market. In 1984, his activities had expanded to compañía production on other campesinos' land.

Casto Terrazas, the son of Fructuoso Terrazas, a former sharecropper in Huaylla Qhochi who was granted 7.44 hectares of land and has not yet partitioned it among his sons and daughters, married Hilaria, the daughter of Cornelio Solís. Their marriage godparents are Gregorio Coca and Marta Solís, Hilaria's aunt and uncle. Although Casto is not a merchant, he produces in compañía with other campesinos. Originally landless, Casto gained access to two hectares of land by marrying Hilaria, and later, between 1980 and 1984, he was able to buy another 10.24 hectares of land. Casto's godfather helps him by transporting his harvest to the market without charge.

The fact that the wealthy use kinship and traditional forms of alliance in support of their accumulation does not mean that the process of class formation is free of profound antagonisms. What it does mean is that these new tensions and antagonisms are expressed in "traditionalist" ways: gossip, character assassination, and conflicts arising over the division of animals or harvest in share agreements (cf. Guha 1989; Scott 1985, 1990; Stern 1987).[31]

Besides differences in wealth, for instance, religious beliefs also divide villagers in Sank'ayani. Seventeen families, seven of whom are wealthy, profess to be evangelicals; the rest are Catholic.[32] The rich use a Protestant moral code of behavior—abstention from worldly pleasures such as alcohol and dance—as a justification for their wealth. They underscore the fact that they were able to save money to buy land, trucks, and crops because they do not have any vices, such as chicha drinking which, they say, is the main reason why most Catholics remain poor. Yet evangelicals do not embrace their new religion in order to break away from reciprocal obligations and fictive ties. On the contrary, they remain fully involved in all life cycle rituals, continue to accept coparents and godchildren married or baptized in the evangelical church, and contribute generously to these festivities with food and bottled soft drinks, which at the time of research were more expensive than chicha. Although rural differentiation is couched in moral and religious terms, most evangelicals converted to Protestantism long after they accumulated wealth, and they are likely to reconvert to Catholicism, too. This was the case with Trinidad Solís, who was a Catholic until 1982, when he became an evangelical. In 1984, after one of his sons had a truck accident that left nine persons dead and several injured, Trinidad went again to confession and took communion during a mass given for the dead in the local cemetery.[33]

Unlike the evangelicals, the Catholics maintain that no one can become rich without being "abusive," implying that the rich have made money because they once stole other campesinos' crops at night and now cheat and take advantage of the poor. Some also say that the rich have made a pact with the devil, who helps people make money if they agree to repay the favor throughout their lives. This pact then forces them to make money by any means.[34] This also justifies the "unsocial" behavior of the wealthy and accounts for the riches of the devil, who lives in a gold-filled palace inside Mount Tunari, the highest peak in Cochabamba.[35] These new tensions are, then, expressed in traditionalist idioms, as much as wealth and class inequalities are expressed in idioms of reciprocity and community.

The idiom of equality also pervades the sindicato agrario Sank'ayani which, unlike other unions in Tiraque, is distinguished by its organization and ability to command the participation of all union members in communal work benefiting the entire community. Leadership positions in the union are chosen by elections on a yearly rotational basis with the understanding that every man has an equal right to become a union leader. Men who have already served in such positions are not reelected. The male-oriented union has also recognized the right of women to participate in its meetings. Even though this right is limited to widows and single women with children, women enjoy a theoretically equal standing with men: they may express their opinions and vote. In this way, the Sank'ayani union contrasts with most unions in the region which do not include women in their meetings except as representatives of their husbands (in which case, they are not allowed to vote).

The campesino union meets twice a month to discuss any issues relating to the well-being of the village, as well as the position the local union should take regarding issues raised by the Tiraque Central

Campesina. The range of problems discussed at these meetings is considerable, as they can relate to the irrigation roster within the community; the management of the local school and its land (which they cultivate communally to raise money for the school); the building and management of a dispensary; the upkeep of the road leading to the community; and issues beyond the village itself. Differences of opinion are thoroughly presented, defended, reviewed, and finally voted on by all those present. What is most striking in this union is that most decisions are carried through with the participation of most of its members. All union members worked in the building of the dispensary, for instance, as well as on the school's land. They also repaired the road leading to the community, although this work benefited local truck owners more than most other members. The truck owners reciprocated by lowering transport fares to and from the community.

Nowadays, few of the truckers and merchants who used to operate in Sank'ayani travel to the village, unless they are hired for a specific purpose. Occasionally, truckers from distant places, such as the cities of Cochabamba or La Paz, show up bringing salt, valley products, and clothes to barter for potatoes. Otherwise, the Sank'ayani truckers—in particular, the Solís family—monopolize many of the transport needs in the village, a fact that entails a greater dependence on the wealthy for most households in the village. Several campesinos indicated that they preferred to use the services of local truckers rather than hiring others, even though the latter might offer a cheaper service, because they thought that, if they did not do so, they risked antagonizing the local truckers and would not be able to rely on them in case they needed their services on other occasions. The multiple social relations established between households within the locality through loans of land and animals, ritual kinship, ayni, credit, and compañía relations are also important reasons why the poor prefer to depend on local truckers rather than to draw on outsiders.

Reciprocal and fictive kin ties and "community" relations made it possible for the wealthy to dominate and exploit their poorer covillagers, and the fear of hard times seems to solidify this control. Yet the poor may, and in fact do, resist this domination in an implicit cultural struggle over the meaning of these relations, since they have crucially different practical consequences for the poor in contrast to the wealthy. Thus, rather than being ideologies imposed to mask inequality, such practices remain vital, constantly being renegotiated and often subverted by campesinos in their relations of work and, more generally, daily life. As residents in the same village or as ritual kin, the poor may lay claims on the rich in the form of a right to receive help in times of dearth, as well as a right to receive payment for labor in kind rather than low wages. Paradoxically, however, these ties of domination and subordination, which are based on unequal forms of borrowing and sharing, allow poor peasants to maintain direct production outside the influence of the market, while they resort to compañía as a means of borrowing inputs to produce cash crops. In this "bargain," they lose partial control of the product of their land and labor and often compromise the sale of the harvest far in advance, giving up the right to a more equal exchange. But this is the price they choose to pay for maintaining a relative autonomy, preserving control over the labor process, and reproducing themselves as peasants in highly differentiated campesino communities.

Chapter 5
The Accumulation of Wealth and Capital

As in other villages, the village-based wealthy families of Sank'ayani rose to join the ranks, and to challenge the position, of a regional merchant class already established in Tiraque. This class is a varied and partly segmented group of families who live in the villages, the town of Tiraque, or other Valle Alto towns. The major difference between the town and village merchants is that the latter still reside in villages where noncommoditized relations of production, mediated by idioms of reciprocity and community, prevail, while several members of the vecino or town-based merchants are commercial farmers employing wage laborers to crop their land even while they share-crop the land of peasants or their own land with landless peasants.[1] Although town merchants also establish ritual kin relations with peasants, social obligations toward them are not as binding as those stemming from residence in the same community. Other distinctions among the regional merchant class are the amount of capital they control, the scope of their operations, and the manner in which they operate; some operate from their houses, while others are mobile, traveling to different peasant villages and market towns.

This segmented class is nevertheless uniform in its mode of wealth accumulation; particularly, in its indirect control over peasant cash crop production through compañía contracts, loans, and advanced harvest purchases. These forms of productive relations are based on, and, in turn, generate, further interpersonal bonds with peasants such as *casero* ties (long-term bonds established between people in barter or commercial transactions) and fictive kinship. Since all members of the merchant class use similar strategies to have access to and appropriate peasant surplus labor and produce, there is fierce competition among them. This competition is most noticeable in the marketplace and in transport. The paradox in Tiraque lies in the fact that within a competitive environment of developed markets and "open roads," merchants are able to establish an oligopolistic control over exchange and transport. As we have seen in the preceding chapter, village merchants and truckers are able to do this not so much in the marketplace, but rather in peasant villages and households through the establishment of an "alliance" at the level of production.[2] Such alliances, in turn, constrain the participation of peasants in the market, since they relinquish half their cash crops and often sell their own share of the crop to their compañía partners. Peasants are also constrained in the hiring of trucks to transport their crops, animals, or manure. In the case of Sank'ayani, we saw that the "capitalist" compañía partner had the option of buying the other half of the crop from his landowning peasant partner, and that village-based truckers were hired by peasants even though they charged more for their services than truckers from other villages or the town. It would seem apparent, then, that unequal exchange in the village has its roots in production. The market dominates peasants precisely because of the intimacy of their relations with the regional dominant class in a situation in which both merchants and the peasantry make use of cultural idioms of community, fictive kin, and reciprocity; both groups collude in their acceptance of these unequal relations, which, in their disguised forms, may appear as equal and reciprocal.

This chapter deals with the regional merchant "elite," focusing in particular on those who live in the town of Tiraque. The elite are the merchants, moneylenders, and truckers or the so-called rural brokers so ubiquitous in the literature,[3] or, to use the local categories, these are the *chhaleras, ranqheras, rescatistas, qhateras,*[4] and *transportistas* or truckers. *Chhala* means barter in Quechua, so *chhalera* refers to an individual engaged in barter exchange. The term *ranqhera* is used to identify individuals involved in the purchase of animals, while *rescatistas* purchase agricultural goods, and *qhateras* are petty market traders who set up stalls in the marketplace. Unlike these latter traders, who are predominantly women, transportistas are men. When examining these characters superficially as individuals, one cannot fail to notice the large differences among them. Among those operating in Tiraque, for instance, there is a woman who buys a sack of potatoes in the market and sells it retail on the streets of Cochabamba, and a trucker, the owner of one or two trucks, who is at the same time a merchant, a moneylender, and an entrepreneur who plants on his own land and on the land of others, in compañía or according to other contractual arrangements. These examples represent the extremes of a continuum. Some social scientists in Bolivia tend to view this continuum as an evolutionary process in which individuals start from lowly beginnings to become powerful merchants and truck owners (cf. Ustariz and Mendoza 1982). While there is a grain of truth in this assertion, there is a danger of oversimplication and of equating activities with social groups.

Social reality is much more complex in Tiraque as, surely, it is everywhere. Two critiques may be made of the evolutionary view. First, people are involved in a multiplicity of income-earning activities. This becomes clear when the household rather than the individual is taken as the unit of analysis. While the husband might be a trucker, the wife a merchant, and a young daughter a chhalera or barter woman, other members of the family might be professionals, schoolteachers, or members of the armed forces. Moreover, dedication to one activity does not exclude engagement in another in a different setting. A woman might be involved in barter exchange in the villages on Mondays, set up a clothes stall in a marketplace on Tuesdays, buy potatoes in another market on another day of the week, and make and sell chicha in her house on weekends. Furthermore, these same individuals and households rely on other sources of income such as cash-crop and livestock production that may, in some households, be as important, or more important, than commerce. Thus, rather than referring to social categories or specialized agents, concepts such as traders, merchants, and transporters refer more to different activities that are often carried out simultaneously by members of the same family or by individuals at different phases in their careers. These are different but related ways that shape and control social relations of production and appropriation.

Second, and more importantly, wealth is not accumulated by working up an evolutionary ladder, but by establishing agreements in production with peasant households. Indeed, for most of the wealthy, engagement in market or transport activities provides a means to have access to labor and commodities through different forms of credit relations as well as sharecropping. Petty traders, such as poor campesinas or working-class women, also operate in Tiraque. But unlike wealthy merchants, these women sell and buy small volumes of products to complement the incomes of their households. The point is that the use of concepts such as brokers, intermediaries, transporters, or marketwomen masks rather than illuminates the marked distinctions that exists between different social groups.[5]

My concern here is to examine modes of wealth accumulation in the Tiraque area. In order to do this, I will first discuss the formation of the new, town-based merchant class and its relations with the peasantry. Since these relations are based on the production, exchange, and transport of peasant crops, I will describe how town-based merchants and truckers operate in the peasant villages, the town, the marketplaces, and the region as a whole, and how they are constantly challenged by emergent village "elites" and by other merchants and transporters from the Valle Alto. In the face of this competition, the merchant-transporters of Tiraque first joined together in a voluntary association and then in a transporters' union. Both organizations failed to control effectively either local transport or local markets. A focus on the activities and strategies of merchants serves to underscore the importance of their alliances with peasant households. These alliances enable them to control cash-crop production, transport, and exchange.

The Town's Nouveau Riche

To examine the formation of a new, town-based dominant class, it is necessary to retrace our narrative to the period immediately after the reform of 1953 and look at several important changes that took place in the region and in Bolivia. The most important was, of course, the departure of hacendados and the transformation of colonos into landowning peasants. This increased the number of households with whom the wealthy could establish relations of production and exchange, and ritual kin ties.

In Chapter 3, I discussed how the national government, by threatening to take land from peasants, urged them to cultivate all available land and participate more in the market "in defense of the National Revolution." These threats and pleas were unnecessary in Tiraque, since most peasants were integrated into the market both before and after reform. As we have seen, what bound peasants more tightly to the market, as well as to traders and merchants, were neither political threats and pleas nor any innate attractiveness of the market, but rather the reorganization of production and the imposed "squeeze" on reproduction. We have also discussed the fact that ownership of land did not turn peasants into "independent" producers. Rather, immediately after agrarian reform, many households did not even have seed, manure, or money to begin production and needed "help" from traders, merchants, and vecinos who could advance these factors of production. This dependence increased with the introduction of chemical fertilizers and pesticides in the late sixties. Peasants also needed the support of vehicles to transport products to and from markets.

Those vecinos from Tiraque who were at that time best positioned to "help" peasants were the middle yungueños whose lands were unaffected by agrarian reform and who had earlier been involved in trade with piqueros and yungas colonizers. These were the Ochoa, Ferrufino, Irigoyen, Quiróz, Sandoval, Estrada, López, Torres, Velarde, and Torrico families. Seven of these families owned trucks. Each of these families carved out an area of operation in the countryside by establishing casero relations with peasants and, most importantly, by becoming their fictive kin. Both these relations create the bonds of intimacy and trust that are necessary for credit (in the form of money, inputs, products, or chicha) to be extended to peasant households, as well as for animals to be given in share partnership, and for planting to be carried out in compañía with landowning peasants or with landless peasants on the merchant's land. Peasants know that through these relations they will have a prominent vecino family on whom they can rely in times of need. This might involve a place to sleep if nightfall surprises them in town; a place to store purchased goods, such as stoves or beds too large to carry on foot to the village; a place to store crops they could not sell at the market; and, occasionally, a place to have their young children raised as the vecinos' servants.

Ritual kinship, then, is important in transforming initially impersonal exchange relations into intimate (yet unequal) relations in which the parties involved can lay claims on each other. These claims are solely based on cultural expectations of fictive kin rights and obligations. Before agrarian reform, few colonos were coparents or godchildren of townsfolk, except for those who became fictive kin of the hacendado. After the reform, through these relations, which are in essence no different from those binding village "elites" to poor peasants, the town-based merchants were able to establish alliances with peasant households, through which they embarked on control of cash-crop production, exchange, and transport in the peasant villages. Unlike wealthy villagers, however, rich townsfolk tended to operate on a much broader regional scale, extending their control over numerous households in several villages. The merchant-transporter José Ochoa, for example, had, until his death in 1964, such links with ten villages where he had 110 godchildren.[6]

Alliances such as these, binding vecino and peasant households, become particularly relevant when they are examined within the competitive context in which merchants operate.

Competition and "Free" Exchange

Since the agrarian reform, noveau riche Tiraqueños have been engaged in competition with merchants and truckers from Punata and other rural towns. This competition increased in the late 1960s and worsened after the 1970s with the steady increase in the number of truck owners among campesinos and vecinos. The growth experienced by the Bolivian economy during General Banzer's regime was partly responsible for this, but the generalized corruption of his regime was what most benefited rural entrepreneurs. Many state-financed loans were diverted to speculative enterprises or were obtained to purchase trucks. Cocaine paste production also provided opportunities for rapid enrichment for many individuals. During this time, more vehicles were imported into Bolivia than at any time previously. It is widely believed, although difficult to corroborate, that several vecino truck owners from Tiraque, and many from Punata, obtained money to buy trucks from their involvement in cocaine production in the 1970s.

The proliferation and competition of merchants and transporters has not, however, improved the terms of exchange of peasant products or decreased transport fares. On the contrary, the terms of exchange—both barter and commercial exchange—tend to be increasingly unfavorable to peasants. Competition has affected the careers of many entrepreneurs, forcing them to refine their strategies for profiting from unequal exchange while at the same time seeking to retain control over peasant cash cropping. To understand these seemingly diverse outcomes, it is necessary to describe how town-based merchants and transporters operate in peasant villages, in the town, and in marketplaces. These outcomes are not only diverse but contradictory: control over peasant production is achieved through involvement in the culture of reciprocity, which is at least partly antithetical to increasingly unequal exchange.

Exchange in Rural Villages

Even though today, more than in the past, peasants take their products to regional markets, they still continue to conduct exchanges in their own villages and in the town. Two modes of exchange take place in the peasant village: barter and commercial exchange. First, peasants from the highland plateau often appear in Tiraque with blocks of salt and medicinal herbs, and peasants from the valleys of Cochabamba bring maize, squash, onions, and carrots to exchange for potatoes. These transactions, involving the exchange of use values that are more or less equivalent, are generally undertaken by peasant families bound together by long-term exchange relations, friendships, and perhaps, fictive kin ties. In this case, it is very unlikely that peasants will refuse to barter, even though they might not want to do so, because refusing a partner's wish to exchange would jeopardize the future of this long-established relation.

Second, truckers also appear in the peasant villages from as far away as La Paz, bringing blocks of salt, clothes, and fruit; and traders, traveling on foot, show up with small amounts of bread and dry goods, fruit, coca, sugar-cane alcohol, and sometimes, agricultural products from the valleys and the yungas to barter for potatoes. These barter transactions, however, stand in marked contrast to barter exchanges among peasants, functioning according to two separate logics. For the traders, barter is just one phase in the circulation of goods, since barter involves the exchange of commodities for use values that are then sold in the market at a profit. For the peasant, barter has a completely different meaning since he is exchanging use values, and money does not enter into the transaction. The peasant logic permeates the actual exchange, since traders indicate that they are acquiring produce for their own consumption, but the exchange of goods, based on an estimated equal volume or equal weight, always entails an unequal exchange of value. A basketful of oranges amounting to fifty units was, on one occasion, exchanged for a basketful of potatoes amounting to one *arroba* (25 pounds). At the time, fifty oranges sold for $b1,500, while an arroba of potatoes sold for $b6,000 in Cochabamba. Similarly, a block of salt that sold for $b1,500 was exchanged for the same weight of potato. In spite of this inequality, of which peasants are fully aware, they willingly enter into barter exchange with traders because in so doing they can save the time and money they would spend if they went to the market solely to get these products. When they are reluctant to exchange, chhaleras find ways to oblige peasants in order to barter with them. Chhaleras carrying food, for example, usually offer some of it to the children of the household. As food cannot be shown without being offered and cannot be rejected, children accept it and then the parents are forced to reciprocate by exchanging produce with the chhaleras.

Rescatistas, or itinerant merchants, also visit the villages to purchase agricultural products and animals from peasant households. These traders do not usually take products to sell in the peasant villages although, occasionally, they take chicha and sugar-cane alcohol to give as presents. This is the stereotypical portrayal of such women, who by making peasants drunk are able to buy agricultural products and animals very cheaply, leaving the peasants further in debt and establishing a relationship of dependence based on debt. For the rescatistas, the principal advantage of buying in the villages rather than in the marketplace is that in the villages there are no scales to weigh the crops and thus they can benefit from differences in measurement. Equally important is the fact that rescatistas are able to establish more intimate relations with peasants in their villages than in the markets. They have more time to sit and talk with them and become acquainted before money or inputs are extended to them in compañía, loans, or advanced purchases. Eventually, they become fictive kin. Once these commercial and fictive relations are established, the rescatista might take presents to her caseros, coparents, or godchildren. No matter how small these presents or favors might be, peasants always reciprocate with presents that are usually larger than the one received. For instance, after I gave the photographs I had taken of them to campesinos of Sank'ayani to reciprocate for the patience they showed in answering the many, often repetitious questions I put to them, they would provide me with potatoes, fava beans, and, once, with a sheep—besides the usual offering of cooked food. When I protested, they answered that I should accept the presents as demonstration of their *cariño* (love) and that, in any case, "it did not cost them anything"—further proof that they do not consider important the labor they spend on cultivation and raising animals.

The amount of produce these traders or merchants obtain from each household is small—maybe a sack or less of potatoes, one sheep, a few pounds of dried fava beans and ch'uño, two or three cheeses, or three or four eggs. But, by repeating the same operations with several households, they can assemble considerable quantities of agricultural produce and animals that they later sell retail or wholesale from their houses and at regional or urban markets. Trading within the villages can be a time-consuming activity, particularly if the merchant does not own a vehicle, because it requires spending several days in the villages, visiting caseros and fictive kin, spending the night with them, and storing the crops assembled piecemeal in their houses. Only after a sufficient volume is assembled do traders hire the services of truckers to transport these products out of the village, or use their own trucks to do so.

Exchange in the Town

Some of these traders and merchants also operate from their place of residence in town, where they receive visits from peasants who ask for money advances or loans and bring products into their houses to sell or to obtain products on credit. Other merchants are not spatially mobile, but because they own a shop, a chichería, or are in charge of a public office in town, they are also able to establish regional exchange and productive relations with peasants without having to leave the town. A prominent vecino, Luis Ochoa, one of the small-claims judges and a local chicha tax collector, operates in fourteen villages in Tiraque as a moneylender, compañía partner, and wholesale merchant from his house in the town square. He has seventy-seven godchildren in these villages. Similarly, Gerardo Bravo, a rentier landowner and wholesale merchant, uses his chichería to establish ties with peasants from several villages.

To this day, chicherías are important locales for contacting and getting to know peasants from different villages. Almost all chicheras are women. They make chicha on a regular basis, having it ready for sale on Fridays and Sundays when most peasants go to the market and the church in town. Once peasants finish selling and buying in the market or after church services are over, they enjoy going to chicherías to meet other people, drink, and dance. Before deciding what chichería they will go to, most visit several in order to taste the quality of the chicha. Chicheras always offer a free glass or a small jar of chicha to arriving customers who, after tasting the chicha, buy another jar and, if they like it, stay for several hours. If they do not like the chicha, they continue visiting other chicherías until they find the one they like best. If acquaintances, friends, or relatives are already in the chichería, newcomers are invited by them to drink large quantities of chicha—an invitation they must reciprocate. Small jars are replaced by larger ones, the larger ones by buckets, and these, finally, by five-gallon oil cans filled with chicha. Drinking and the opportunity to be with other people helps customers lower social defenses. They tend to become more talkative, revealing things they would normally keep to themselves; some become unruly, and fights are not uncommon.

Among their generally drunken customers, chicheras are always sober. They make a considerable effort and use different means to make their customers drink, but always manage to drink very little, if at all, although they are also invited to do so by their customers. Chicheras also talk with their customers and overhear conversations, whereby chicheras become well-informed individuals. They learn about the latest gossip, market prices, about who did what to whom, who owes money, who had a good harvest, and so on. Their control of information and sobriety confers relative power on chicheras. Many use the chichería as a means of establishing sharecropping, moneylending, commercial, and ritual kin relations with their peasant customers. Loans involve direct money disbursements or serving chicha on credit. These are generally repaid with agricultural produce after the harvest in the amount and value previously agreed upon. Thus, without having to leave their homes, merchants and moneylenders use the chichería as an informal setting in which to establish ties of domination with peasants.

Exchange in the Marketplace

In the villages and towns there is apparently little competition once a merchant establishes intimate bonds with peasant households, but competition among merchants becomes more noticeable in the marketplace. This competition seems to stand in direct relation to the size of the marketplace: the larger the market and the number of merchants, the more intense the competition and the less unequal the exchange, which remains unequal, nevertheless. Keeping in mind that much of this inequality stems from well-known structural and political factors, such as the asymmetry of the rural sector vis-à-vis the industrial sector, supply and demand, and municipal price regulations, I will now focus on the strategies adopted by traders and merchants to outcompete each other and increase their profit margins in the marketplace.

Both commercial and barter exchanges take place in all regional markets. Such markets attract similar categories of peasants, traders, and merchants, including truckers. Participants from each specialize, as it were, in specific transactions and produce. Among peasants, women generally sell animals and barter small amounts of agricultural products usually saved for consumption, while men usually sell cash crops. Traders engaged in barter take the same goods to the regional markets as they take to the villages. They either sit in front of their neatly piled goods while they wait for their peasant customers to come to them or walk around looking for customers, with their goods in baskets, calling out as they go, "Chhalaway, caserita" ("Let's barter, caserita"). In general, the standard measure for barter is a *chhala* (or about six pounds), but rather than weighing the goods being exchanged, vendors place these goods in containers such as plates, pots, baskets, or the palms of the hands. Since all of these measures vary, the actual volume exchanged depends to a large extent on bargaining and on what each individual considers a fair exchange. The size of the market, the number of traders, and the poverty of peasants shape their bargaining power. In the small markets of Aguirre and Cañacota, where barter is the principal mode of exchange, a small number of chhaleras receive larger quantities of agricultural products in each barter transaction than in other markets. To use the example of Cañacota once again, poor peasants exchanged potatoes and fava beans for *arrope* (the residue of maize after processing chicha), which is generally not sold but given away to friends or fed to pigs.

Qhateras form another category of market trader. They both sell and barter different kinds of produce, such as vegetables and fruits not locally produced, and dry goods, pots and pans, clothes, school supplies, batteries, and so on. They arrive early at the markets so that they have time to set up their goods on the ground under tall, square umbrellas. These women use small hand scales, seldom showing the correct measurement, to weigh the goods they sell at prices higher than in the city.[7]

Ranqheras and rescatistas (wholesale merchants) go to markets to purchase animals or agricultural products. Ranqheras go directly to that part of the marketplace set aside for the purchase and sale of livestock. There is fierce competition among livestock dealers because, except in Punata, not many animals are brought to the market for sale. Each ranqhera always wants to be the first to make a deal with the peasants bringing sheep and pigs to sell. As soon as she spots one coming from several blocks away, she runs toward the peasant, gets hold of the rope tied around the animal's neck or leg, feels the animal for fat and diseases, and makes an offer. In the meantime, another ranqhera makes a better offer and starts pulling on the rope. Sometimes there are two or three ranqheras fighting over the same animal. Ranqheras are also alert for approaching trucks to see whether there are animals on them. If there are, the women jump on the running truck in order to have priority over the other ranqheras.

Livestock prices vary during the course of the year, reaching their lowest price during the "hungry season" before the harvest, when more animals are brought to the market and the rainy season begins. At that time, many peasant households sell their sheep and pigs because they cannot afford to feed them and because they need the cash. The number of households selling animals increases supply and decreases prices by 30 to 40 percent.

Rescatistas, or buyers of agricultural products, are as busy and competitive as ranqheras in making their transactions in the market areas set aside for the sale of potatoes, fava beans, peas, and barley. They also wait for peasants to arrive on foot or in trucks, and attempt to get to them before others do. Often, they start bargaining with peasants before they even have a chance to unload their cargo. Once it is unloaded, the rescatista checks the quality and the size of the produce, makes an offer, and, if the owner agrees, places an amount of money as downpayment on the sack. In this manner, the rescatista makes sure that the peasant will not sell the produce to somebody else, while she is free to select more produce. Only when she is sure that no more goods will be brought to the market does the rescatista begin to relax. Then she goes to each one of the peasants who sold her barley, fava beans, or potatoes and pays the remainder of the amount of money she owes. After weighing the sacks of potatoes on a scale, the rescatista transfers them to her own sacks, which are then placed on her truck, or on a hired truck, to take to other markets or to the rescatista's storehouse.

Itinerant merchants travel to different marketplaces, often covering long distances to take advantage of differences in weights and measures and regional variations in prices. The lack of a standardized system of weights and measures is a common feature in rural Bolivia. Instead, a combination of old Spanish, English, and metric systems work to the advantage of the merchant. As a report from the Ministry of Agropecuarian and Peasant Affairs (República de Bolivia 1978:1) states,

A diversity of units of weight, volume, and area are still being used in the countryside which give rise to great confusion, since most people do not usually know their equivalencies. This lack of knowledge, nevertheless, works to the illicit advantage of a few to the detriment of the majority—like the rural merchants who engage in land, agricultural, or livestock transactions with peasants.

The unit of weight of a sack of potatoes, for instance, is the carga, which is the equivalent of 216 pounds in the markets of Cochabamba and Punata. This weight, however, varies between and within regions, ranging from 200 to 250 pounds. In the market of Tiraque, the weight of a carga of potatoes is 200 pounds, whereas it is 250 pounds in the market of El Puente, and in the peasant villages, unweighed sacks weigh around 240 pounds. These variations are due to the fact that peasants use the arroba as a unit of volume, and in each region and, often in villages within the same region, the weight of the arroba varies. To add to this confusion, a sack of potatoes generally consists of eight arrobas (which themselves vary in weight) although in some villages the sack contains ten arrobas. Similar differences exist with the unit of weight for grains and fava beans. These are sold by the arroba. But while the arroba of fava beans, for instance, weighs forty pounds in the Tiraque region, in Cochabamba it weighs twenty-five pounds. Rural merchants benefit from these weight differences, since price differences per carga or arroba in one region are not very significant. The price of a carga remains the same whether it weighs 200 pounds or 250 pounds. As one transportista from Punata who travels 60 kilometers to El Puente market put it: "These extra arrobas make our trip here worthwhile."

Several factors affect the price of agricultural products. Leaving aside structural factors, such as those stemming from the unequal relation between industry and agriculture,[8] the most important stem from the interplay of municipal efforts to control the market and the merchants' strategies to evade such measures. By municipal decree, all potatoes reaching the city of Cochabamba should be sold in a public *tambo*, or government-controlled storehouse, where weights and prices are regulated.[9] Other municipal policies to lower prices have involved, at different times, the prohibition on exporting potatoes from the department of Cochabamba or the promotion of potato imports from other departments or countries to maintain a high level of supply, and price controls. The latter policy was imposed during the period of fieldwork, but prices could only be controlled in the few instances when municipal inspectors were present to enforce this regulation. This gave rise, instead, to speculative hoarding and a thriving black market ultimately benefiting merchants and adversely affecting consumers.[10] Rather than taking potatoes to the public tambo to sell, rescatistas took them to city wholesalers who paid higher prices, knowing that they would make up for this by selling retail potatoes of different quality[11] or by selling in other departments where prices were higher.

Prices paid by consumers in Cochabamba and other departments naturally influence the price of agricultural products in the countryside. Yet each rural market has its own price-setting dynamic. Several factors determine the amount of money rescatistas are willing to pay in each market: supply and demand, number and type of buyers and sellers, and prices in the market where merchants intend to sell (Ustariz and Mendoza 1982). Peasants, on the other hand, have as their point of reference the previous week's average price, plus an additional sum that they always add to keep up with inflation. The price finally agreed upon is reached after extensive bargaining. In the potato market of Tiraque, for instance, the rescatista always challenges the price peasants ask, claiming that their potatoes are not good or that the sack contains too much soil. Rescatista women are expert bargainers; they joke and tease campesinos until they are able to set a price that is closer to the one they intended to pay. This is the reason the wives of campesinos often prefer to sell cash crops themselves, claiming that "men are not all that bright and rescatistas take advantage of them." The market "opens" once the first carga of potatoes is sold and the price at which it is sold, serves, at first, as the reference price for all further sales. As more potatoes are brought to the market, however, the price tends to drop, and by the end of the morning or early afternoon, the price of a carga of potatoes is generally a few thousand pesos lower. In September 1983, for instance, peasants began asking $b30,000 to $b38,000 for a sack of potatoes in the early morning, but by noon the average price had fallen to $b25,000.

Prices also fluctuate seasonally[12] and regionally with the agricultural cycle and ecological diversity. Harvest seasons are not the same for all regions. In some localities lower altitude and irrigation allow peasants to harvest potatoes as early as October, so that when, in Tiraque, for instance, old potatoes are still being sold in the market, in neighboring Colomi peasants are selling new potatoes at higher prices. In September 1983, a carga of potatoes sold for $b32,000 in the city of Cochabamba, for $b26,000 in Colomi, for $b29,000 in El Puente, and for $b27,000 in Tiraque.

Since itinerant merchants profit from all these regional variations in prices and weights, it is important for them to travel to different markets which are held on different days of the week. Mobility and the ownership of a truck are thus important factors in the success of the enterprise and the accumulation of wealth.

Competition on the Roads

So far I have dealt primarily with traders and merchants, referring only in passing to transporters cum merchants. Since transportistas do not constitute a homogeneous grouping, and since they are important characters in Bolivia, it is necessary to describe them here in more detail. I will begin with transportistas in general, and then describe the activities of those who operate in the countryside.

The term transportista refers generally to owners of motor vehicles and to drivers, the majority of whom are today members of the powerful national confederation of transporters (Confederación Sindical de Choferes de Bolivia, or CSCB). The organization of transporters became important in Bolivia only after the revolution of 1952,[13] and was widespread during General Banzer's regime (1971–78), after the Ministry of Transport and Communications passed resolution 49/71 on April 1971 regulating public transport in Bolivia and mandating that all public transport "must only be carried out by professional drivers organized in unions affiliated to the Confederación Sindical de Choferes de Bolivia" (República de Bolivia, 1972).[14] Two years later, General Banzer elevated this resolution to a decree (No. 10715, February 1, 1973) thus making unionization obligatory for all truck, bus, and taxi owners and drivers (República de Bolivia, *Gaceta Oficial de Bolivia* 1973:16833). As the Secretario de Conflictos (the federation's arbitration secretary) in the Cochabamba Federation of Transporters told me, the number of transportistas increased considerably in Bolivia during 1971 and 1978. He referred to this time as the period of the coordinators, Banzer's hand-picked union leaders, and as the worst phase "in the history of the transporters unions because the coordinators accepted everybody into the unions as long as they were paid a bribe."

In 1984, 70,000 members were affiliated to the CSCB, about 80 percent of whom were "investors" or wealthy individuals, such as landowners, professionals, bureaucrats, or members of the armed forces, who owned taxis and buses, but did not themselves drive their vehicles. Among truck owners only about 15 to 20 percent were nondriving owners.[15] The remaining owners drive their own vehicles, providing services in urban, long-distance, or interprovincial transport. All transporters operate as individual entrepreneurs.[16] Those involved in long-distance transport travel distances greater than two hundred kilometers, use buses or large, new trucks that carry both freight and passengers, while interprovincial transporters travel on smaller, old trucks or buses within the countryside or from rural towns and villages to cities. These truckers carry crops, manure, wood, fertilizer, animals, goods in general, and passengers. They usually travel with their wives and an assistant, a young man, often a compadre's son, who rides on the back of the truck and helps with the loading and unloading of freight and passengers. Like truckers from Tiraque, most interprovincial truckers are merchants, sharecropping partners, and also moneylenders.

Class, capital, and power also create additional differences among transporters and shape the outcome of their enterprise. For individuals who buy a second-hand truck but lack operating capital except for the truck itself, a miscalculation of costs or an accident that destroys the uninsured vehicle[17] can result in total loss or bankruptcy. For those transporters who control substantial operating capital, own more than one new vehicle, transport long-distance freight, or engage in commerce and other speculative enterprises, trucking can indeed be lucrative.[18]

All of these differences translate into divergent interests and demands. Operational costs, for instance, are relatively high for all transporters, mainly because of poor road conditions and the rapid depreciation of vehicles. The average life of a truck is about 350,000 kilometers (Estudio Integral del Transporte 1980), or five to six years. Yet, depreciation affects owners of new vehicles more seriously than owners of second-hand vehicles, who generally pay for their depreciated vehicles in cash. Instead, owners of new vehicles have to repay the cost of the truck[19] in dollars, at high interest rates and over a short period of time (usually three years). On the other hand, excessive capacity (trucks leave urban centers practically empty, except for passengers, but return filled to capacity) and the time spent in the cities to unload trucks and return to the countryside are factors contributing to the high operational costs of interprovincial truckers. Fixed costs are low but variable costs, especially those of spare parts, are higher and are the cause of bitter complaints on the part of all transportistas, since importing firms operate in dollars and quote their prices according to the daily black-market exchange rate. As one transporter put it: "We operate in dollars but earn in pesos. . . . Commercial houses [importers of vehicles and spare parts] exploit us. . . . After paying for a whole year for my vehicle with great sacrifice, I hardly own the wheels of my truck!"

What binds vehicle owners together is their alliance in the CSCB, where they support each other's demands and bargain among themselves to obtain privileges. Interprovincial transporters support the demands of the more powerful long-distance or urban vehicle owners as long as they remain free to establish their own, non-government-regulated fares in the countryside. In 1982, for instance, interprovincial truckers joined in a general strike to force import firms to accept the payment of debts at the official exchange rate, which only benefited owners of new vehicles bought on credit. They join forces, too, to obtain benefits and privileges from the state.

The most important of these concessions was General Banzer's unionization decree. This measure brought together urban, interprovincial, and long-distance transporters, including salaried drivers (who aspire to become full-fledged transportistas) into a supraregional organization. As members of the CSCB, transportistas articulate their demands, limit the access of others into the more powerful urban and long-distance unions, and hold strategic control over transport. They are thus able to exercise considerable political power in Bolivia because they are able to paralyze the country every time they stage a general strike.

Since the 1970s, the state has granted numerous privileges to transporters. They have benefited especially from their long-term alliance with the military, which brings them import privileges and subsidies. Indeed, all military regimes have, in one form or another, favored transporters at various times by granting long-distance and urban unions permission to import vehicles with reduced or no import duties, by backing purchases on credit of new vehicles with Central Bank guarantees, and by extending subsidies, such as cheaper gasoline,[20] and income tax exemptions. General Banzer, for instance, passed a law in 1971 (Decree No. 9669) exempting unionized transporters from the payment of income taxes. As a result of these concessions, largely motivated by political considerations on the part of the military, the transportistas' unions have been the staunchest supporters of the military regimes.

The power of the CSCB was momentarily threatened after 1978 when the social forces compelling General Banzer to step out of office sought, among other things, to curtail the power of the CSCB. Local newspapers of that period are filled with denunciations of the transporters' arbirtrary fare increases by almost every sector of the population. In Congress, too, members of the newly organized parties passed resolutions denouncing the CSCB as illegal and unconstitutional. Campesino unions often mobilize to block the roads to protest against exhorbitant increases in transport fares. In a widespread mobilization in November 1979, campesinos set up road blocks in several regions in Bolivia to prevent the flow of agricultural goods into the urban centers. In several localities, they also attacked transporters and burned their trucks. For almost a week, the country was paralyzed. Transport stopped, with resulting food shortages in the cities. The campesinos were protesting both against the economic measures taken by the government[21] and against the transportistas, who had raised their fares after an increase in the price of gasoline. In a show of support, the Central Obrera Boliviana (COB) called a one-day general strike, expelled the CSCB from its ranks and, at the same time, promoted the organization of an independent (but short-lived) Federation of Salaried Drivers (*Presencia,* July 13, 1980). The conflict was resolved through the efforts of the COB, which mediated between the Bolivian government, the Confederación Unica de Trabajadores Campesinos de Bolivia (CSUTCB), and the CSCB. The government agreed to give a preferential gasoline price to the transportistas, stipulated that freight and passenger fares could only be increased by 30 percent, and promised to attend to the CSUTCB's long-term demands.[22] The democratic experiment was short-lived, lasting only two years. These years were punctuated by three military coups which nullified the results of three national elections. Not until 1983, with the return of a democratic government under the presidency of Siles Suazo, was public road transport declared open to anyone who wanted to engage in it. Yet, the transporters' confederation was not abolished. On the contrary, it staged numerous strikes demanding fare increases and the import of tires for union members at the official exchange rate, demands that the government was forced to accept. Ironically, this concession led several nonunionized transporters in Tiraque to join the local union so that they would be eligible to purchase cheaper tires for their trucks.[23]

Powerful as the CSCB is in Bolivia, the Tiraque-based union failed to maintain the cantón Tiraque effectively under the control of its unionized transporters. Nevertheless, union membership allowed them to share some of the privileges accorded to transporters by the state.

The Transporters' Union in Tiraque

To check competition and retain control over an area of operation, merchants and transporters made use of several strategies to keep competitors out. These ranged from outright threats and intimidation to the voluntary association and unionization of truckers.[24] Thus, in 1963, Tiraqueños formed a truckers' association (Asociación de Choferes de Tiraque General Barrientos) to establish rights of operation over the entire cantón Tiraque. The stated aim of this organization was "to put an end to the disorder created in Tiraque by foreign [non-local] owners of vehicles who trample over the rights of the sons of the town" (AAT: Correspondencia, February 4, 1963). The actual purpose was to defend the interests of Tiraqueño transporters and merchants. The association did not succeed, however, in keeping outsiders away from Tiraque, mainly because at the time there were not more than twelve truckers in the town. Tiraqueños then made several attempts to organize a local union in order to become part of the CSCB. This would have put them on equal terms with the truckers of Punata, who had been organized in a transport union since 1962.

Not until 1971 did Tiraqueños succeed in these efforts, simply because they could not raise the minimum of twenty-five members required by the confederation for union organization and Tiraque was not a provincial capital—two preconditions for establishing a local provincial union. A ministerial resolution on mandatory unionization and the designation of Jaime Ferrufino, a trucker from Tiraque, as coordinator of the Cochabamba truckers' federation, finally led to the approval of a Tiraque transporters' union—the Sindicato Mixto de Transportistas 10 de Octubre—in 1971. Thirty-five truck owners, including four from Punata, two from Cochabamba, three from the peasant villages, and the remainder from the town of Tiraque, formed the union.[25] Their goals were to regulate the operations of local transport according to a schedule of rotating days and areas of operation; to establish minimum fares within the region; and to "invite" the truckers of Punata and Colomi to respect the jurisdiction of the Tiraque truckers.[26] Since the union's regulations follow the general guidelines set up by the CSCB, it is necessary to describe how the organization of transporters functions in the country as a whole.

The Confederación Sindical de Choferes de Bolivia is formed by ten departmental federations and 160 unions. Besides protecting and defending the interests of transporters, the principal responsibility of the CSCB is to set conditions regulating membership and the benefits and obligations of members. To become a member of the union requires the payment of a fee, a commercial driver's license, and five years' experience. An important prerequisite to becoming a member of some of the more powerful unions is to have connections with high-level union leaders. Each member is allowed to own two vehicles. In practice, however, many have more vehicles than the specified number and circumvent this restriction by registering family members as owners of vehicles.[27] Members are entitled to very few social benefits from the union, apart from minimal provisions for medical care. They do not receive a pension upon retirement.

Thirty-two unions belong to the Cochabamba Federation of Truckers. Seven of these are urban transport unions; two are interdepartmental; seven are associated unions of mechanics and drivers; and sixteen are interprovincial unions that, with few exceptions, have their headquarters in provincial capitals. One of these exceptions is the Tiraque union. Six of the interprovincial unions also form Transpeco, a larger organization regulating long-distance transport. This is the only organization in Cochabamba that collects freight and distributes it (according to alphabetical order) among member truckers. Since there are more trucks than available cargo, most truck owners are assigned a trip only once or twice a month; only those who occupy leadership positions within the union or are friends of these leaders transport freight more often.[28] Interprovincial transporters operate under the guidelines of each provincial union, which regulates transport within a specific region.

In Tiraque, these regulations involve setting a rotational schedule for the sequence of departure of buses and trucks from the town to the marketplaces, or to the city of Cochabamba. On other days, truckers are free to work within the region on the days they please. Bus owners make on average about ten round trips to Cochabamba and four to Punata per month. Truckers make an average of four round trips per month to Punata and two to Cochabamba on a scheduled basis, and they make a variable number of additional trips, carrying manure, wood, or potatoes on a contractual basis. In contrast to the interdepartmental truckers, those operating at the interprovincial level have to seek their own cargo and passengers. It is thus important for them to operate within a region that they know well, because they must get to know local traders, merchants, and peasants in order to develop an assured clientele. Since most of these truckers are also merchants and the sharecropping partners of peasants, they tend to operate only in particular areas within a region.

Transport fares for freight and passengers, established by the CSCB in conjunction with the Bolivian government, vary according to distance, the region, and whether the vehicle travels up or down the mountain roads.[29] In practice, however, fares are often much higher than the official ones. This is mainly because the government (which regulates transport fares in the cities and for interdepartmental and provincial transport between departmental capitals and rural towns) leaves the fares from rural towns to peasant villages unregulated, and so it is up to the local unions to decide what the minimum charge should be. This leaves their members free to charge whatever they please above the basic fare as long as their clients are prepared to pay it. In Tiraque, for instance, the fare that campesinos have to pay to transport a sack of potatoes from their villages to the town of Tiraque or Punata is often higher than the fare charged from the town of Tiraque to Punata or from Tiraque to the city of Cochabamba. This is not the case when they travel as passengers. In August 1984, for instance, the cost for transporting a carga of potatoes was $b750 from Tiraque to Punata, $b2,500 from Sank'ayani to Tiraque, and $b4,000 from Sank'ayani to Punata.

Fares are even higher for the transport of an entire truckload of potatoes or manure, and are set according to the arbitrary calculations of transportistas. Until recently, these fares were usually paid after the harvest in potatoes, but nowadays, truckers demand payment in cash at a rate that is becoming prohibitively high for peasants. The transport of a truckload of manure from Punata to Sank'ayani, for instance, used to cost from one to one-and-a-half sacks of potatoes, or its equivalent, if paid in cash. In April 1982, this fare was $b800 (about the equivalent of a sack of potatoes). By August 1984, this fare was increased to $b140,000, and to a staggering $b120 million in September 1985 (see Table 14).

Provincial or local unions, like those from Tiraque and Punata, reach agreements delimiting areas of operation for their members. According to these agreements, the areas in the vicinity of the town of Tiraque and those on the mountains to the northwest and northeast are reserved for local transporters, while Punateños and all transporters are free to operate in those areas located alongside major public routes, such as the Cochabamba to Santa Cruz road or the Cochabamba to Chapare road. Outside transporters are not allowed to travel to a village located within the jurisdiction of the Tiraque union to pick up passengers and freight or to deliver manure, unless they are contracted to do so by a villager. They can, however, travel to the

TABLE 14. Increase in Transport Costs for Manure from Sank'ayani to Punata Relative to the Price of a Sack of Potatoes, 1982–85.

Year	Transport Cost of Manure ($b)	Price of Potatoes ($b/100 kg)	Truckload/Sack Potatoes Ratio
1982	800	792	1:1
1984	140,000	110,000	1:1.3
1985[a]	120,000,000	15,000,000	1:8

Source: Author's fieldnotes.

[a] These prices reflect the impact on prices brought about by the economic measures taken by the government of Victor Paz Estenssoro in August 1985. The week after these measures were passed, the price of potatoes in Tiraque dropped from $b24 million to $b15 million, while transport costs for manure increased from $b70,000 to $b120 million.

villages to engage in occasional exchange transactions. Finally, all transporters are free to travel to and from any marketplace.

This freedom of movement and the opening of a marketplace in Tiraque in 1971 seriously affected local truckers, since it attracted more competitors from other regions to whom peasants could sell their crops without having to travel to the markets of Punata or Cochabamba, and without having to depend as much on local truckers and merchants. Prominent Tiraqueños, including truckers, were involved in the establishment of the local marketplace mainly to oppose the functioning of a peasant-controlled market opened the previous year on the outskirts of town.[30] In opposing this market, the truckers unknowingly acted against their own interests. On the one hand, the new marketplace brought the market closer to the peasant villages, thus reducing transport costs for those who used to take their crops to Punata or Cochabamba. On the other, it attracted more merchants and truckers into the region on market day, thus increasing competition for Tiraqueño merchants and transporters. Before 1971, these transportistas used to make from three to five round trips from the peasant villages to Cochabamba or Punata on market days; since 1971, however, vecino truck owners seldom go to the villages to pick up passengers and freight destined for the Tiraque market, because peasants generally ride on the vehicles owned by rich campesinos in their villages and merchants from other towns travel on trucks from Punata, Cliza, or Cochabamba. While these truckers have passengers and cargo for the entire round trip, the transportistas from Tiraque would have to make one way of the round trip to Cochabamba without cargo, which, they argue, is not sound economics. They do, however, travel to the markets of Punata and Cochabamba on Tuesdays, Wednesdays, and Saturdays.

Contrary to the expectations of the transporters of Tiraque, then, unionization failed to keep the entire cantón under their control. Since the agrarian reform, the area in which the merchants and truckers of Tiraque once operated actually diminished considerably. Several factors besides the competition posed by merchants and truckers from other towns and the local villages contributed to this: the loss of Vandiola; the construction of a new paved road to Santa Cruz which bypasses the rural towns; the growth of Punata as the most important regional market town; and the weakening of the ties with the towns of Arani and Vacas to the point that, by the 1980s, very few Tiraqueños ever went to these places. Today, merchants and truckers of Tiraque operate and establish ties of fictive kinship with peasants in only twenty-one out of fifty-eight peasant villages, comprising a relatively small area within the cantón Tiraque. Conflicts are not infrequent among transporters, who resent the presence of others in their "domains" or the "unfair" competition of truckers who charge lower fares than those established by the union, or offer better fare bargains to peasants for the bulk transport of manure. Nonunionized transporters, many of whom are from peasant villages, pose the most serious threat to the union, however, and to the interests of town transporters. These rich villagers not only compete with unionized truckers in transport,[31] but also in the provision of cash or inputs needed for cash-crop production by poor peasants. We may recall that the wealthy in Sank'ayani successfully replaced outside transporters and merchants who used to operate in the village.

The Family Enterprise

Shortly after the opening of the marketplace in Tiraque, prominent vecinos (who had replaced the hacendados affected by reform), many of whom had been founding members of the Tiraque transportistas' union, began to emigrate from Tiraque. Few acknowledged increased competition as the main reason for their decision to leave; most justified their departure on the grounds that they sought better educational opportunities for their children. From 1974 to 1980, at any one time there were no more than fifty trucker families. During these six years, however, twenty-eight individual families of truck owners had moved out of the region and been replaced. Twenty-two moved to the city of Cochabamba, where they continued to be involved in urban (taxis or buses) or long-distance transport, mainly to Chapare. Although those involved in long-distance transport make fewer trips per month than those operating within Tiraque, they make more money per trip than any of their rural counterparts.

Luis Torrico, for instance, who owns two trucks, could make a gross income of $b245,000,000 (or about US$817) per month in 1984 just by making two trips between Cochabamba and Chapare.[32] Since Luis occupies a leadership position in the Chapare transporters' union, he can probably make more trips in one month than can rank-and-file union members. Other Tiraqueño transporters, while keeping a truck, invested in other equally profitable enterprises in the city. José Velarde, for example, bought a rice processing plant. Others moved away to Santa Cruz, La Paz, Tarija, and even to Argentina and the United States. Yet all of them kept the land and houses they had in Tiraque, returning to oversee the sowing and harvesting of their crops. These they plant in compañía arrangements with landless or landed peasants. They also return to celebrate the festivity of the Virgen de las Angustias and to pay homage to their dead relatives on Todos Santos (All Saints' Day).

Most of the families of this second migration were wealthy. After the reform, they accumulated enough wealth in Tiraque to invest in the purchase of land or expand control over arable land through compañía and similar contracts; to invest in agricultural and livestock production; and to invest in commerce and moneylending. They also had sufficient assets to finance the purchase of new and larger trucks to engage in long-distance travel after they moved out of Tiraque. Before their departure from Tiraque, these families had consolidated their social position in the region. They had enjoyed high social status and occupied important positions in the alcaldía and in the truckers' union, and they had an extended network of fictive kin. In short, they had replaced the departing hacendados of the 1950s.

Left behind were a few prominent Tiraqueños, along with upwardly mobile merchants and transporters who were seeking to establish themselves as the leading families in the region. These families, however, were not related through marriage, so genealogical links had yet to become important in the operation of their enterprises. Among the upwardly mobile transporters who stayed in Tiraque, four replaced their trucks with buses and were able to make money in transport without having to travel as much as truckers and without having to compete with new truckers. They know that their buses will be filled to capacity on the round trips to Punata and Cochabamba. In the fourteen round trips they make each month, these bus owners earned an average gross income of $b1,094,610 (or US$353) in 1984, while truckers who carried wood from Tiraque to Punata made in twenty monthly round trips an average of only $b800,000 (or US$258).[33] Table 15 shows the monthly gross earnings of four bus owners compared with that of a trucker.

TABLE 15. Gross Earnings from Transport, April 1984.

Transporters	Monthly Gross Earnings ($b)
Bus Owners	
1. Fructuoso	1,149,000
2. Clotilde	1,151,040
3. Alberto	1,152,400
4. Gerardo	926,000
Trucker	
5. Nemecio	800,000

Source: Author's fieldnotes.

All the transportistas listed on the table have other sources of income; three of them, in particular, were able to change their vehicles after they established alliances with peasant households in different villages. Fructuoso and his wife Julia, for instance, hold monopolistic control over an entire village as well as over peasant households in six other villages. They operate as merchants, moneylenders, and compañía partners. Besides their bus, they own land in Tiraque and a chichería in town.

Clotilde, known in Tiraque for her stinginess, also plants in compañía on her own or on peasants' land. She does not lend money, since she does not trust peasants. Now in her sixties, she spends most of her time in Cochabamba, except when traveling in her bus to and from Tiraque. All three of her sons own trucks or buses that they bought with money made in the United States.

Alberto is a young transportista who bought his first truck in 1980. His parents-in-law have been involved in commerce and sharecropping for many years in several villages, although they have never owned a truck. Now, two of their sons-in-law and one son are transportistas and this has helped them expand their family enterprise. Three of their daughters are merchants. They also own a chichería in town.

Gerardo is the least successful of the four bus owners listed in Table 15, mainly because he has never had enough money to engage in exchange, moneylending, or sharecropping on a large scale. Born to a poor, landless family in Tiraque in 1940, Gerardo has never married, and the lack of a wife who could take care of the commercial side of the enterprise may be one reason for Gerardo's lack of success as a transportista. Gerardo joined the army in 1963, serving until 1974. He then migrated to Argentina and remained there for two years. He was able to save enough money to buy a second-hand truck when he returned to Tiraque in 1976; he also joined the local transportistas' union. In 1980, Gerardo spent some time in Chapare, where he bought four hectares of land. After he returned to Tiraque at the end of 1981, he exchanged his truck for a bus. In 1984, Gerardo transferred his membership to the transporters' union of Chapare, to which he traveled with his bus until it was lost in a road accident.[34] As we shall see in Chapter 6, Gerardo is a controversial figure in Tiraque, involved in both the Central Campesina and in local politicking.

Nemecio, the trucker in Table 15, was a carpenter until the revolution of 1952. After harassment by peasants for his affiliation with the Falange Socialista party, he migrated to Argentina for three years. Upon his return in 1960, he bought his first truck. His wife is a merchant, and two of his sons are truckers; one son is also a mechanic. They own land in Tiraque, plant in compañía, and lend money. The family owns a chichería in town. Nemecio is also the cadastral tax collector for the cantón Tiraque. In addition to the twenty round trips that either Nemecio or one of his sons makes to Punata carrying wood, they sometimes transport truckloads of potatoes during the harvest season or truckloads of manure in the planting season. They also buy old trucks and repair and sell them, making a considerable profit in the process.

The most successful family among the new generation of truck owners is probably the Flores family. Carlos Flores was the son of a rural schoolteacher from Punata who married a woman from Tiraque in the early 1900s. When Carlos reached adulthood, he acquired a small plot of land in Vandiola and married Ester Paz from Tiraque. In Vandiola they planted hot peppers, and Carlos, who owned three mules, also worked as a *fletero* (mule pack driver), transporting goods for other colonizers. The Flores family had five sons and two daughters; when their older sons matured, they also were able to work as fleteros. Carlos was put in charge of the coca customs house in Santa Rosa for several years. When Vandiola was abandoned after the agrarian reform, the Flores family moved back to Tiraque, where Carlos bought a small plot of land in the village of Tarugani. His three oldest sons began working as assistants to truck owners and later became truck drivers. After working as drivers for several years, they were able to buy their own second-hand trucks and thus became full-fledged transportistas.[35] David and Matías, the two eldest sons, moved to Cochabamba, where they became affiliated to the Chapare trucker's union. The third son, Felipe, decided to stay in Tiraque, where he has been very successful.

In 1970, Carlos bought his first truck, which he and his two youngest sons, Miguel and José, drove. Carlos, Felipe, and David were founding members of the Tiraque truckers' union. All the men in the Flores family except one, who is a rural schoolteacher in Santa Cruz, are transportistas. The two daughters are single: Carmen is a rural schoolteacher, and Julia was in charge of the Registro Civil in Tiraque until 1983. Carlos died in 1981, and his truck was inherited by Miguel, who dropped out of military school that same year. José worked as a driver until 1984, when he bought a Mercedes-Benz truck. Miguel and José are also members of the transportistas' union.

In 1970, Felipe, the third son, married Beatriz Camacho, first a chhalera, and later a potato rescatista from Tiraque. On recounting her life history, Beatriz says that when she married, she used to make more money as a rescatista than her husband made as a driver. In 1976, Felipe bought his first truck, which allowed them to expand the extent and volume of their commercial enterprise. Two years later, Felipe bought thirty-five hectares of land in Tarugani, and since then, he has bought land there and in other areas, amounting to some sixty hectares. Felipe claims that he plants more potatoes (100 sacks) and gets higher yields than anybody else in Tiraque. Although it is difficult to corroborate this claim, Felipe has certainly become a capitalist farmer, since he not only farms his land with wage labor, but also invests large amounts of capital in production. Like his brothers, he borrows this capital from the Banco Agrícola.[36] Yet he works on his land shoulder to shoulder with the wage laborers he employs, dressed as a campesino, wearing rubber sandals and a poncho (something that no other vecino would do). Beatriz accompanies her husband when they go to work the land, and, with the help of peasant women, she cooks for the laborers. They argue that it is important to be present and work alongside the laborers if they want to make sure that all work well. They also produce in compañía with peasants, providing seed and/or fertilizer. In addition, the family owns from ten to twenty oxen, some of which Felipe distributes among campesino families through a shares system, while he fattens others and resells them at double their price after two months.

Beatriz still works as a rescatista. Every Friday she buys between 90 and 120 sacks of potatoes in the Tiraque market, from peasants in their villages, and in her own house. She sells these potatoes, the crops from their own land, and their share of potatoes and other agricultural products that they produce in compañía, to a distant relative in Cochabamba. He, in turn, resells them in the department of Beni, where the price of a sack of potatoes is higher than in Cochabamba. For several years, the Flores family members were the only local representatives of Bayer fertilizers and insecticides and operated a small shop in their house. They have two houses in Tiraque, and they are now building a three-story house in Cochabamba to which they are planning to move soon.

Felipe traded in his truck several times, each time buying a larger one. During the period of fieldwork, he had a ten-ton Ford that he drove himself. Unlike other truck owners, Felipe seldom has the truck parked for long periods of time. On market days, he makes two or three round trips a week to Punata and Cochabamba, as well as at least two trips per week with manure during the planting season. He also, on occasion, carries wood. On average, he makes some seventeen trips a month. Besides this, when he is not busy farming the land, Felipe makes trips from Chapare to Cochabamba and beyond, carrying fruit. In 1982, Felipe had a serious accident with his truck. His cousin and his younger daughter died in the accident, and Beatriz broke both legs. Several other people were injured, which meant that Felipe had to pay their hospital and medical bills.[37] The truck was so badly damaged that it took him a year to have it repaired. Beatriz could not work as a rescatista for a long time. But the expenditures resulting from the accident and their inability to operate as transporters and merchants did not impoverish the family, a fact that serves to illustrate the importance of their other enterprises. As Felipe states, at present he makes more money in cash crops and livestock production than he does as a trucker. The truck is useful, he claims, because he does not have to depend on others to take fertilizer and manure to his land and to transport the harvest and the potatoes they sell. Indeed, the truck enables him to avoid relations of dependency for fertilizer and for access to markets, relations that would cost him a sizable portion of his crops. The truck also helps Felipe get to know more peasants and landless townspeople, whom he can then hire as laborers and with whom he can ultimately enter into compañía relations.

Felipe has held several public positions. When the Tiraque truckers' union was founded, he was elected transport secretary. Three years later, in 1974, he was elected secretary-general, a position he still holds, despite the union's rules that no one can hold office for more than two years. But Felipe also maintains close relations with the leadership of the Cochabamba transporters' federation. In addition, Felipe served as president of the school's parents' committee for several years. Surprisingly, he has never been elected to occupy any position in the alcaldía. Instead, his brother Miguel was elected mayor of the town, an office that he occupied from 1980 until 1982, when he was removed after a conflict erupted between transporters and townsfolk, schoolteachers, and campesinos over an increase in transport fares. Miguel was accused of defending the transportistas rather than representing the interests of Tiraqueños in general.[38]

Taken together, these six short, selective biographies illustrate a number of themes shared by the emergent dominant families as well as by the more established families in the region. These include the interweaving of family members in different yet complementary activities; the formation of family-run, multiple enterprises that combine "alliances" with peasants, trade, transport, and money lending; the important part played by women in the success of the family enterprise.

In conclusion, it may be observed that competition within this segmented class of merchants and transporters takes place not between specialized agents, such as merchants and transporters, but across a wide range of economic activities between contending families. As we have seen, the best strategy for limiting this competition is to establish and maintain intimate alliances with poor peasants, producing with them in compañía, buying directly from them, and providing transport services for them as "partners." These enterprises thus rest squarely on peasant labor, the basis for the accumulation of wealth in the region. The fact that Felipe Flores was planning to move out at the point at which he was able to transform wealth into wage capital illustrates a larger and crucial process, namely that whereas the extraction of wealth takes place in the countryside, its transformation into capital is associated with the migration of the wealthy to the cities.[39]

Chapter 6
The Culture of Power and Politics

Contrary to what I had expected, given the structural relations of dominance and dependence binding peasants to the regional merchant class, political alignments and social cleavages unite and divide Tiraqueños in ways that do not always correspond to class alignments or interests. Peasants seldom openly oppose merchants as a class. Instead, they tend to divide into factions and align with nonpeasant groups. In only two contexts have campesinos united around a common cause: during the early revolutionary years of the 1950s, when they mobilized against hacendados and, more recently, when campesinos mobilized to confront the state. This they did by opening their own markets or by boycotting the market, blocking roads and demanding government intervention to obtain better prices for their crops.

My argument is that what makes peasant resistance difficult for Tiraqueños are the intimate relationships peasants establish with particular households in order to produce cash crops. This connection prevents peasants from moving effectively against their compañía partners and fictive kin, with whom they have direct, productive relations and to whom they often sell their crops. In contrast, both wealthy and poor campesinos and vecinos can and do mobilize against the state, that is, in a setting where they are confronting neither their partners nor their fictive kin, but rather the "faceless" yet powerful forces that affect, in different ways, the livelihood of all. More often than not, however, these mobilizations have not been successful, but have ended in repression, as occurred in the road blockade of 1974, in unfulfilled promises on the part of the state, or in the factional division of campesinos. In fact, it was during one of these mobilizations against the state that new factions (those existing at the time of fieldwork) were formed, placing in opposition a new generation of campesino leaders and an older generation that had emerged during the post-1952 revolutionary years and during General Barrientos's regime. After that time, politicking in Tiraque may be characterized by periods of quiescence—underlined with latent factionalism—and punctuated by conflict and overt division, with leaders rallying vecinos and campesinos from various villages to confront leaders in the opposite faction. Although a relatively small number of recurrent protagonists actively participate in these conflicts, the events in which they become involved have, in one way or another, affected the entire region.

In this chapter, I analyze social and cultural constructions of class and identity by examining the ways in which local modes of representation of self and others are negotiated and contested in discourse and daily life. The case will be made by using two different but related examples. The first deals with political conflicts and factional disputes, focusing on the historical formation and reformulation of factions and on the use of the concept "campesino" (peasant) as a "class" idiom for political incorporation. In the second and contrasting case, I describe the ritual celebration of the Virgen de las Angustias (patron of successful townspeople), in which vecinos participate to gain social status congruent with their wealth. This example will also show how vecinos make use of the concept "indio" (Indian) as an "ethnic" idiom for social closure—a closure that both delineates and reflects intraclass antagonisms between town and village "elites." [1] Both cases will serve to illustrate how class and cultural antagonisms and alliances interweave in complex ways. The argument is that, whereas common cultural values and ideals both underlie and restrain political disputes and confrontations, these values are interpreted, manipulated, or used differently by different people in different contexts and situations. While nouveau riche villagers and townspeople draw closer together as members of a dominant merchant class, at the same time ideological and subjective ethnic distinctions keep them apart. Further, I argue, these political practices and cultural constructions of class and identity are structurally related to ongoing processes of rural differentiation, class formation, and articulation with larger forces. In fact, these different interpretations of social reality are similar to the "traditional" values, institutions, and forms of labor mobilization and exchange used by an emergent class to exploit the peasantry. An analysis of conflict and ritual will then unravel the paradoxes and contradictions of class and culture. As Sider (1986:8–9) puts it, "Culture enters the dynamic of class because . . . it is where class becomes dynamic; where the lines of antagonism and alliance come together and apart." To capture this dynamic, it is important to examine not only conflicts between classes but also within classes, as well as inter- and intraclass alliances and oppositions.

Campesinos Confront the State

As we saw in Chapter 3, rural communities came into being in Tiraque and in the central valleys of Cochabamba as a result of campesino mobilization and struggle over land and against the hacendados. These communities incorporated former colono, sharecropper, and piquero households that were highly differentiated households even before agrarian reform. Since then, too, ongoing processes of class formation have further differentiated these households. In spite of these differences, communities developed as "aspects of struggle" and, as such, they often become "active" communities, thus succeeding "in being neighbours first and social classes only second" (Williams 1973:104–7). But, as Williams also reminds us, "This should never be idealized, for at the points of decision, now as then, the class realities usually show through."[2] It is important, I argue, to keep this in mind when discussing community mobilization and consciousness. A disregard for these distinctions has led some social scientists to refer to "peasants" in a way that profoundly ignores crucial class differences among households. The fact that in Tiraque, as probably in many other regions, wealthy and poor villagers, campesinos and vecinos unite in alliances—alliances that are often formed under the campesino banner—does not mean that the outcome of their collective action will have similar results for different social protagonists. This will become clear when we discuss campesino political mobilization and factionalism in Tiraque.

The latent factionalism[3] present in situations in which campesinos mobilize to confront the state can be seen in two contrasting episodes: the opening of a campesino-controlled market in 1971 and the boycotting of the markets in 1982. The first episode reveals efforts to resist local authorities and influence market location and unequal competition by bringing the market closer to the rural villages and attracting more merchants. This provides the background for understanding the formation and composition of the factions dividing Tiraqueños during the period of fieldwork. The second case illustrates the futility of attempts to confront merchant capital in the marketplace by leaving untouched the class alliances that characterize production. These episodes show both the articulation of peasants with the market and the impossibility of their effectively either withdrawing from it or influencing it. The market, presumably the area in which they are free to come and go, sell or buy, negotiate price and quantities, is in fact the place where peasants continually rediscover their vulnerability and their powerlessness.

Campesinos Open a Marketplace

In 1970, the alcaldía of Tiraque decided to increase revenues by charging campesinos a tax on the agricultural products they sold outside the region. To collect this tax, employees from the alcaldía stood outside the town on the road to Cochabamba, stopped trucks, and forcibly charged peasants fifty Bolivian cents per sack of potatoes and twenty-five cents per quintal of barley;[4] truckers were also asked to collaborate in the collection of this tax by identifying the owners of potatoes in their trucks for the tax collectors (AAT: Ordenanza Municipal, 1970). To avoid the payment of this new municipal tax, campesinos from three neighboring villages in the valley of Tiraque (Plano Bajo, Plano Alto, and Millumayo) opened a marketplace in Lomapata in the immediate vicinity of the town of Tiraque (three kilometers away) but outside the town and near the villages. They were led by a pro-market committee of seven men.

One man, Marcos Inturias, was at the time the secretary-general of the Central Campesina; the others, however, were young men (the sons of former colonos in the haciendas Urmachea and Millumayo) who had been too young to take leadership positions during the implementation phase of agrarian reform. The training ground for these emergent leaders was a conflict over a landing strip that had been built in 1966 on the former hacienda Millumayo so that the plane General Barrientos used for his travels in the Bolivian countryside could also land in Tiraque. This conflict had erupted at about the same time as the opening of the market. The land belonged to the former colonos of the hacienda, who had made it available with the understanding that the former hacendado would compensate them with an equivalent amount of land. Since he failed to do so, the peasants decided to plow the landing strip after Barrientos's death. This led to a confrontation with the vecinos, who insisted that a landing strip was necessary for the town. The landing field was built, plowed, and rebuilt several times; the mayor appealed to the army to declare Tiraque a military zone and to the air force to take control of the landing strip. This time the campesinos resisted through legal means, hiring a lawyer to argue their case. They won a lawsuit in 1971. At first, only the former colonos of Millumayo participated in the event, but as the conflict grew, campesinos from neighboring villages also became involved. Soon after this confrontation, these leaders organized the market in Lomapata.

The family of Marcos Inturias donated lands for the marketplace. Other committee members built adobe houses around the market grounds, and, in order to attract merchants, campesinos lowered the prices of their cash crops and declared the market a *feria franca*, implying that merchants did not have to pay municipal taxes. The market was a success: it attracted merchants and truckers from other regions, deprived the alcaldía of the right to collect taxes, and threatened the local truckers' control of transport in Tiraque.[5] But the market gave campesinos a degree of independence from town control that the mayor and vecinos were not willing to tolerate. To counter what they viewed as a threat, prominent vecinos (a trucker and two small claims judges) organized a committee, including two old campesino leaders and one of the founders of the Lomapata market,[6] to establish a marketplace in the town of Tiraque. The mayor also appealed to the army, accusing Inturias of being a "communist instigator" (AAT: Correspondencia 1972). This was a serious accusation indeed during the repressive regime of General Banzer. Truckers actively supported the opening of the market in town and contributed to its success. On the day of its inauguration in January 1973, local transporters provided free transportation to campesinos and merchants attending the market. The outcome of this struggle was the gradual decline and closing of the Lomapata market, once again favoring the town of Tiraque over its rural hinterland.

This struggle over the marketplace blurred class conflict since factions were composed of vecinos and campesinos, rich and poor. The alliance of campesino leaders with prominent vecinos has persisted until the present time. The split among the principal campesino leaders has never been mended. Rather, as we shall see, the rift has tended to deepen.

Campesinos Boycott the Market

In 1976, campesinos from the area of Tiraque organized the Association of Potato Producers (Asociación de Productores de Papa, or APP) which later became a department-wide organization and received legal recognition in 1978.[7] The objectives of this organization were to produce and sell potatoes with cheaper inputs and higher market prices; to import fertilizers and insecticides; to obtain fair prices based on actual production costs; and to "bypass brokers, who increase the price of potatoes, in defense of the peasant economy and the interests of consumers" (APP: Acta de Fundación, August 28,

1976).[8] After the military coup of General García Meza in 1980, the APP was considered a "leftist organization" and was therefore banned.

Although some members of the association continued to carry out underground meetings, it was only in February 1982 that the APP reorganized publicly. Delegates from the entire department of Cochabamba met in Tiraque to elect an ad hoc committee that would lead the APP until elections were called. In this and subsequent meetings, the delegates voted to boycott the market by not selling potatoes, and to request that the government increase the price of a sack of potatoes to the level of the price of fifty kilograms of chemical fertilizer.[9] The measure, implemented in April 1982, put pressure on the departmental authorities who met in Tiraque with the APP to negotiate a solution. The prefect of Cochabamba promised to allow an increase in the price of potatoes (up to $b1,400 per sack) in the city and to import duty-free fertilizer at the official exchange rate if the APP lifted the boycott.

Although the prefect did not keep his word, the APP lifted the boycott once campesinos realized that, for several reasons, it was not going to be successful. First, the decision to boycott the market seriously affected campesinos from regions where potatoes were ready for harvest and sale. Second, other so-called campesinos did not respect the boycott, taking truckloads of potatoes in their own trucks to sell in other markets. They, as well as other sharecropping partners, ultimately benefited from the boycott, since they were able to profit even more from the higher prices their crops obtained in a market with less supply. A final reason for lifting the boycott was that all the members of the APP ad hoc committee were summoned to Cochabamba to face charges of leftist affiliation raised against them in Tiraque.

The failure of these mobilizations illustrates three crucial problems: first, the powerlessness of campesinos when they choose to confront the state rather than the dominant classes in the region; and second, the contradictory nature of the APP, which is formed by poor, middle, and rich campesinos, as well as wealthy town-based merchants. (This situation is replicated in the villages, in the village unions, and in the Central Campesina.) Contrary to its rhetoric, the APP best represents the interests of rich campesinos, many of whom are, in fact, merchants, transporters, and capitalist sharecropping partners. In 1984, for instance, the association decided to import fertilizers and insecticides directly from Europe and Japan in order to circumvent the commercial importing houses. This, however, required members to deposit money (the equivalent in Bolivian pesos of twenty-five U.S. dollars per sack of fertilizer) in a bank six months in advance, a requirement that most peasants could not fulfill.[10] Finally, both the opening of the market outside the town of Tiraque and the boycott took place during the periods of repressive right-wing dictatorships, and in both instances, progressive leaders were accused of being "communists." These confrontations, then, bring to light the relationship of local politics to wider national and global forces.

The history of the campesino movement has been intimately related to developments in Bolivian national politics since the revolution of 1952. As we saw in Chapter 3, the state and national political movements sought, on various occasions, the political support of campesinos. Tiraqueños did not stay outside these events. They joined the campesino militias in support of the National Revolution; they were also sent to Santa Cruz and Beni to fight the right-wing members of the Falange Socialista Boliviana party. They divided into opposing camps in the champa guerra, and also participated in the 1974 road blockade.

General Banzer's "carrot-and-stick" policy toward campesinos (implemented after the 1974 blockade in which many of them were massacred) rewarded those loyal to the government and persecuted those considered dangerous elements, thus furthering the conflict among campesino leaders by creating greater personal animosities between those in control of the Central Campesina and those outside it. In Tiraque, Marcos Inturias (see below), often intimidated by the government's hand-picked campesino coordinator of the Central Campesina and his followers, was finally forced to emigrate to an agricultural colony in Santa Cruz, where he has remained ever since. At the same time, the Central Campesina received a tractor and agricultural tools from the government in recognition of the loyalty of its leaders. After the organization of an alternative, yet clandestine, campesino confederation, positions became even more polarized and factions formed around the opposing campesino leaders. Since that time, the main object of factional dispute has been control of the Tiraque Central Campesina, although the two factions have taken opposing stands in almost all of the conflicts that have taken place in the region.

Class, Factions, and Coalitions

Although class divides Tiraqueños, they often appeal to a "class" idiom—*campesino*—to build a following in factional disputes. This term, which literally means peasant, was first introduced in Bolivia after the agrarian reform to refer to the rural population, substituting an "unbiased" term for the pejorative "Indian." We may recall the local definition of campesino. Nowadays, to be a campesino in Cochabamba is to have access to land, to speak Quechua and, probably more important for men, to know how to drive the ox-drawn plow. Residence in a community and/or membership in a campesino union are also important, though not exclusive, criteria. These constitute public, openly stated notions of *campesinidad* (of being peasant), which are often appealed to in order to legitimate one's right to be considered a campesino, or to challenge the right of others to define themselves as campesinos. But local representations of campesinidad are also manifested in visible yet unspoken forms, such as the sandals and weathered feet and hands of men, women, and children; the rough, homespun slacks and *corazas* (short ponchos) men wear over manufactured clothes when working in the fields or the ponchos they wear on cold days; the thick, homespun polleras, shawls, and hats women wear on their braided hair. In both senses, however, the concept campesino is far from clear, for it encompasses differentiated groups. Furthermore, vecinos, who usually do not perceive themselves as campesinos, share many social and cultural characteristics with them. All vecinos speak Quechua, most have access to land and know how to plow, and some are members of sindicatos campesinos. Many vecinas don polleras and shawls and put their hair in braids. It is precisely because of the ambiguity of the concept that what it involves to be a campesino is contested in public and, simultaneously, used as an inclusive category to incorporate both poor and wealthy campesinos and vecinos in factional conflicts and in political mobilizations against the state.

Superficially, it would seem that political ideology and rhetoric divide Tiraqueños more than do class distinctions. In fact, the self-definition of factions, politicking, and the argument for political dispute are expressed in ideological and rhetorical terms. One of the factions defines itself as "nationalist," but members of the other faction call it "rightist." Three of its campesino leaders are men in their fifties who moved to leadership positions during the later stages of the MNR government and General Barrientos's regime, alternating during that time as secretaries-general of the Central Campesina. All three were members of the MNR regional party cell and were outspoken supporters of Barrientos. Although they have not occupied any position in the Central Campesina since 1970, they remain the undisputed leaders of the nationalist faction. The other leaders are younger men who were attracted to this faction during or after the Lomapata event and who occupied the position of secretary-general or coordinator in the Central Campesina during the military governments, in active cooperation with these governments.

Members of the other faction refer to themselves and are recognized as "leftist." Marcos Inturias was the main leader of this faction until he was forced to leave the region. He was the son of a former colono and had attended the University of San Simón at Cochabamba for two years. According to local accounts, Inturias's political awareness, education, and integrity made him a leader with a difference. His style provided an alternative model of political leadership for a younger generation of campesinos from his own and neighboring villages. After Inturias left the region, the younger campesinos became leaders of this faction, occupying minor leadership positions in their villages during Banzer's regime and moving into significant positions in the Central Campesina during the post-Banzer democratic governments. These new leaders had their politics formed not so much in the revolutionary years of agrarian reform, or in the schools and universities, but in witnessing the direct intervention and violence of military regimes. In general, they are more independent of the state than the former leaders.

Campesinos' political rhetoric, manifested in public speeches, conforms to certain practices that serve to distinguish leaders from nonleaders, campesinos from vecinos, and nationalists from leftists. Although both campesino leaders and vecinos are bilingual speakers of Quechua and Spanish, only campesinos exclusively use Quechua when they address a public issue. The Quechua they speak differs from colloquial Quechua, however, borrowing extensively from Spanish, which makes the language characteristically redundant and repetitive. The Quechua they speak is, therefore, different from that of the rank-and-file campesinos. Vecino leaders select the language they use according to their audience: if it is formed by a majority of vecinos and the issue relates only to the town, they use Spanish; but if the issue concerns the region and the audience consists of campesinos and vecinos, they speak Quechua. This Quechua, too, is different from the speech of rank-and-file campesinos.[11] Members of the nationalist and leftist factions also make use of specific figures of speech to distinguish each other's political ideologies. The leftists tend to address other campesinos as *compañeros* (comrades); the nationalists tend to use *hermanos* (brothers) to emphasize their nonleftist orientation.

The internal cohesion of factions tends to be based more on leaders' shared experiences than on the sharing of a well-defined political ideology. Some campesinos have changed factional allegiance several times in their careers and, because of this, they are called *pasa-pasa* (individuals who change political affiliation often) by other campesinos. Desertion from one faction and incorporation into the opposing one is generally due to personal conflicts between leaders. Most of the campesino leaders are well off. They come from villages located in the valley of Tiraque, near the town or from the town itself, and they are related to each other through kinship, affinal, and compadrazgo ties that crosscut their factions. The fact that most of the campesino leaders are from neighboring villages located in the valley of Tiraque and near the town has made this the most conflict-laden area in the region. The split between leaders from the same village has led to fission of "communities," for instance, with Plano Bajo divided into Plano Bajo and Urmachea, Pista split into Pista and Millumayo, and Chapapani divided into Chapapani and Villa Progreso.

Leaders in both factions tend to build a core group of supporters who ordinarily remain loyal to them, even when the leaders decide to change their factional membership. Some leaders build their core group principally among their brothers or other close kin or affinal relatives; others recruit loyal followers among campesinos from their own village; still others rely more on campesinos from both neighboring and distant villages. Besides this core of loyal supporters, leaders recruit larger groups of followers only for those occasions on which larger numbers are needed, such as for a show of force or for an election in the Central Campesina. In contrast to the core group, this group is less committed and more passive. Its members tend to follow the directives of their own village leaders who, in turn, align with the factions' leaders. These alignments are short-lived and tend to shift, since they are made around specific issues and depend on localized particularities, such as who controls the union in a village at a particular time.

The alliances between the leaders of each faction and their followers rest upon shared experiences, friendship, and, to a lesser extent, shared political ideology. This bond is strengthened by the implicit understanding that they will share some of the political "spoils." Failure to do so weakens the alliance and often results in the desertion of some individuals. Similar motives cement relations between leaders and their core followers. Political capital may be tapped from different sources. The most important sources originate with the state, the political parties, the development institutions working in the region, the churches, the *gringos* (foreigners), and the personal networks of relations with departmental and national campesino leaders.

The leaders of the Cochabamba-based Federación Campesina are important potential allies in regional disputes, and members of both factions seek to establish personal ties with them. During the military regimes, the Tiraque nationalist faction had no problem establishing such relations, since the Federación's leadership was also nationalist. But in periods of democratic government, the leaders of the Federación were "leftist." Yet, division also exists among these leaders. Capitalizing on this, the Tiraque nationalists seek the support of at least one of the Federación's leaders who might be attempting to build his own power base within the department of Cochabamba. Other non-Tiraqueños may also become potential allies: foreigners residing in Tiraque (a doctor and his wife), a visiting anthropologist, those who occasionally show up to supervise ongoing development projects, and those who want to start new projects. Campesino leaders of both factions try to be the first to establish relationships with such persons, perceiving them as potential, although often unaware, allies who may help by taking people around in their jeeps to carry out different errands and who may act as cultural brokers in the city.

The state has been the major provider of political resources, especially during military regimes. These resources may be extended directly to leaders or through the official party, the state institutions, and the Tiraque Central Campesina. State prebends are conspicuous during electoral campaigns. At election time, the official party might give money to leaders in recognition of their political loyalty and for "buying" campesinos votes, or use state development institutions and personnel to influence peasant voting patterns through the provision of favors and even through the establishment of fictive kin relations. Out-of-power political parties extend resources to campesino leaders directly or through private development institutions working in the region in order to obtain votes. All these institutions, subsidized by political parties or the state, extend different resources to Tiraqueños. These range from the construction of irrigation systems and canals, to interest-free or low-interest capital to initiate agricultural projects or set up dispensaries, to technical assistance, and to the distribution of basic food staples to women's clubs. The state institution for community development organized women's clubs in several villages in Tiraque, distributed basic food staples to campesino households,[12] and, during the period of field research, was involved in a large irrigation project financed by the West German government. The Catholic and Protestant churches also provide a variety of resources to their followers. The Catholic Church, for instance, organized women's centers through which mothers of infants received basic food staples in twenty-seven villages. They also opened a dispensary in town and provided preventive health care for village infants. The evangelicals have a free boarding house for poor peasant children in town.

Cooperation among all of these state, private, and religious organizations is almost nonexistent. Instead, they compete among themselves to establish spheres of influence in the region in order to capture campesino support, votes, or, as one campesino put it, "to justify their salaries and funding which they receive in the name of campesinos." While campesino leaders and factions capitalize on this competition for their own benefit, the strategies of these institutions are similar: organized on the basis of opportunism at the top and clientage at the bottom, they create more divisions in the region and add new arguments for contesting interests and claims, implicitly working to defeat the goals of progressive institutions.

Although all the resources made available to Tiraqueños by these institutions can be obtained directly, control of the Central Campesina Tiraque and of the Irrigation Committee is critical for capturing most of them, since through these two organizations uncommitted campesinos can be brought to support the faction that controls them. The Irrigation Committee is a powerful campesino organization set up to supervise the distribution of water to all those villages and households whose members contributed labor in the construction of the irrigation canals. Committee leaders are elected by members of their villages but, since its inception, the committee has been under the control of the nationalist faction. Thus, the main object of factional dispute, and of mobilizing support, has been the control of the Central Campesina which, depending on the national political climate, has been led by leaders of either the leftist or the nationalist faction. Control over the Central Campesina is important, too, because it allows one faction to bring about changes in the personnel of most other political offices in the town of Tiraque, such as the alcaldía, the civic committee, the civil register, and the Association of Potato Producers (APP). The two factions also become involved in and take opposing stands regarding most of the conflicts in the region.

From 1971 to 1978, the nationalist faction controlled the Central Campesina. After General Banzer stepped down, and during the brief democratic interval (1978–80), members of the "leftist" faction controlled the alcaldía, the Central Campesina, the APP, and the Irrigation Committee. After the coup staged by General García Meza in 1980, control of these offices was taken over by members or sympathizers of the nationalist faction, and the APP was banned. A transporter, Miguel Flores, was elected mayor, and his sister took charge of the civil register. The nationalists remained in office until shortly before the reinstitution of democratic government in 1982.

The first indication that the political process was opening up in Tiraque was the reorganization of the APP in February and the staging of a department-wide boycott of markets in April 1982. The leftist faction used the APP as a springboard to seek the control of the Central Campesina and to replace the mayor and other officeholders. They did not have to wait long for the occasion. It came four months later, in August, after the Tiraque transportistas, having failed to pressure the government to authorize an increase in fares, unilaterally increased fares in a manner that many Tiraqueños thought to be excessive.

It was, however, the non-Tiraqueño schoolteachers, living in the town only during the week, who took the lead against the transporters in the conflict that erupted over the increase in transport fares. This dispute involved all Tiraqueños although, as usual, they were divided in two factions. The teachers organized a "Resistance Committee Against the Arbitrary Increase in Transport Fares" that consisted of four campesinos of the leftist faction and three vecinos who sided with this faction. They presented a document to the prefect of Cochabamba, radio stations, and the press, declaring a state of emergency and warning transportistas against increasing fares lest drastic measures be taken against them.

The next day, after Tiraqueños heard this document read on the radio, along with accusations against the Flores family (who were referred to as "thugs" who threatened schoolteachers, controlled the transportistas' union and the alcaldía, falsified documents, and charged excessive rates in the civil register), the square was lively with gossip, criticism, and complaints that the issue of the fare increase had divided the town. Matters grew worse after a transporter and a member of the Resistance Committee got into a fist fight, and the threats and gossip increased; it seemed that the conflict was going to get out of hand. Members of the Resistance Committee made another visit to the prefect, the Teachers Federation, the Central Obrera Departamental, and the news agencies in Cochabamba to complain about the fight and about threats made against the schoolteachers by the transporters. To put an end to the conflict, the prefect ordered that a new mayor be elected in Tiraque to replace Miguel Flores.

A town meeting, to be held on the square, was called for the following Sunday both to deal with the accusations and threats that had been exchanged between some of the truckers and the schoolteachers and to elect a new mayor. The meeting was led by Hernán Salas, a vecino who owns a small plot of land on the outskirts of town and occasionally works as a mason. The audience was formed largely by campesinos, transportistas, and few vecinos, although most watched the event from a distance. Supporting the transportistas was the nationalist faction, while the schoolteachers had the support of the leftist leaders. The meeting began with the transportistas demanding an explanation for the "lies that had been broadcast and reported in the press about the Flores family which," they argued, "damaged its honor." They also accused the schoolteachers of not providing adequate instruction to children, since teachers missed too many classes. "Because they spend so little time in Tiraque," it was said, "they do not have the right to become involved in regional problems and, if they want that privilege, they should reside in the town permanently." As the accusations and counteraccusations grew heated, Salas said that the matter would be discussed later, and that they should proceed with the election of a new mayor. The audience nominated four candidates. Votes were cast as the name of each candidate was called out and people in the audience raised their hands. Salas, the candidate of the transportistas, won the majority of the votes, although he did not want to accept the nomination and wanted even less the office, claiming that he had land to cultivate and other occupations that would not leave him any time for the alcaldía. But those who nominated him—the nationalist faction—insisted that he could not refuse, and Salas was forced to accept the results of the election. The issue that had caused this confrontation—transport fares—was never discussed in this meeting, which ended with people slowly drifting away in groups, many going to the chicherías to continue talking, while others remained in the square to comment on the events.

Several conclusions may be drawn from this conflict, the first to occur during the period of fieldwork. First, it brought to center stage the politically important actors and basic political alignments in the region. Except for transportistas and schoolteachers—the principal actors in the conflict—alignments did not correspond to class or group interests, but campesinos and vecinos sided with either one of the opposing groups. Second, the conflict revealed the interplay of two different political strategies. The transportistas and their allies preferred to limit the conflict to regional boundaries and to rely on threats, bullying, and manipulation to win their case. The faction led by schoolteachers sought to extend the dispute beyond the region by publicizing it and seeking the support of different individuals and institutions from the city of Cochabamba. Third, the transportistas and their supporters, the nationalist faction, were better organized for the confrontation, making sure that a majority of their own followers were present to cast a large number of votes for their candidate. In contrast, only a handful of leftist campesino leaders were present to support the schoolteachers. Since the campesinos did not recruit followers for the election, there were not enough of them to offset the nationalist vote; thus the group that started on the offensive ended on the defensive. Two further major points may be made about this confrontation. One is that the conflict remained restrained, in spite of the many accusations, threats of physical violence, and even fist fights, revealing an underlying cultural understanding regarding how these battles should be fought. Another, related point is that the behavior of the schoolteachers enraged many Tiraqueños, since the teachers were not from Tiraque and did not live in the town. They were thus not part of the "community," and had no right to become involved in its affairs. Town residence, it is important to note, is an ambiguous standard; being "native" to the town is also at issue in such designations.

Hernán Salas did not remain long in office. In four months he resigned, and after an election, he was replaced by Demetrio Zapata, a Tiraqueño who has lived most of his adult life in La Paz. As a nonresident vecino, Zapata stood outside the factions and conflicts dividing the region. Yet, as a native of the town, his friends were the prominent vecinos with whom he tended to side when conflicts emerged. Most vecinos were delighted with the new mayor, whom they perceived as contributing to the "development" of Tiraque. Demetrio Zapata had established a wide network of key contacts in La Paz, which he tapped immediately after becoming mayor. He managed to convince a politician to introduce a bill in Congress to make a new province out of the Segunda Sección Tiraque. Although the bill was not discussed in Congress for a long time, Zapata kept it alive in the minds and dreams of Tiraqueños. He eventually succeeded in gaining the bill's passage in 1986. He also obtained financial aid from the embassy of the Republic of China (Taiwan) to install a new lighting system in the streets of the town, and as a sign of gratitude, he changed the name of its main street to Sun Yat Sen (an interesting change in a region where most people do not know where China is much less who Sun Yat Sen was). A few months later, the British Embassy donated a clock to be installed in one of the church towers. Zapata's main objective, however, had been to persuade these ambassadors to donate money for building a road to the abandoned yungas of Vandiola. In this effort he was not successful.

By the end of 1982, when a democratically elected president, Hernán Siles Suazo, took charge of the national government in October 1982, the leftist faction organized and won a none-too-well publicized election for the Central Campesina. All leadership positions were occupied by campesino leaders of this faction, except for one position that was occupied by a vecino transporter, Gerardo Rocha. This was the first time since the organization of the Central Campesina that a vecino was elected to occupy a leadership position in it. Rocha was also elected president of the civic committee, and from his newly gained positions of power, he sought unsuccessfully to wrest control of the transportistas' union from Felipe Flores. This union is more difficult to manipulate than any other, because only the unionized transportistas, most of whom are vecinos, have the right to vote in the union's internal elections.

In the face of these events, together with changes in the national government, nationalist campesino leaders remained relatively quiet for some time, apart from the criticism they directed against the new secretary-general of the Central Campesina, Pedro Alfaro, for his "self-election." Ironically, it was the near-collapse of the social order, rather than the customary coup, that provided the nationalist faction with the opportunity to oust the leftist leaders from the Central Campesina.

By mid-1983, Bolivians became painfully aware that the new democratic government could not solve the acute economic crisis the military had left as its legacy. The government could not control the consequences of this deepening crisis: increasing inflation, speculation, and the hoarding of basic foodstuffs, which, in turn, led to a never-ending sequence of strikes, road blockades, hunger strikes, and marches staged by every sector of Bolivia's population. The government was virtually paralyzed, so the Central Obrera Boliviana (COB) stepped in to promote Juntas Vecinales (neighborhood organizations) to enable people to acquire basic foodstuffs. In 1983, the combined effects of a drought in the highlands and intermontane valleys and floods in the lowland regions contributed to a further deterioration of the economy. Crops were lost; entire sheep and llama herds were devastated; and whole altiplano villages were abandoned by peasants who migrated to the cities, where they became beggars. To alleviate this situation, the European Economic Community, as well as Japan, the United States, and other countries, donated foodstuffs, fertilizer, and seed to Bolivia.

The effects of the drought were not as devastating in Tiraque as they were in the altiplano. Yet Tiraqueños were entitled to receive flour donated by the European Economic Community and fertilizer donated by the Netherlands. The reception and distribution of the flour created a major conflict in the region. The flour was channeled to Bolivia through the Movimiento de Izquierda Revolucionaria (MIR), one of the parties in the coalition government, which distributed it through popular organizations such as the workers and peasant unions.[13] The MIR favored those organizations that were under party influence, of which the Tiraque Central Campesina was one. The flour thus reached Tiraque through this organization, whose leaders were responsible for its distribution among the villages. Soon after the flour began to arrive and be distributed, rumors began to circulate that the secretary-general and other leaders were not distributing all the flour but were keeping some for themselves. The sources of the rumor were the leaders of the rightist faction, who did everything they could to keep the rumor alive, challenging leftist control of the Central Campesina. These "self-elected" leaders, the nationalists argued, "were stealing flour from campesinos." Moreover, they had accepted a transporter, Gerardo Rocha, into the Central Campesina. Arguing that Rocha was not a campesino because "he did not know how to drive the ox-drawn plow," they challenged his right to occupy a leadership position in the campesino organization. For these reasons, they claimed, the Central Campesina leadership had to be re-elected. And the nationalist faction organized an ad hoc committee to be responsible for demanding a new election.

Even before a date was fixed for the election, both factions began to campaign. Leaders organized neighboring villages or unions into subregional campesino organizations, or *subcentrales*, that served as subregional power bases for the contending factions.[14] Leaders also organized two Juntas Vecinales to acquire staple foodstuffs at low cost from national and international agencies. These Juntas Vecinales also served as showcases for each faction to demonstrate publicly, vis-à-vis the opposite faction, its efficiency in obtaining and delivering goods. Finally, both factions sought the support of noncampesino allies such as schoolteachers, vecinos, transportistas, leaders of the Federación Campesina, and the personnel of private and state institutions. Some of these allies collaborated by providing transportation for the leaders in their proselytizing campaigns in the villages or by transporting campesinos to the town of Tiraque on the day of the elections.

It would seem that in the midst of a national crisis, Tiraqueños were oblivious to wider problems, since they were involved in petty acrimonies that intensified the contention of local factions. But the election not only serves to outline the "manipulative strategies" (Vincent 1978) of factions, but also to unravel the relation of class and consciousness, as well as the interplay of regional and wider political forces. In 1983–84 the crisis-relief foodstuffs donated by industrial nations created, as well as alleviated, problems. These goods tended to end up in the hands of those who least needed them and also tended to increase campesinos' dependence on the political parties, churches, and other institutions that acted as intermediaries in their delivery. The food assistance policy not only made people dependent, but also provided resources that were tapped by dominant groups for their own economic or political profit. In the case of Tiraque, this food provided still more opportunities for fomenting corruption, graft, political division, and conflict among both campesinos and vecinos.

The fragmentation brought about by the increased dependency

and the greater resources available for factional manipulations can be seen in the elections for leaders of the Central Campesina in December 1983 and in January 1984. The electoral campaign intensified in December after both factions agreed with the Federación Campesina to hold the election on December 24. The incumbent leaders of the Central decided, however, to advance the date of the election to December 22 while the nationalist faction held another election on December 24, resulting in two different and opposing leaderships for the Central Campesina. Both elections took place in the town square and, on both occasions, there were about two hundred peasants present, most of whom were from the villages loyal to the faction that was holding the election. Thus, within two days there were two elections in the Central resulting in two leaderships. Each claimed to be the legitimate campesino representatives in the Central as they had been elected in free elections and each sent a different delegation to a campesino meeting in Cochabamba and to a peasant congress held in La Paz.

This state of affairs persisted until the rightist faction, on the pretext that its election had not been properly sanctioned by the Federación Campesina, was able to convince the latter to oversee new elections, which were scheduled for January 13, 1984. When the leftist leaders were notified, however, they opposed them. They sent a document to the Federación declaring that elections had already been held on December 22; they also declared the Tiraque Central independent from the Cochabamba Federación, and warned against sending representatives to supervise new elections. In spite of this show of bravado, on January 13 members of both factions waited around the Tiraque square for the arrival of the Federación's representatives. When it became obvious they would not show up, the leftist leaders of the Central Campesina held a meeting in the town hall, while the rightist leaders held another meeting in the marketplace. The rightists then decided that they also had the right to meet in the alcaldía which meant that they had to remove the leftists by force. Since they outnumbered the leftists, the rightist faction gained control of the alcaldía after a fist fight (the transporter Gerardo Rocha receiving most of the blows).

From that moment on, the confrontation between the two factions was more open, although it mainly involved isolated fights between an individual of one faction with two or three of the other. A man returning home alone at night or drinking alone in a chichería became an easy target for attack by members of the other faction. Most men thus avoided being alone. The wives of the leftist leaders, in particular, made a point of not letting their husbands out of their sight.

The conflict climaxed early one Friday evening when one of the nationalist leaders, returning home after spending a day in the market and chicherías, was attacked by the younger brothers of Pedro Alfaro (the secretary-general of the leftist faction). The nationalist leaders decided to retaliate by attacking a house in the village of Millumayo, where they suspected Alfaro had hidden the flour he was rumored to have kept for himself. Carrying guns, they went to the house, where they were met by Pedro and his family, the men brandishing a few old guns and the women holding broken bottles in their hands. For almost four hours, the shooting could be heard from the town, but even then, the struggle was restrained. As one campesino put it: "No one was hurt as we were shooting to scare each other rather than aiming at each other." Although most of the nationalist leaders took part in the affray, many did not want to get involved in the defense of a cause marred by corruption that would eventually affect their own reputations. Finally, the rightist faction was able to enter the house, where they found, depending on whose account is believed, between 40 and 110 bags of flour.

This event was decisive in forcing the Federación Campesina in Cochabamba to oversee the election of new leaders for the Tiraque Central, which took place the day after the shootout. Five high-ranking leaders of the Federación went to Tiraque for this third election. The leftist faction was completely demoralized after the "flour affair." Pedro Alfaro had been in hiding since the shootout, and the other leaders, who had also been accused of stealing flour, were too shell-shocked and concerned with their own images to be able to build up their forces to oppose the nationalist faction. The nationalists, in contrast, had been very active since early morning, rallying the support of a large number of voters. Three truck owners from the villages, as well as two vecinos, used their vehicles to bring peasants from distant villages to the town. About two hundred voters finally gathered in the square. For the first time in this electoral sequence, some vecino transportistas affiliated to a campesino union took an active part in the election.

Knowing the political background of the nationalist leaders, the Federación's secretary-general (a leftist himself) announced that campesinos who had occupied public offices during military regimes could not be candidates for election. Complying with and, at the same time, circumventing this request, the rightist leaders hand-picked candidates from among their campesino allies who had never occupied public offices before. A new leadership was thus elected. Although the outcome of the election did not gratify the leaders of the Federación, they had no alternative but to accept it. Thus, the nationalist faction was able to legitimize its control of the local Central Campesina with the intervention of the Federación's leftist leadership.

As was the case on other occasions, this change in the leadership of the Central Campesina led to the replacement of personnel in other public offices. Three days after the election, the alcaldía was calling for an election to replace Gerardo Rocha as president of the civic committee. The new president of the committee was a young vecino nominated by the rightist leaders. Shortly after, the civil register had a new officer, the son-in-law of a vecino, who was a friend and ally of the nationalist leaders. A year later, in 1985, and in spite of the divisions between the two competing factions, the two joined forces to stage a road blockade to protest government policies. Against all expectations, Pedro Alfaro (the former secretary-general of the leftist faction) was the main organizer of the blockade and so was able to rebuild his political standing in the region. At the time this blockade was organized, the leftist faction took advantage of the absence of the nationalist secretary-general from Tiraque to elect a new secretary-general for the Central Campesina. Campesinos, however, confiscated five kilograms of cocaine from a woman who crossed the blockade. When the cocaine mysteriously disappeared, the campesino leaders began to distrust one another, leading immediately to a redefinition of faction membership. Once again, factions were reformulated, leadership changed, but everything remained almost the same.

In attempting to analyze the political conflicts and alignments in the region, one can discern certain characteristics common to the events described above. First, a relatively small number of protagonists were usually involved in the conflicts. These were the faction leaders, that is, the campesino leaders and their vecino allies. Since the 1970s, campesino leaders have always participated in the conflicts and have been repeatedly nominated and elected to occupy positions of leadership in the region. Only on a few occasions, however, have vecinos openly involved themselves in conflicts. Even though they support one or another campesino faction, they are seldom seen in public with their campesino allies. Other vecinos and campesinos tend not to participate in these conflicts, except on the occasions they are drawn into them, in which case their participation generally involves gossiping about the event and criticizing the leaders.

A second characteristic was the social space in which these conflicts took place. This space comprised the town and the villages located in the valley near it. Many of the confrontations took place in the town square, the most visible space in Tiraque. This characteristic is closely related to the nature of the conflicts, which often involved public issues such as transport fares or the control of political office—issues that the contending parties attempted to "publicize" and bring into the public sphere by seeking the support of others within and outside the region. In other words, there was a concern to bring into the open the issues under dispute. But by confining the conflict to the town square most of the time, both the left and the right disenfranchised the hinterland villages.

Finally, although in many instances it seemed that the conflict was going to get out of hand, it in fact was kept within bounds. Occasionally, confrontations resulted in a few bloody noses and black eyes, but even when the conflict climaxed in the shootout, campesinos shot in the air, intent only on scaring each other. The fact that people are beaten up, accused of stealing, yet not killed points to the underlying integration of the two factions. In contrast to these theatrical and partly ritualized political practices, campesinos deal with other types of conflict in a very different manner.

Issues considered to be more substantive, such as murder or robbery are sometimes punished by death. Thus, for example, when a campesino was found for a third time stealing oxen, the members of one village took the law into their own hands and killed him. Yet instead of publicizing or bragging about it, the entire village closed in upon itself and remained determinedly silent about the attack. Perhaps the wives of the factions leaders were the only ones to understand the nature of the conflicts resulting from regional politicking. Many of them repeatedly opposed the involvement of their husbands in local union activities and in regional politicking, which they considered time-consuming practices that distracted their husbands from productive activities. The tensions within households created by the men's involvement in regional politicking were, of course, based on the fact that while men "played" factional politics, the workloads of women and children increased considerably.

Regional politicking, then, involves the partly ritualized confrontation of competing factions in which leaders make public statements about themselves. Political rhetoric, as manifested in public speeches and practices, serves to distinguish leaders from nonleaders and campesinos from vecinos. But this is not always the case, since criteria for self-definition are often situational and ambiguous, resulting in confusing and contradictory messages. Fluency in Quechua and the ability to drive the ox-drawn plow are, it will be recalled, the distinguishing qualities used to define a campesino in the region. Nationalist leaders used this definition to exclude Gerardo Rocha from the campesino category and to challenge his right to hold a position in the Central Campesina. But most vecinos share these qualities, and some are members of campesino unions. Members of the Flores family (transporters and merchants), for instance, often make use of the same criteria to define themselves as campesinos when in fact they are not. Indeed, José and Felipe Flores told me that Luciano, who still lives in a rural village, was not a campesino because "he does not work in the fields with the sweat of his brow like we do, spending, instead, much of his time in the city representing others in court." Following denunciations made by other groups against rural merchants, Tiraqueños also make explicit statements against them, although some of them are merchants, transporters, and compañía partners themselves. Yet these public denunciations on one occasion are often contradicted on another when they identify themselves with a particular social group as, for instance, in parades where truckers, merchants, war veterans, and campesinos march in different groups. In these events, some campesino leaders who are also truck owners march behind the transportistas' union banner rather than with the Central Campesina. But in other contexts, which are also public, "campesino" becomes an inclusive category that unites members of different factions—wealthy and poor, vecinos and campesinos—to mobilize against the state in order to protest any state policies that are detrimental to all. The local definition of campesino is thus ambiguous, and its meaning is often negotiated and contested in public arenas.

The profound importance of ambiguity and the restraint with which the political and ideological struggle is fought in the midst of increasingly tense disputes shows how class antagonism and common values interweave.

Class, Ethnicity, and Social Closure

While the local definition of "campesino" is often used as a banner to forge broad inter- and intraclass alliances and oppositions, ethnic concepts such as *indio, cholo,* and *blanco* (Indian, cholo, and white) provide the language for social exclusion, separating townsfolk and villagers in general and, most particularly, the town "elite" from the village "elite." Ethnicity is thus yet another cultural form that defines lines of antagonism and alliance.

Even though the lives of vecinos and campesinos intricately intertwine in daily life, for they establish long-term compadrazgo ties, sharecropping agreements, and shifting political alliances, one cannot help but notice the tensions that exist between the town and the villages, between vecinos and villagers. And these tensions usually keep them from intermarrying and from participating together in religious celebrations. Apart from some of the very poor, vecinos do not marry villagers, even if the villagers move to town. In addition, villagers do not participate in the religious festivals celebrated in the town, and vecinos seldom participate in the festivals that take place in the villages.[15] These distinctions are also maintained after death; the layout of graves in the town's cemetery provides a perfect example of these apparently immutable differences: vecinos are buried in the best-kept, central part of the cemetery, while villagers are buried at its margins.[16]

The social divide between vecinos and villagers is not, however, based on perceived images of "class," but on "imagined" representations of ethnicity that are encoded within a hegemonic discourse that tends to associate the countryside with everything that it perceives as being the cause for Bolivia's underdevelopment: the "lazy" and "unruly" Indian and the "arrogant" cholo parvenu.[17] Within the parameters set by this discourse, both "cholo" and "indio" are pejorative terms, to be mentioned only in private unless there is a clear intention to insult. One exception is the concept *cholita*, the diminutive of chola, which is a noninsulting form used to address women who wear polleras (broad, gathered skirts). Even though, since the revolution of 1952, the term campesino has replaced "Indian" in both official and public discourses, dominant images and associations of the countryside—and the people who live in it—with "backwardness" and "Indianness" persist.

An account of some of the things I was told in private will illustrate this point. One afternoon, while we were sitting on the stoop of his house in town and a new truck went by, Don Roberto, said: "Ahí va el indio Trinidad" ("There goes the Indian Trinidad"). This statement was surprising to me in two ways. On the one hand, Don Roberto refers to himself as a mestizo—he even sometimes jokingly calls himself a "cholo." He has a dark complexion and has been landless and poor all his life. On the other hand, Trinidad, who is from Sank'ayani, is one of the richest men in Tiraque: He owns more than one hundred hectares of land, is a moneylender, and establishes sharecropping agreements with numerous peasant households. Furthermore, he has a fair complexion and green eyes. But he still lives in his village and speaks very little Spanish; therefore, despite his wealth, he remains in the eyes of vecinos an "Indian."

More surprising were the statements made by vecinos who defined themselves as "white" about people who lived in rural villages. In fact, most vecinos were at pains to validate their "white" ancestry by indicating that their parents or grandparents were "Spaniards" who had come from the cities of Cochabamba, Sucre, or La Paz, or from Tarata, an important rural town in colonial times. They thus added luster to their ancestry. Don José, for instance, a well-to-do vecino, told me that his grandparents had come from Tarata. But his assertion was later challenged by another vecino, distantly related to José through marriage, who whispered to me: "Do you know that José's grandparents were tribute-paying Indians?" After about one year of almost continuous residence in the town, I visited campesinos in their villages for extended periods of time. I was then asked by more than one vecino how I could possibly live among those "ignorant" and "dirty" campesinos. In one of his visits to the town, a former hacendado even bothered to come to my room to warn me against the campesinos with whom I associated, telling me that I should not trust them. These representations of the dirty and untrustworthy "other" correspond with hegemonic representations of the countryside—dominant images that do not distinguish between "Indian" and "campesino," and which are expressed in statements such as: "Los campesinos son buena gente hasta que se les sale el indio" ("Peasants are nice people until they reveal their Indianness"). Dominant representations of the "Indian" are then imbued with essential characteristics that people seemingly inherit and preserve for many generations, traits that may lie dormant but can easily be "awakened" in particular situations. The fact that "Indians" are now officially called "campesinos" does not change their essential nature. In both dominant and local representations of ethnic identities, the urban setting—city or town—is associated with "whiteness," whereas the essence of "Indianness" is situated in the countryside or rural village. Yet when the words "indio" or "cholo" pass from private to public arenas and become insults, they tend to lose their essential connotations. As insults, these words imply that people are behaving like "Indians" or "cholos."

The ambiguities inherent in local cultural representations of self and others become even more revealing when we situate them within the context of ongoing processes of class formation and cultural differentiation. As we have seen, since the transformation of landless tenants and sharecroppers into landowning campesinos, they have become dependent on a new rural merchant class. Although these families are wealthy and wield considerable power in the area, they nonetheless come from, and many still live in, rural towns and villages. Furthermore, they not only remain enmeshed in rural life, but their wives, mothers, or mothers-in-law may still wear polleras. They thus remain close to their origins and to the countryside, and, simultaneously, they remain distant from dominant Western culture. It is in this context that ethnic representations become important to one's own standing vis-à-vis others who share similar origins. Encoded within a hegemonic and essentialist image of race, a vision that associates Indianness with the countryside and whiteness with the city, local constructions of identity are further elaborated and manipulated in specific arenas that are meaningful only insofar as the audience is regionally based. In a wider context, those who represent themselves as white in Tiraque are not recognized as such, because they are still associated with the countryside.

Unlike their predecessors, who were not only wealthy but also occupied important positions in the alcaldía and other public offices and, most importantly, were "white," the nouveau riche vecinos are perceived as cholos. We might recall how these families competed among themselves to become the leading families in the region. They establish and maintain intimate alliances in production with poor peasants, buying directly from them and providing transport services for them. Some of them also attempt to control key political positions in the alcaldía, civic committee, and transporters' union, extending a wide network of fictive kin relations and political allies. Wealth and power by themselves, however, do not confer whiteness, because this is a prerogative that has to be granted by others. There is one major occasion on which this privilege may be sought: the ritual celebration of the Virgen de las Angustias, the patron of the town.[18]

The festival attracts a large number of prominent townsfolk no longer living in Tiraque, their friends, and guests from Cochabamba, such as leaders of the truckers' federation and confederation, lawyers, businessmen, and bureaucrats invited by vecinos in the expectation that their presence would add luster to their names. The festival is celebrated in *romerías* (groups of devotees to the virgin) of Tiraqueños residing in and out of town, who sponsor the fiesta. Being a member of a romería involves great expense. Guests are offered meals twice a day and inexhaustible quantities of chicha, cocktails, and beer for four consecutive days. The hiring of a band, which plays four days and nights almost without stopping, the purchase of large quantities of flowers and candles for the church, and firecrackers that are set off on the square are large additional expenses. But, despite the expense, vecinos and former townsfolk indicate that they cannot refuse to participate in the fiesta, since to do so would be an offense to the virgin. Most of the *romeros* (devotees) are not poor, however. Many are truckers (who claim it was through the virgin's benevolence that they were able to buy their vehicles), lawyers, military officers, agronomists, and schoolteachers (cf. Lagos 1993). The parish priest preaches against excessive expenditure and drinking. Each year he proposes to change the fiesta into a "religious" one, but to no avail, because it would mean depriving the nouveau riche of the opportunity to make an open statement about their wealth, hospitality, and savoir-faire.

Villagers are not invited to participate in the townsfolk's celebration, although those related through ritual kinship to vecinos are expected to help in the cooking and serving of food and drinks. Some do go to town during the festivity, but only to watch the fireworks and see the townspeople dance, drink, and participate in numerous processions around the town square. Recently, campesinos from two villages located near the town organized two romerías; they did not compete with the vecinos' romerías, although they were also making a public statement about their own wealth. Perhaps one day they will; for the moment, the fact that they have their own celebration, independent of the vecinos', means that they accept the cultural exclusion imposed on them by townspeople.

Wealthy Protestants, such as the evangelicals from Sank'ayani, remain apart from the efforts of Catholic vecinos to gain social prestige. Evangelicals are well aware that as campesinos they are not welcomed in the vecinos' celebrations. Because of this, or in spite of it, they look down on Catholics for their "worldly and vice-ridden" practices. Although some evangelicals join Catholics in occasional chicha drinking bouts, most accept and practice their version of the Protestant moral code of behavior: abstention from worldly pleasures such as alcohol and dance. By doing so, they set themselves apart from the vecinos' system of prestige, and they perceive their moral superiority as transcending the cultural barriers imposed on them by other members of the merchant class who, by the mere accident that they are "native" to the town, consider themselves "white" and therefore superior.

Thus, despite the dramatic transformations that have taken place in Tiraque and despite the fact that some villagers are wealthier than most vecinos, a long-standing discrimination remains apparently unchanged. Social closure rests on a colonial model of reality, imposing symbolic barriers to social climbers of village origins. But there is a crucial difference. Nowadays, wealth and, most importantly, land ownership do not whiten the skin (cf. M. Harris 1964).

These antagonistic constructions of difference are not intrinsically different from the public statements made by the competing leaders in regional politicking. The difference lies in the fact that competition in the political arena is exacerbated by the availability of varied and competing sources of political capital and by conflicting kin, compadrazgo, and class loyalties. In both instances, however, the fact that some individuals define themselves and others as campesinos, white, Indian, or cholo, and that they may be categorized by others differently, obscures social reality. But these contradictory public and private statements and ambiguous, subjective evaluations of self and others regarding class and identity are also effective means for social exclusion. Similarly, the meaning of "campesino" is contested in the region and, at the same time, overrides differences of class and identity, uniting and dividing vecinos and villagers in factional disputes. But when the audience is the state, poor and wealthy, vecinos and villagers, whites, Indians, and cholos represent themselves as an imagined class—campesinos—rather than as an imagined ethnic group. In doing so, they coalesce different interests and cross-cutting identities into a common one to mobilize against the state and global forces. By choosing this mode of representation, they squarely place themselves within a "modern" discourse, rejecting, at the same time, pervasive dominant images that relate the countryside with Indianness.

Conclusion: The Paradoxes of Autonomy, Power, and Culture

If capital in our countryside were incapable of creating anything but bondage and usury, we could not, from the data on production, establish the differentiation of the peasantry, the formation of a rural bourgeoisie and a rural proletariat; the whole of the peasantry would represent a fairly even type of poverty-stricken cultivators, among whom only usurers would stand out, and they only to the extent of money owned and not to the extent and organization of agricultural production. Finally, from the above-examined data follows the important proposition that the independent development of merchant's and usurer's capital in our countryside *retards* the differentiation of the peasantry. . . . Actually, the real masters of the contemporary countryside are often enough not the representatives of the peasant bourgeoisie, but the village usurers and the neighboring landowners. It is, however, quite legitimate to disregard them, for otherwise it is impossible to study the internal system of economic relationships among the peasantry.

(Lenin 1899/1956:188–89)

Autonomy is a powerful and vital ideology. It is powerful because it underlies the actions and discourse of subordinate groups who seek to create sociocultural spaces within and outside power relations. Like all ideologies, autonomy is a vital one because it is rooted in reality or, at least, in the perceived possibility of severing ties from dependence and subordination on power holders. If this were never possible, the ideal for autonomy would simply cease to feed the dreams and hopes of subordinate groups. As Eagleton (1991:15) indicates, "Successful ideologies must be more than imposed illusions, and recognizable enough not to be simply rejected out of hand." There is no doubt that subordinate groups succeed in creating relatively autonomous spaces that sometimes allow them to control the labor process and to establish alternative sociocultural relations and identities. Yet, rather than being discrete domains rooted in an unchanging past, the daily lives, political practices, and the discourse of the subaltern and the dominant are intricately intertwined. Thus autonomy, conceived both as ideology and as agency, is always imbricated in power in a *social process* that is simultaneously active and transformative. In other words, autonomy is an arena of struggle—of resistance, accommodation, and domination—where both dominant and subordinate groups come together and apart in specific historical contexts. And what makes for historical specificity is the transformation of social relations and the changing relations between the state and civil society, both of which shape power relations and the culture of politics and representation in new ways.

* * *

In tracing the historical formation of a landowning peasantry and a merchant class, I have shown that direct control over land and other means of production among petty commodity producers allows for a certain degree of independence in the labor process. Yet the conditions of the possibility to control it are constrained just as much by wider forces as in the impossibility for households to produce and reproduce independently of other households. Rather, every household depends on other households to maintain a precarious and often illusory autonomy. Indeed, the ideal for autonomy on the part of peasants has always been threatened by a chronic lack of money, and debt, or dependence based on loans, has shaped class relations in Tiraque. I have argued that the emergence and reproduction of merchants in Tiraque have been contingent both on the existence of a "free" peasantry, not tied to the hacienda, and of other petty commodity producers, such as artisans, who, even though they are "independent" producers, still must depend on others to produce goods for the market. Both landowning peasants and artisans are ultimately dependent both on the state and on dominant social groups for their social reproduction. These two classes are thus mutually determining, each to the other and each for themselves, with indebtedness, or the risk of it, being an important and basic nexus between the two.

In contrast to Lenin's suggestion that we should disregard the practices of moneylenders, my study shows that an examination of peasant needs for money and sharecropping provides the crucial analytical entrée for understanding the labor process in rural villages, relations of production and appropriation, commoditization processes, and unequal exchange in a "free" market context. The historical process through which colonos were transformed into landowning peasants, and ground rent was transformed into a particular form of capitalized rent, has not led to the emergence of a proletarian class. Rather, poor peasants remain poor peasants because they can borrow land, labor, and inputs from other peasants, and from the wealthy.

The trajectory followed by members of these two social classes has by no means been linear. Rather, the struggle for autonomy on the part of the rural poor has been fraught with difficulties, setbacks, and vulnerability. Those who were able to purchase plots of land and become piqueros before agrarian reform still remained dependent in various ways on hacendados, merchants, and the state: on hacendados for access to additional land to farm or to pasture their animals, for money in the form of token wages, and on their good will to place their sons as colonos when land was not sufficient to distribute among them; on merchants for loans advanced on future harvests; and on the state for their right to private property by paying a cadastral tax and personal services. The newly acquired freedom and relative autonomy of this emergent class were precarious, since the risk of losing the land was indeed an ever-present reality. Thus, it is not surprising that when the rural poor struggled for land in Bolivia, they built broad alliances, incorporating highly differentiated households of landowning peasants, hacienda tenants, and artisans who united in collective actions against a perceived common enemy: the merchant hacendado. And this long struggle, which culminated in the violent seizure of hacienda lands and animals, and in the arrest, beating, and sometimes killing of hacendados, was also punctuated by periods of quiescence and accommodation. With agrarian reform, landless colonos and sharecroppers were transformed into, and began to be called, campesinos. This definitional change, however, is not a semantic one but involves rather a structural transformation, making these independent producers vulnerable to new forms of domination and exploitation. Since then, regional politics has been shaped as much by intra- and interclass alliances and oppositions, and by accommodation and cultural collusion, as by resistance to wider hegemonic forces and the state.

Whereas most peasants today do not depend on the wealthy for their access to land—since they own it, even though the state reserves ultimate patrimony over it—they still depend on them for money to produce, or for assistance to help confront unexpected expenditures and family crises. To limit this dependence on the rich, peasants have intensified cash-crop production. This, however, both increases the costs of production, by requiring more intense use of chemical inputs, and also ties them tighter to markets they cannot control and within which they have little bargaining power. To try to lessen their increased needs for credit, peasants engage in a variety of strategies. They leave their homes to work for wages as seasonal laborers in Chapare, where they frequently contract syphilis or other diseases, or they do day work in Tiraque for wages or in-kind payments. None of these strategies turns them from peasants to proletarians, since they also enter into sharecropping agreements, through which they obtain fertilizers and insecticides to produce cash crops, thus reducing the always-threatening risk of indebtedness. But they simultaneously relinquish a substantial part of the crop in exchange for preserving a partial autonomy. Reproducing themselves as peasants, they also reproduce dominant groups.

The careers of nouveau-riche families have been similarly discontinuous and nonlinear. Incapable of transforming the sociocultural ties that bind them to the poor, the various dominant families emerging in Tiraque have not transformed themselves into agrarian capitalists. Family fortunes rose and fell as they engaged in risky and frequently speculative enterprises. Often overextending themselves, their fortunes could be reversed by wider forces beyond their control. In Tiraque, the 1952 revolution truncated the fortunes of a rentier-merchant class and frustrated the hopes of many upwardly mobile families, but at the same time laid the groundwork for the emergence of a new dominant class in the rural towns and villages. Superficially, these new, wealthy families seem strikingly similar to those families forced to leave Tiraque after the revolution and agrarian reform. Both were involved with agricultural production and diverse speculative enterprises, and both developed their own ways of creating and exploiting peasant vulnerability. Structurally, however, the basis of power of the new "elites" has changed profoundly with the transformation of colonos into landowning peasants and the reorganization of production. Power now lies not in political control over land, but in the appropriation of peasant labor and produce through "traditional" forms of work and exchange relations, and in the intimate relations of dominant groups with peasant households.

Indeed, postrevolution emergent village "elites" do not distance themselves from their neighbors (not even those who have converted to Protestantism). Rather, they tend to remain in their villages, reinforcing bonds of common residence with fictive kin. Similarly, the town-based wealthy families seek to extend these forms of intimate relations with peasant households in several villages, relying on village culture and customs to consolidate their hold over production and exchange. Unlike the practices of social climbers documented by anthropologists in other parts of Latin America (cf. Cancian 1965; W. Smith 1977; E. Wolf 1966), the nouveau riche of Tiraque do not violate traditional expectations or abandon ceremonial expenditure. Rather, they continue to be enmeshed in village life and cultural practices, even though these may have meanings and practical consequences for them that are quite different from the meaning and consequences these have among the poor. This is precisely the secret of exploitation and domination in the region of Tiraque, and the reason for the use of cultural practices such as reciprocity and barter, community, and ritual kinship. The intimacy of these relations makes it difficult and risky for peasants to move against the merchant class, because to do so would imply moving against their covillagers, sharecropping partners, or coparents and godparents on whom, paradoxically, they depend to reproduce themselves as landowing peasants. In their daily practices, both merchants and landowning peasants are thus actively negotiating class antagonisms, aligning and dividing themselves along cultural definitions of class and ethnicity. In so doing, Tiraqueños interpret and elaborate dominant discourses to shape a changing reality, their relations with each other, and their relations with the state.

The reliance of rural merchants on accommodation and cultural collusion to exploit and dominate a peasantry is, however, a limitation, since they cannot transform their accumulated wealth into capital in the region and seldom outside the region. Not unlike their predecessors, they, as much as the peasantry they dominate, are ultimately dependent on larger capitalist forces and the state, and their fortunes may also be reversed by these same forces. Peasants know that their livelihood and its limitations depend on their wealthier covillagers, kin, and fictive kin, and, ultimately, on the state—as their many failed attempts to confront the state indicate. They also know that the land they forcibly seized from hacendados was afterward claimed by the state as its patrimony, and then legally granted back to the peasants who took it in the first place. Some even know the intimate connection between the state and the world economy. As one campesino leader who lived in a hinterland village put it: "Our exploiter is the International Monetary Fund."

Peasants, as I have shown, must both confront the state and dominant groups and simultaneously sustain them. This fundamental structural ambivalence feeds both their dreams and their despair.

Appendix: Bolivian Exchange Rates, 1982–85

	Bolivian Pesos ($b) per 1 U.S. Dollar[a]	
Date	Official Exchange	Black Market Exchange
1982		
January	25	40
February	44[b]	44
May		96
June		100
July		140
August		200
September		270
November	200	n. a.
December		300
1983		
January		300
February		400
October		900
November	500	1,400
1984		
January		1,850
March		2,600
April 1		3,500
April 13	2,000	6,700
April 26		3,100[c]
May		3,400
July		3,700
August		5,000
September		10,000[d]
October 16		14,500
October 20	8,500	15,000
November 8		18,000
November 15		20,000

Date	Bolivian Pesos ($b) per 1 U.S. Dollar[a]	
	Official Exchange	Black Market Exchange
November 22	9,000	n. a.
December		27,000–30,000
1985		
January		40,000–120,000
February	50,000	
August		1,000,000

Source: Author's fieldwork.

[a]Several reasons account for exchange rate variations: official devaluations, speculation, and government attempts to control illicit cocaine production and exchange.

[b] Every increase in the official exchange rate signifies a devaluation of the Bolivian peso.

[c]Exchange rate went down due to closing of Bolivia's Central Bank.

[d]Troops moved into the Chapare to stamp out cocaine processing operations.

Notes

Preface

1. In colonial times, *cholo* referred to individuals with one white grand-parent. By 1900, the term had become a pejorative one, to be mentioned only in private unless there was a clear intention to insult. An exception is *cholita*, the diminutive of chola, which is a non-insulting form for addressing women who wear *polleras* (broad, gathered skirts).

2. Locales where chicha is served.

3. Except for the names of these individuals, I use pseudonyms through-out the text.

Introduction

1. This and subsequent translations are mine.

2. Much has been written about rural communities in Latin America. See, in particular, Wolf 1955, 1957, and 1986. Roseberry (1989:14) argues that we should conceptualize community "not as a given society—or culture-outside-of history, but as political association formed through processes of political and cultural creation and imagination—the generation of meaning of contexts of unequal power." On the issue of the cultural invention of com-munity and tradition, see Anderson 1983 and Hobsbawm 1983.

3. For a different perspective, see Cook and Binford (1990), who suggest the possibility of "endofamilial accumulation."

4. The literature on the development of capitalism has been punctuated by "crucial critical moments" (Vincent 1990) in which the validity of domi-nant concepts has been repeatedly challenged and partially displaced. Even though recent studies recognize that capitalism does not develop in a linear fashion and that it can both destroy and create a peasantry (cf. Roseberry 1983, 1989; Wolf 1983), the persistence and re-creation of peasantries contin-ues to generate heated debates among Marxist social scientists. For excellent reviews of these issues, see R. Harris 1978 and Deere 1987. Also see Bernstein 1979; Deere 1990; Friedmann 1980; Mintz 1973.

5. The concept of commoditization refers to the effect commodity re-lations have on the economy of the peasant household (Bernstein 1979). For recent debates concerning the impact of commoditization on the labor

process of peasants and petty commodity producers, see Chevalier 1982; Friedmann 1980; Long 1986; C. Smith 1984; G. Smith 1986.

6. Depending on the theoretical stance adopted by scholars, peasants have taken many guises. In the literature they appear as a category functional to the accumulation of capital, as a mode of production, as "disguised" proletarians, as "wage labor equivalents," as petty commodity producers, or simply as peasants. For these different conceptualizations, see Bartra 1974; Bernstein 1977, 1979; de Janvry 1981; Goodman and Redclift 1981; Montoya 1982; Roseberry 1978; Warman 1978, 1980; E. Wolf 1966. Some writers even suggest that the concept be dropped altogether, since, they argue, it does not have any analytical validity (cf. Ennew, Hirst and Tribe 1977; Friedmann 1980; Leeds 1977). The debate is far from being resolved insofar as the theoretical discourse is divorced from empirical reality and remains tied to a hidden agenda that denies historical agency to peasants: proletarians are a "class for itself," and peasants a "class in itself." While some Marxist "quotationists" refer to Marx (1852/1963) to support this argument, they overlook the historical specificity of the case Marx was making about the political practice of peasants in France.

7. The term encompasses truck, bus, and taxi owners and drivers.

8. Albó 1974; Cajka 1979; Centro de Investigación y Promoción del Campesinado (Cipca) 1979; F. Iriarte 1981; Peinado 1971; Simmons 1974. These studies provided valuable comparative material.

9. In this, I follow Vincent (1977), who suggests the importance of considering all those "forgotten" categories of people such as the landless, women, artisans, merchants, and moneylenders for the study of agrarian societies.

Chapter 1. An Introduction to Tiraque

1. For an analysis of the impact mining had on various regions in Alto Perú, see Larson 1988, Assadourian 1982, Rivera Cusicanqui 1978.

2. Prior to the Spanish conquest, states and various ethnic groups attempted to control diverse areas, located at different altitudes, by setting up colonies in order to have access to a variety of resources (Murra 1972). Platt (1982:24) mentions that the Charka and Karakara Confederation in Northern Potosí set up colonies, probably to produce coca, in the yungas of Tiraque.

3. The boundaries of the Segunda Sección Tiraque were defined when the province of Arani was founded in 1914. Prior to that time, the territory formed part of the province of Punata.

4. These figures are based on information collected by me in a regional survey. The population census of 1976 shows a total population of 14,811, with 1,373 residents in the town (República de Bolivia, 1977). The quantitative information presented in this section was obtained in a survey of cantón Tiraque carried out in July and August of 1984. The cantón was stratified into seven zones on the basis of ecological and geographical similarities. Lists of household heads were then obtained from leaders of campesino unions in each zone, from which 96 households or replacements were selected by random sampling. My thanks to Elba Luppo and Julio Zubieta for helping in the survey design and the processing of these data. The number of campesino unions in Tiraque varies through time (sometimes in surprisingly short pe-

riods of time), since unions that are usually based in one or two villages often split due to political conflicts (see Chapter 6).

5. During colonial times, *vecino* was the term used to define town residents who owned a house in town, could bear arms, and formed part of armed militias (Molinié-Fioravanti 1982:136).

6. The Department of Cochabamba is the major potato producer and exporter in Bolivia, and Arani is the second most important potato-producing province in the department.

Chapter 2. The Emergence of a Merchant Class and Landowning Peasants

1. It is important to clarify here the role coca plays in Andean culture. First, coca is a basic element in every social relationship of work, exchange, ritual, and divination. Second, coca is consumed by placing a few dry leaves in the mouth where it is left until all the juice is extracted from the leaves. In this form, coca acts as a nonaddictive, mild stimulant. Thus in no way does this form of coca use compare to cocaine consumption in industrial nations. Coca is also rich in vitamins. See Allen 1988, Carter 1983, Latin American Bureau 1982, and Nash 1979 for a more detailed discussion of coca in the Andes. For the impact of illicit cocaine production on Bolivian society, see Healy 1986.

2. The Peruvian historian, Heraclio Bonilla, points out that coca was the third largest item of expenditure incurred by mine owners in the nineteenth century (personal communication).

3. Simón Bolivar enacted the first reform to dissolve the Indian communities established under Viceroy Toledo in 1564. Bolivar's decree was soon abolished, since the republican state depended on Indian tribute as its most important source of revenue. A second, and more successful, assault on the Indian communities began in 1866, followed in 1874 with the *Leyes de Exvinculación*. The last *Revisitas* (censuses of Indian communities) of the 1880s registered the implementation of these laws.

4. With the foundation of the province of Arani in 1914, Tiraque became the capital of the Segunda Sección Arani, with the same territorial jurisdiction.

5. The archival records used for the reconstruction of Tiraque's social history were located in several public offices: court records in Tiraque's court house contain information on land and money-loan litigation; archives in Tiraque's municipal council are an invaluable source for the reconstruction of the region's history and the political and economic career of town residents. Most of these documents consisted of loose papers, sometimes placed in uncatalogued file folders. In this court house, as in others, the documents were thrown on the floor of a mice-infested room. I was obliged, therefore, to collect data "randomly." Although many documents are incomplete, they still provide rich information. Other sources included the office of the Registro de Derechos Reales in Cochabamba, which documents land transactions, sharecropping and lease contracts, mortgages and land litigations from 1888 to the present (*Libro Principal del Registro de la Propiedad and Libro de Gravámenes e Hipotecas*). These books are catalogued by province and year. Information from these archives was collected in two ways. A census of all the

documents from the Libro de Gravámenes e Hipotecas was taken, although some years were found to be missing. These were few and scattered, and did not affect the reconstruction of data series. In addition, with the use of a name index, the land transactions of about thirty families were collected. Archives in the Tesoro de Hacienda and Notaría de Hacienda at the Prefectura of Cochabamba provided information on Indian and general population censuses, Indian land transactions, and cadastral censuses. The Archivo Histórico Municipal in Cochabamba also contains notarial records.

6. In 1938, the name of the Concejo Municipal was changed to Alcaldía.

7. The census describes them as "rentiers."

8. In Bolivia these servile household obligations were called *pongueaje* for men and *mitanaje* for women, and those who provided it were called *pongos*.

9. Mitre (1981) indicates that the railroad connecting mining camps with the Pacific coast redefined the regional economy. The reduction in transport costs that this entailed meant that imported agricultural and industrial goods competed with local production. On the decline of the hacienda in nineteenth-century Cochabamba, see Jackson 1988, 1989.

10. Before the 1880s, the main sources of credit in the region were the Church and individual moneylenders who charged annual interest rates ranging from 12 to 60 percent. After 1880, private and state banks provided long-term loans at lower interest rates, ranging from 10 to 12 percent. But only hacendados were entitled to receive them; thus, moneylenders covered the bulk of the loans. For instance, for a total of 154 loans extended in the province of Arani for the period 1890–1902, 112 were provided by moneylenders and only 42 by banks (RDR: *Libro de Gravámenes e Hipotecas*). This source contains documents referring to land and other property mortgages on account of money-loans, bail, lease and sharecropping agreements, and the establishment of productive enterprises where the partners mortgaged their properties in guarantee.

11. See Simmons (1974) for a history of this hacienda.

12. In fact, this is the explanation given by one former colono when asked how he obtained money to purchase a small parcel of land.

13. Dandler 1967, Larson 1988, Leonard 1948, and Patch 1956 refer to the existence of piqueros prior to the agrarian reform of 1953 in various regions in the Valle Alto. According to Dandler (1967:91), hacendados sold land to former colonos to reduce the supply of labor on the hacienda, to pay debts, and in response to diminishing returns on agricultural production. My information on piqueros in Tiraque was collected from interviews and a survey of land transactions recorded in the Libro de Propiedad in DR (see note 6).

14. The Revisitas of the 1880s registered the implementation of these laws. Every Indian community was visited by the Junta Revisitadora in charge of registering individual ownership of fixed plots of land (six *fanegadas*, or 17.38 hectares) to every household in the community. Land in excess of this reverted to the state. In many regions, the Junta Revisitadora encountered open opposition from village Indians, obliging members of the Junta Revisitadora to request the protection of an armed guard (PC: "Informe del revisitador del cantón Quirquiavi, Provincia Arque," May 27, 1897). Platt (1982) documents similar reactions in Northern Potosí.

15. Since the Revisitas, the *Libro de Indígenas* at the Notaría de Hacienda,

Prefectura de Cochabamba, has registered all land transactions in the former Indian villages.

16. This hacienda was first formed with the Indian lands left "vacant" by the Revisita. Its size later increased with additional land purchases (Blanco 1901; RDR: Libro Principal del Registro de la Propiedad 1940).

17. In a strict sense, Vandiola plantations were quite different from the plantations described in other regions in Latin America, since productive relations were not based on slave or wage labor and goods were produced for internal consumption rather than for export. For a distinction between haciendas and plantations, see Wolf and Mintz 1957.

18. Records of birth and marriage kept at the parish of Tiraque provided much of the information about the origin, principal declared occupation, and racial classification of the family members. These records were also used to reconstruct, expand, or corroborate geneaologies, and to gather information on fictive kin ties.

19. PC: Notaría de Hacienda. "Registro de adjudicación de tierras del Estado," n.d.

20. The collection of municipal taxes was granted through public auctions to individuals able to provide a money guarantee, or to medium or large landowners who could mortgage their land. All the taxes collected were then retained by the collector.

21. This information was compiled from lists of moneylenders kept at the Archivo Alcaldía Tiraque for tax purposes.

22. This is a very strong insult for which I was unable to find a translation.

23. The information that follows was compiled from loose papers and incomplete files in AAT and JT, and corroborated in interviews with Tiraqueños.

24. Kelley and Klein (1981) make a similar argument in their study of the rebirth of inequality in Bolivia after agrarian reform.

25. This will be discussed more fully in Chapter 3.

26. For a similar argument on the expansion of haciendas in the highland plateau, see Rivera Cusicanqui (1978). Rodríguez Ostría (1983) provides a different explanation.

27. Abercrombie (1991) indicates that "whites" define their identities by asserting their non-Indianness.

28. According to Klein (1982), by 1950 all sectors of the Bolivian economy were stagnant and undercapitalized. The mines, for instance, had not experienced any significant capital investment since the economic crisis of the 1930s. Basic food imports climbed from 10 percent of total imports in 1920 to 19 percent in 1950 when 72 percent of the total population was engaged in agriculture, and the industrial sector employed only 4 percent of the economically active population.

29. These were the military governments of Colonels Toro and Busch (1936–39) and Colonel Villarroel (1943–46). David Toro and Germán Busch were two young officers during the Chaco War who led the government of "military socialism" after the war. Colonel Gualberto Villarroel was a member of RADEPA, a secret military lodge organized among ex-prisoners of war. During Villarroel's term, the miners organized the National Federation of Miners, and the rural poor congregated in the first National Congress of Indians to be held in Bolivia. At this congress, Villarroel announced several reforms related to the working conditions of colonos on haciendas, including

the abolition of the pongueaje system. These reforms were never put into effect. A mob hung Villarroel in front of the presidential palace in 1946. After his death, colonos in the higland haciendas near the mining camps staged several strikes (Harris and Albó 1976); there were rebellions in Ayopaya, Cochabamba (Dandler and Torrico 1984), and in Achacachi, La Paz (Albó 1979); see also Rivera Cusicanqui 1984. This period of rural mobilization has not yet been fully investigated.

30. See Dandler (1967) for a detailed account of the many vicissitudes colonos encountered in their efforts to organize and challenge the hacendados. Although it has not received so much attention, colonos in the municipal hacienda Vacas also organized to rent the land from the Municipal Council of Cochabamba (RDR: *Libro de Gravámenes e Hipotecas* 1940).

31. *Originario* was the name given to Indians who held land in the Indian villages in Vacas until the Revisitas of the 1880s, when they were granted individual land titles.

32. In the 1970s and 1980s, further unsuccessful attempts were made to build the road.

Chapter 3. Revolution, Agrarian Reform, and the State

1. Scholars disagree about the role played by the peasantry immediately after the revolution and whether their mobilization was a grass-roots movement or one promoted from above (see, for instance, H. Buechler 1966; Carter 1965; Healy 1983; Heath et al. 1969; Heyduk 1971; Leóns 1977; Patch 1956; Simmons 1974). As Dandler (1967) points out, the position of each investigator is influenced by the setting where research was carried out, since the participation of peasants varied from region to region. No doubt, the most revolutionary settings were the Valle Alto and Valle Bajo of Cochabamba (Dandler 1984), and regions near La Paz and Oruro (Albó 1979; Harris and Albó 1976; Rivera Cusicanqui 1984). These differences also reflected the hesitation and lack of consensus on the part of the government as to what action to take regarding the peasantry (Dandler 1984).

2. Modeled after the labor unions, sindicatos agrarios from one region are grouped into a *subcentral* which, together with other subcentrales, depend on a regional Central Campesina. Centrales from the entire department, in turn, form the Federación Campesina Departamental and all of these combined form the Confederación de Trabajadores Campesinos de Bolivia.

3. The archival material for this section was collected from the office of Servicio Nacional de Reforma Agraria, which records all information on properties affected by the agrarian reform law. In the office of Registro de Derechos Reales in Cochabamba there is also the Libro de Propiedad Agraria (1960-present), documenting land transactions on properties affected by the agrarian reform.

4. According to SNRA records, there is no doubt that this hacienda was affected by the reform, but the peasants claim that they had not been granted land. The hacendado refused to talk about the subject. I pursued the case further with the Federación Campesina in Cochabamba, which suggested a meeting between the hacendado and the sharecroppers to reach an informal agreement. I also consulted with a lawyer who indicated that the case could

only be taken by an agrarian judge, and that he did not know any who were not corrupt. The problem appeared insoluble.

5. Except for unreliable gossip, I was not able to determine why one household received such a large parcel of land, larger than any plot former colonos in the hacienda had held in usufruct.

6. Conflicts among campesino leaders seeking to control entire regions were particularly notorious in the central valleys of Cochabamba (Dandler 1984) and in the region near La Paz (Albó 1979).

7. For a description of this period in Bolivian history, see Dandler 1984; Dunkerley 1984; Klein 1969; Mitchell 1977.

8. Barrientos is well-remembered in the mining camps for the massacres of miners in 1965 and 1967 in Siglo Veinte, the largest mining camp in Bolivia. Domitila Barrios de Chungara (1978), herself the wife of a miner and member of the Housewives Committee, gives a vivid account of these events.

9. The building of a landing strip generated a drawn out conflict in Tiraque after Barrientos' death. See Chapter 6 for a more detailed account of this conflict.

10. The number of dead in Tolata has been estimated to reach 100 people (Albó 1987a; *Cuadernos Justicia y Paz* 1975). There are no figures for Epizana, Totora, and Melga. For a description of this period, see Dunkerley 1984; Flores 1984; Lavaud 1984; Rivera Cusicanqui 1984.

11. For detailed studies on the history and development of campesino organizations, see Healy 1989, G. Iriarte 1980. Hurtado 1986 and Rivera Cusicanqui 1984, also discuss the peasant movement but concentrate on *katarismo* (as the Aymara Indianist movement Tupaj Katari is known) and on its influence mainly on the peasant unions of La Paz and Oruro and on the CSUTCB.

12. In a study of the decrease in production in the highland plateau, Clark (1968) concluded that this was due to the general and short-lived market disarticulation that took place in the countryside as a result of agrarian reform. Another factor that has had a long-term and increasingly negative effect on some crops has been the economic assistance Bolivia has received under the PL 480 Program from the United States since 1956. Under this program, Bolivia buys from the United States very cheap, subsidized wheat that in 1984, for instance, sold in the market at prices far below local production costs. Faced with this competition, wheat producers have reduced production and Bolivia has to rely more and more on the import of this grain (Burke 1971; *Los Tiempos*, 1984).

13. AAT: Correspondencia, Federación Sindical de Trabajadores Campesinos de Bolivia, Circular No. 12, 1955.

14. There are a significant number of studies, undertaken in the 1960s, that show both the differential outcome of agrarian reform in various areas of Bolivia and the generalized increased participation of peasants in markets: Barnes de Marschall and Torrico 1971; H. Buechler 1966; J-M Buechler 1972; Carter 1965; Clark 1968; Heath et al. 1969; Heyduk 1971; Leóns 1977; McEwen 1975; Simmons 1974.

15. The campaign was first carried out, and continues to be carried out until today, by the state agency for agricultural extension. In 1970, Yacimientos Petrolíferos Fiscales Bolivianos, the state-owned petroleum company, launched a second promotional campaign when it was planning to produce

chemical fertilizers in Bolivia. The project was never carried out and Bolivia remained dependent on the import of fertilizers and other chemical inputs (USAID/YPFB 1969). The Bolivian subsidiary of Grace Company also promoted the use of fertilizer by supplying it to rural merchants (Deere 1971). In the 1960s, the Alliance for Progress established an experimental farm in Tiraque to "modernize" agriculture (Simmons 1974).

16. The BAB, established in 1942, underwent reorganization in 1954, 1963, 1974, and 1976 in order to solve the high delinquency problem that the bank had experienced since its inception. Between 1967 and 1971, peasants had the lowest proportion of delinquent loans (6.5 percent), while farmers and cattle ranchers had the highest (30 and 27 percent, respectively). Associations had a 30 percent delinquency rating.

17. This information was compiled from BAB, Boletín Estadístico 1980 and 1982.

18. In 1978, General Banzer decreed a moratorium on outstanding loans and interests (Bertero 1986).

19. Recent studies on peasant livelihoods underscore the need for households to diversify their economic activities, see, for instance, Deere 1990; Collins 1988; Long and Roberts 1984; G. Smith 1989.

20. Figueroa 1982 and González de Olarte 1984, provide quantitative breakdowns of volume and expenditure on purchases on an annual basis. Although my aim was to obtain similar information, I found it next to impossible to calculate expenses, since purchases of consumption goods vary according to household means and the agricultural cycle. As one woman put it, "Compramos cuando tenemos; si no, nos arreglamos" ("We buy when we have money, if we don't have it, we manage"). By this she meant that if they could not buy propane gas, they used wood for cooking, and if they did not have money to buy other goods, they would get them through direct exchange or go without them. Unless the researcher could multiply herself or himself into as many researchers as households exist in a village and spend a whole year with each unit, I do not think that information obtained through questionnaires could provide adequate data. Campesinos, like most consumers who do not keep track of such purchases, simply cannot remember them. When pressed, they will give a rough estimate or make up a figure.

21. Data compiled by Mendoza (1982) from 1979 to 1982 and by me for 1982–84 during the whole period of field research. Prices for agricultural, agroindustrial and manufactured goods were recorded in three markets (Punata, Tiraque, and Cochabamba). These prices were collected during a time when Bolivia was experiencing the highest inflationary crisis in the last thirty years. To compute the relative variation of prices, these were converted into U.S. dollars according to black market rates of exchange. This is how Bolivians themselves estimate real prices. From $b40 in January 1982, the Bolivian peso devalued to $b1,200,000/US$1 in January 1985 (see Appendix).

Chapter 4. Production, Sharecropping, and Class

1. The information on this union was gathered in a census, and by participant observation and archival research. The census represents 93.3 percent of the total population. Five households had to be omitted: two questionnaires had to be discarded because of unreliable and incomplete information,

and members of the other three households could not be reached because they reside in other villages for most of the year. A word of warning regarding the census is necessary. The census was taken in December 1983 and January 1984, after a year of severe drought that had devastating effects on many households. The drought was so severe that it reduced the harvest of potatoes by 40 percent in Bolivia. Compared to good or regular years, production and exchange figures seem low, but since conditions of dearth prevail in village life, they could still be considered as typical. Campesinos also provided underestimated figures, but field observation allowed for a partial correction of this problem.

2. A large body of literature that analyzes households and domestic enterprises of petty commodity producers, has contributed to our understanding of these relations (cf. Collins 1986, 1988; Crummett 1987; Deere 1990; C. Smith 1986a; G. Smith 1989). Some scholars, however, indicate either explicitly or implicitly that whereas social differentiation among peasantries is an integral part of their class position, this differentiation does not necessarily translate into class distinctions. Following Chayanov, some scholars emphasize the cyclical nature of differentiation (cf. Shanin 1973); others minimize the internal differentiation of peasantries and underscore, instead, power relations between peasantries and the state (cf. Warman 1978) or between differentiated peasants and landowners (cf. Gould 1990; G. Smith 1989). A more recent body of literature points to the need to concentrate on gender differentiation within households to better understand processes of class formation (cf. Deere 1990; Folbre 1986; D. Wolf 1990).

3. Several scholars address the issue of household boundaries, suggesting that the community (cf. O. Harris 1982a; Sider 1986; Warman 1978) or the confederation of households within and outside the village (G. Smith 1989) are more appropriate units of analysis.

4. *L'uki*, a bitter variety of small potatoes, is used in ch'uño, which is made during the coldest days of June and July. Potatoes are spread out on the ground and left there for two nights and two days. During the night, the temperature is low enough for the potatoes to freeze. In the day, the Andean sun is warm and dries out the potatoes. Once they are dried and turn black, women and children stamp on them to remove the skin. *T'unta* is a similar freeze-dried potato that is dried in the same manner but then placed under running water for two days to remove the tannin. It is then left to dry for another day. In an economy of frequent dearth, freeze-dried potatoes are most important for preventing famine.

5. Campesinos from the Valle Alto look down on their highland counterparts, who are often pejoratively called *laris*, because of their perceived backwardness vis-à-vis their more sophisticated and more fluent Spanish-speaking vallunos.

6. Potato seed from the highlands are much coveted by campesinos from the valleys because valley crops are prone to diseases.

7. Potatoes are native to the Andes and come in many varieties. In Tiraque the most common potato varieties cultivated are *Imilla blanca, Sani imilla, Waycha paceña, Runa, Puka imilla, Qhollu*, and *luk'i*.

8. Compared with other estimates, including my own, these figures are higher because Cipca includes more days for phytosanitary treatment of plants than peasants. In Sank'ayani, for instance, households spend about 170 days/hectare to cultivate potatoes.

9. According to campesinos, the reason they cut the foliage is "for the potato skin to get thicker," and to speed the maturation of tubers, which, if left too long in the ground, might rot. They also cut the leaves to facilitate harvesting.

10. The classification of potatoes is as follows:

Chapara Very large
Qolqe First quality (literally, means money in Quechua)
Qolqe murmu Second quality (seed used for sale)
Murmu Third quality (seed for own use)
Ch'ili murmu Fourth quality (small seed for own use)
Ch'ili Fifth quality (small)
Ch'uño Sixth quality (for freeze-drying)
Descarte Seventh quality (not good, used for household consumption)

11. Hoopes and Sage (1982:4) indicate that potato harvest yields are low and are getting lower in Bolivia, declining by 35 percent in the period 1970–80. In the same decade, total potato production rose by 20 percent, but only because the area under cultivation rose by 77 percent.

12. See, for instance, Cipca 1979; F. Iriarte 1981; Jones 1980. These studies provide detailed descriptions of potato production and costs in Cochabamba. Jones raises many of the problems discussed below regarding costs of agricultural production.

13. In his detailed economic analysis of compañía contracts in Cochabamba, Jones (1980:293–94) relates different types of contracts to the life cycle and financial development of the partners. Espejo Luna (1982) emphasizes compañía as a credit relation. Simmons (1974) also describes compañía in Tiraque and explains it as an insurance against risk and as credit. Sharecropping has always been an elusive social relation for both historians and social scientists. See Byres 1983 and Pearce 1983 for comprehensive reviews of the literature.

14. Lehmann (1986) describes a similar sharecropping agreement in Ecuador, which he explains as a way of spreading costs and risks of production. See also Robertson 1987 and G. Smith 1989.

15. In fact, this is the way the Instituto Boliviano de Tecnología Agropecuaria, the government extension agency, works with campesino households. According to the local agent, this was the only way he could "induce" campesinos to experiment with new techniques and with more "adequate," yet more costly, amounts of fertilizer and insecticides.

16. The unit of sale for potatoes in the communities is the *chimpu*, the amount of potatoes that fill a sack owned by peasants. This always weighs more than 100 kilos. See Chapter 5 for a detailed discussion of the strategies used by merchants to benefit from unequal exchange.

17. Much of the following discussion refers to the entire cantón Tiraque unless otherwise stated.

18. This figure does not include women who moved to their husbands' villages after marriage.

19. The tambor weighs 120 pounds and yields about 2 kilos of cocaine paste.

20. In the villages located near the road to Chapare, from which campesinos move seasonally to Chapare, most men and women from 15 to 40 years

of age have contracted syphilis and other diseases that have now reached endemic proportions in the yungas (Ian Herteleer, M.D., Tiraque, personal communication).

21. Fifteen of these loans were extended to three men. In addition to these loans, other sources of credit were the Banco del Estado, which extended nineteen loans, and commercial houses, which extended four loans for the purchase of trucks and tractors. Since the BAB does not provide statistical data on loans at the level of the cantón, I have used data from the Libros de Hipotecas y Gravámenes, Derechos Reales, which show the individuals who have mortgaged their houses or land to obtain loans from the BAB and other banks between 1952 and 1984. These records give information on the main occupation of the borrower, the interest rate, the amount and purpose of the loan, year and the name of the lending institution. Information for the agricultural year 1984–85 was obtained from the BAB regional office at Punata.

22. Eight of these loans were received by trucker-farmers.

23. After 1984, moneylending declined because of rampant inflation. No matter how high the interest rate was set, it still lagged behind the rate of inflation (see Appendix).

24. Literally, small claims judges. Actually, their work is more akin to that carried out by a public notary, since they write and notarize private documents involving land and water transactions, sale of other goods, partition of inherited land, recognition of heirs, and occasionally money loans. One of these judges kept copies of loan transactions only if the individuals involved were willing to pay for the additional copy.

25. Using data from Jueces de Mínima Cuantía in the Valle Alto, Ladman and Torrico (1981) undertook a study of informal credit markets and found that moneylenders worked with a smaller percentage (about 5 percent) of rural households than I found in Tiraque. Yet it may be that their data involved only loans with legal interest rates (about 4 percent per month), since it is unlikely that higher-rated loans would be registered with the jueces. Their study probably did not include anticresis.

26. Underscoring the conceptual distinction between work and production, Sider (1986:93) states: "The community may control the organization of work and the reproduction of this organization, but the organization and structure of *production* itself—the whole process of determining what will be produced, with what intensity, for what kinds of return, and under what constraints, is in large part imposed upon them." See also Warman 1978.

27. Deere (1990) argues that the persistence of peasants in contexts of increasing differentiation is possible because of the engagement of household members in multiple income-generating activities.

28. At first, it was difficult to obtain a straight answer from these men about how they were able to buy land when they were still colonos, since they emphasized that they were poor and that what they cultivated on their usufruct plots was hardly enough to cover basic subsistence needs. This was a problem I encountered when questioning all former colonos who also had been piqueros. They tended to refer only to their activities as colonos and to leave out other economic activities, such as commerce and barter. It was only when they were asked where they got the money to buy the plot of land that they would refer to their engagement in other activities. According to Trinidad Solís, he made his money by cultivating plots of land the hacienda reserved for pasture and obtained very good results.

29. Simmons (1974) has documented similar reasons for the granting of large plots of land to union leaders in Tiraque.

30. See Blanes 1983 and Gill 1987 for descriptions of the problems colonizers encounter in the newly established lowland colonies.

31. For recent critiques of these studies, see Abu-Lughod 1990; Bayly 1988; Brass 1991; Comaroff and Comaroff 1991; Isaacman 1990; Lagos 1993.

32. In Tiraque there are four protestant sects: Pentecostals, Christian Unity, Seventh-Day Adventists, and Jehova's Witnesses. The evangelicals of Sank'ayani belong to Christian Unity, which has a chapel, a boarding house for campesino children, and a radio in the town of Tiraque. These were financed by West Germans. Missionaries come from the United States, Canada, and Australia.

33. The movement of people from one religion to another and back again is quite frequent in Tiraque. Often an evangelical who is about to die calls on the Catholic priest to confess and to receive last rights.

34. See Nash 1979, Platt 1983, and Taussig 1979 for other treatments of the devil in Andean belief and ritual.

35. The most powerful truck owner in Cochabamba is a man from the town of Quillacollo, where he still lives. He owns about 28 trucks. His area of operation is in the western highlands of the department, where he built secondary access roads to distant communities and, for a long time, was able to control the transport and commercialization of crops and animals in the region. His power and economic success are widely known in Cochabamba and are attributed to his dealings with the devil, who allegedly helped him by causing accidents among the other truckers who ventured into the truck owner's domain. His sister is married to a rich campesino from Sank'ayani.

Chapter 5. The Accumulation of Wealth and Capital

1. My use of the term *peasant* rather than *campesino* in this chapter is to underscore the cultural domination of towns over villages, and the fact that, in the perception of town residents, villagers remain "Indians." See Chapter 6.

2. For the ongoing debate on the formal or real subsumption of peasant households by capital see, for instance, Amin and Vergopoulos 1977; Bartra 1974; Bernstein 1976, 1977; Cook and Binford 1990; Deere 1987; Kay 1975; Roseberry 1978.

3. Anthropologists were first concerned with brokers when, drawn into the study of complex societies, they were confronted with the problem of articulation between different levels of sociocultural integration or between the community and the nation state. See, for instance, Adams 1970; Geertz 1960; Long 1975; Stavenhagen 1975; E. Wolf 1956.

4. There is no precise English equivalent for these terms, but their meaning will be understood from the contextual description.

5. For recent studies of marketwomen in the Andes, see Babb 1989 and Seligmann 1989.

6. I was able to arrive at this figure by analyzing the records of births and marriages in the parish of Tiraque.

7. During the fieldwork period, few dry goods could be found in the city

of Cochabamba because of speculative hoarding. Yet everything was available in rural markets, where there were no municipal inspectors to control prices. These prices were often ten times higher than the top prices established by the government.

8. During my stay in Bolivia, a time of rampant inflation and precipitous devaluation of the Bolivian peso, consumer prices fluctuated with the exchange rate of the Bolivian currency which, in turn, was closely related to the supply of laundered *cocadólares*, as the money made in the illicit cocaine trade is called locally (see Appendix).

9. Jones (1980:225–30) indicates that in Cochabamba the small size of the tambo delays merchants, who have to wait whole days to unload trucks. This bottleneck, he argues, reduces the number of merchants in the rural markets, thus driving down prices in the countryside.

10. The prices consumers pay for agricultural products are also inflated by the large number of traders and merchants (from four to seven) intervening in the circulation process.

11. After harvest, peasants classify potatoes according to size and quality, placing them in different sacks that sell for less or more money. In the city, merchants sell large and small potatoes of different quality at a price per pound not related to these characteristics. I am indebted to Domingo Mendoza for bringing this strategy to my attention.

12. In the highlands of Cochabamba, the annual price cycle of potatoes tends to peak from October to January, during the first harvest, reaching its lowest price from March to May, during, or immediately after, the jatun tarpuy, or large harvest (see Jones 1980: 226). Between 1982 and 1985, the annual price variation of potatoes in Bolivian pesos increased steadily with inflation, but when these prices were converted into U.S. dollars, prices bounced erratically up and down. These fluctuations responded to the exchange rate rather than to seasonal supply variations (see Appendix).

13. The earliest organization of motor-vehicle owners in Cochabamba was the Asociación de Chauffeurs, based in the city of Cochabamba in 1928 (PC: n.d.).

14. The director of the Dirección de Transporte Automotor justified the decree by saying that "the state cannot promote vicious competition which goes against the interests of transporters, and against the interests of the public which would be affected by an increase in fares" (*Presencia*, November 29, 1973).

15. Interview with the CSCB's secretary-general and the confederation's consultant. I was not able to corroborate these percentages. The last population census (República de Bolivia 1976) shows that 3 percent of the economically active population were *conductores* (drivers), of which 54 percent were wage laborers. However, the means of transport employing these drivers was not specified.

16. Except those drivers who work for a few international transport companies and for the national enterprise of transport (Empresa Nacional de Transporte Automotriz), organized in 1984 to provide limited urban service.

17. Only new vehicles purchased on credit from importing firms are insured, because the vehicle remains the importer's property until complete payment is made. Purchasers cannot sell or transfer the vehicle until then (Slater 1969:114). Annual interest rates increased from 9 percent in 1979 to 36 percent in 1982.

18. This explains contradictory statements in the literature regarding trucking as an enterprise. Two early studies surveying business practices among transportistas in the department of La Paz concluded that trucking does not bring large returns (J-M. Buechler 1972; Slater 1969). In contrast, Healy (1979) reports that transporters in the department of Chuquisaca make considerable profits.

19. New, large trucks are costly. Prices range from 70,000 to 120,000 U.S. dollars.

20. Bolivia is an oil-producing country, and gasoline is cheap in comparison to prices in other countries.

21. These involved a devaluation of the Bolivian peso by 20 percent and a freeze in the price of agricultural products.

22. The main objectives of these demands were (1) the establishment of peasant-controlled markets to sell directly to consumers and buy from producers; (2) the creation of a peasant-controlled bank to extend long-term loans to peasants; (3) improvements in technical assistance and peasant participation in the design of development projects; (4) the establishment of free roads to put an end to the control over road transport on the part of unionized transporters, and (5) the promotion of peasant truck cooperatives (*Boletín Agrario*, No. 1, 1980; *Presencia*, December 4, 1979).

23. In March 1984, tires sold for $b800,000, but transportistas could get them through their unions at $b100,000.

24. Simmons (1974:36) presents the case of a peasant truck owner from a village in Tiraque who carried a submachine gun with him to protect himself against threats made by truckers of Punata. They feared that this new transporter-merchant would compete with them in the villages where they operated.

25. By 1984, the number of union members had increased to 58. Of these, 29 were from peasant villages and two were widows of former union members. These women, however, do not drive the vehicles.

26. Libro de Actas, Sindicato Mixto de Transportistas (Tiraque), January 4, 1973.

27. In 1977, fourteen transportistas in Cochabamba owned 787 vehicles (Appleton 1978).

28. In 1980, there were approximately 958 members. In some unions, such as Transpeco, nepotism, bribes, and favoritism become important factors for membership or for the assignment of cargo (Cordeco 1980). This study also points to other problems related to road transport and its control by transporters' unions.

29. In theory, these fares are based on an estimated annual rate of depreciation (10 percent) for vehicles and other operational costs. In practice, however, fare increases are often determined by political considerations in response to pressures from the CSCB and counterpressures from other organized groups.

30. This event will be discussed more fully in Chapter 6.

31. By law, nonunionized transporters were not allowed to render a public service, that is, carry freight and passengers, unless they were transporting their own produce and not charging for their services. In practice, however, it was impossible to put these regulations into effect in rural areas except by intimidation.

32. Long-distance truckers are paid by the *quintal* (46 kilograms) of freight

they transport; Luis's trucks can carry a combined total of 700 quintales. In December 1984, fares from Cochabamba to Chapare were set at $b35,000 per quintal, and at $b48,000 per quintal from Cochabamba to La Paz.

33. These amounts might not seem large relative to incomes in the United States, but compared to the Bolivian minimum wage, these earnings were high indeed.

34. At the time of the accident, the bus was carrying kerosene. The vehicle burned and two passengers died.

35. This is the most common pattern in the development of young truckers. They begin learning to drive while working as assistants, so that they may become salaried drivers. Others learn to drive during their military service. It takes them from 6 to 15 years of driving before they are able to buy their own vehicles, unless they migrate to find work in other regions or countries. Recently, cocaine processing has become an easy, fast way to earn money for the purchase of vehicles.

36. As indicated in Chapter 3, most of these loans were directed to truckers.

37. If they cannot avoid it, transporters prefer to pay hospital, medical, and funeral bills for their injured or dead passengers rather than face more costly court trials. Since most vehicle owners (apart from those buying their vehicles on credit) are not insured, an accident may thus threaten the enterprise.

38. Chapter 6 provides a more detailed discussion of this event.

39. Sider (1986:92) refers to this process of accumulation as "capital formation at a distance."

Chapter 6. The Culture of Power and Politics

1. The problem of ethnic identities in the Andes is, of course, complex and fraught with subjectivity. In this chapter, I am discussing one aspect of social life in which ethnicity becomes salient. See Abercrombie 1991, Crandon-Malamud 1991, and Weismantel 1988 for different ways of interpreting this issue.

2. Roseberry 1989 and Stern 1983 make a similar point. Sider 1986, C. Smith 1986b, and G. Smith 1989 argue, instead, that an awareness of "community" may sometimes be perceived as class-consciousness.

3. There is a large body of anthropological literature on factions. For an excellent review of this literature, see Vincent 1978.

4. This tax had been abolished in the 1950s when José Rojas (campesino leader of Ucureña; see Chapter 3) ordered peasants not to pay it in retaliation for the large number of votes in favor of the Falange Socialista Boliviana party in the town of Tiraque (AAT: Correspondencia, January 31, 1972).

5. At about the same time, other peasant-controlled markets (or ferias francas) opened in the region in the villages of Tuturuyo, Cañadas, Rodeo, and Ramadas in 1982, and in the villages of Cañacota and Boquerón Khasa in 1984. Since these villages are located farther away from the town of Tiraque, vecinos did not oppose them mainly because these areas lie outside their sphere of influence and would not affect their interests. Rather, these markets could affect merchants and truckers from Punata and other market towns.

6. These two older leaders had occupied the position of secretary-general in the Central Campesina several times during the MNR and the Barrientos governments. The third had had problems in Lomapata; he was generally distrusted because he took his crops to Punata rather than selling them in the new market where, it was alleged, he cheated peasants by weighing potatoes to favor merchants.

7. First organized with the assistance of a government agricultural extension agent, the APP has been assisted by private development institutions, the support of which other institutions would like as well. In 1984, the APP had some 12,000 members in the entire department of Cochabamba.

8. See Cipca (1979:133–140) for a description of other APP objectives.

9. At the time, the price of a 50-kilogram sack of fertilizer was $b2,000, while the government had established a top price of $b700 for a sack of potatoes.

10. In 1979, several campesinos, some of whom were members of the APP, organized a Committee of Transport and Commercialization (Comité de Transporte y Comercialización) to replace urban transporters operating in the region of Morochata, located in the western highlands of Cochabamba. As Ustariz and Mendoza (1982:116–23) show, the committee benefited a group of village social climbers who used the organization to advance their political and economic careers.

11. See Albó (1974) for an analysis of situational speech patterns in Cochabamba.

12. These staples, consisting of flour, lentils, powdered milk, rice and oil, are part of the U.S. assistance program for developing countries. The letters on the sacks indicate that they come from "The People of the United States."

13. Fertilizers were channelled and distributed by the agricultural bank and other institutions.

14. Prior to this time, there were already two campesino subcentrales in Tiraque (Koari and Iluri Grande), formed by villages located too far from the town where the Central Campesina meets regularly. These subcentrales still depend on the Central Campesina in Tiraque. In a few months in 1983, however, seven new subcentrales, some very close to the town, sprang up in the region. Some of these remained independent from the leftist-controlled Central.

15. The only exception is the celebration of San Isidro that takes place in the countryside in March. The "owner" of the saint is always a vecino who provides food and drink to villagers from the vicinity. They, in turn, reenact the role of former colonos, planting together on the land reserved for the hacendado's crops.

16. Villages situated at a distance from the town of Tiraque have their own cemeteries.

17. For an excellent analysis of dominant images of the countryside in England, see Williams 1973; and see Roseberry 1989 for a study of images of the peasant in Venezuela.

18. The virgin was brought to Tiraque in 1922 by a hacendada, Gavina Siles de Terrazas, who, with her husband, bought the hacienda K'aspikancha after accumulating merchant capital in the region of Tiraque at the turn of the century. See Chapter 2.

Glossary

Ahijado: Godchild.

Alcaldía: Town or city hall.

Al partir: Animal share system, mainly used for oxen.

Anticrético or anticresis: Contract involving immovable property (land or houses) given in usufruct for a specified amount of money that is repaid at the termination of the contract.

Aporque: Process of raising of furrow around young plants and loosening the soil around them.

Arrendero or arrendatario: Individual who leases or sharecrops land from others.

Arrimante: Landless men and women attached to colono households in haciendas.

Arriendo: Land lease.

Arroba: Unit of weight that varies for different agricultural products. Its weight also varies between regions. An arroba of potatoes weighs 25 pounds.

Arrope: Residue of maize after processing chicha.

Ayni: (Quechua) Term defining a reciprocal relationship.

Ayllu: (Quechua), pl. ayllus. Andean corporate kin group. There has been substantial controversy over this term, much of it arising from the fact that many do not consider the term in a historically specific context.

Bayeta: Rough wool cloth.

Campesino: Literally, peasant. In Bolivia, however, the term is ambiguous.

Carga: Unit of weight used principally for potatoes but also used for other agricultural products. The weight of a carga of potatoes varies within and between regions. In the city of Cochabamba, a carga of potatoes weighs 100 kilograms, or 216 pounds.

Casero: Name used reciprocally by two individuals who have established long-term barter or commercial relations. The term is also used in casual exchanges between sellers and customers in shops and markets in urban centers.

Central Campesina: Regional-level campesino organization, encompassing all local campesino unions.

Chhala: (Quechua) From chhalay: barter. Unit of barter exchange amounting to some six pounds.

Chhalera: (Quechua) Woman dedicated to barter exchange.

Chapara: (Quechua) Very large potato.

Chawpi mishka: (Quechua) Second potato harvest.

Chicha: Alcoholic beverage made of maize.

Chichera: Woman who makes and sells chicha.

Chichería: Locale for selling and drinking chicha.

Ch'ili: (Quechua) Very small potato.

Cholo: During early colonial times, the term denoted individuals with one white grandparent; nowadays, a pejorative term usually applied to nouveau-riche mestizos.

Cholita: Diminutive of chola.

Chimpu: (Quechua) Sack to store potatoes after harvest. It weighs some 240 pounds.

Ch'uño: (Quechua) Freeze-dried potatoes.

Cocadólares: U.S. dollars earned in the illicit trade of cocaine.

Cocaleros: Coca producers.

Colono: Landless men and women settled on haciendas.

Compadrazgo: Fictive kin tie established between one's parents and godparents.

Compañeros: Comrades; companions.

Compañía: Sharecropping agreement.

Concubinato: Common-law marriage.

Con precio: A sheep-share system.

Cueca: Folkloric dance.

Dotación: Land granted to a household by campesino unions from the portion of land not distributed among households by agrarian reform.

Fanegada: Measure of land equivalent to 28,978 square meters.

Feria franca: Rural market exempted from municipal taxes.

Fletero: Mule pack driver.

Gringo: Foreigner. Often the term is also used as a nickname for people with fair complexions and light hair.

Guaniri: (Quechua) Person in charge of placing manure in the furrow.

Hermano: Brother.

Indio: Indian. Nowadays, the term tends to be a pejorative form of address.

Jatun tarpuy: (Quechua) Large, or annual, harvest of potatoes.

Juez de Mínima Cuantía: Small claims judge.

Katarismo: Refers to an "Indianist" movement in highland Bolivia. Its name comes from Tupaj Katari, one of the leaders in the Indian rebellions of the late eighteenth century.

Laris: (Quechua) In Cochabamba, pejorative term used to refer to highland peasants.

L'uki: (Quechua) Bitter variety of potatoes used for making ch'uño.

Mestizo: During colonial times, the term denoted individuals with one white parent. Nowadays, it refers to individuals of mixed white and Indian ancestry.

Minka: (Quechua) Communal work.

Mishka: (Quechua) The first, or early, harvest of potatoes.

Mitanaje: Rotative labor obligation in the hacienda involving colono women who must work in the hacienda house for a period of time.

Mujiri: (Quechua) Person in charge of the seed in the planting of a crop.

Muju: (Quechua) Seed.

Muko: (Quechua) A paste made with corn flour and saliva in chicha preparation.

Murmu: (Quechua) Medium-sized potato.

Originario: Indians who had landholding rights in Indian corporate communities.

Paga: In-kind payment for agricultural work in lieu of a wage.

Pasa-pasa: Term used to define an individual who changes political affiliation often.

Patrón: pl. patrones. Term to refer to hacendados. Boss.

Piquero: Prior to agrarian reform, this term designated landowning peasants.

Piquería: A locality where all peasants are piqueros.

Playa: (Quechua) Marketplace.

Pollera: Wide, gathered skirt worn by campesino women and "traditional" urban women.

Pongo: Name given to hacienda tenants when they worked in the hacienda house.

Pongueaje: Rotational labor obligation in the haciendas involving men who had to work in the hacienda house for a period of time.

Prefecto: In Bolivia, governor.

Prestación vial: Rotative labor service owed to the state for the construction of public roads.

Pututu: (Quechua) Horn used by peasants to call important meetings or events.

Qhatera: (Quechua) Market traders who set up stalls in marketplaces.

Quintal: Unit of weight amounting to 46 kilograms.

Qolqe: (Quechua) Silver or money. Also refers to a particular size of potatoes that are commonly sold.

Qolqe cajita: Little money box. This term is used to refer to pigs held in shares.

Ranqhera: Rural livestock dealer.

Rescatista: Rural merchant specializing in the purchase of agricultural products.

Romería: Group of individuals organized to celebrate a religious festival.

Seña: Downpayment for securing the advanced purchase of crops.

Sindicato agrario: Campesino union organized after agrarian reform in every village.

Subcentral: Subregional campesino organization.

Tambo: (Quechua) Storehouse located in the cities for the storage and sale of agricultural products, mainly potatoes or coca.

Tambor: Bundle of dried coca leaves wrapped with tree bark; it weighs 60 pounds.

T'inka: (Quechua) Involuntary donation of crops, animals or money; a bribe.

Transportista: Transporter. The term encompasses truck, bus, and taxi owners and drivers.

T'unta: (Quechua) Freeze-dried and water-leached potato.

Valluno: People from the central valleys of Cochabamba.

Vecino: Rural town resident.

Yungas: Steep tropical valleys.

Yungueños: Landowners and/or workers in the yungas valleys.

Yunta: A pair of oxen harnessed to a plow.

References

Archives

Archivo Alcaldía Tiraque (AAT), located in the town hall of Tiraque, is an invaluable source for the reconstruction of the social history of the region. Apart from bound volumes containing the council's minutes taken between 1900 and 1921, the rest of the documents consist of loose papers, sometimes placed in uncatalogued file folders. These documents include municipal ordinances (Ordenanzas Municipales), mail sent to and received by the mayor (Correspondencia), lists of moneylenders, municipal tax collectors, and merchants, and complaints and petitions made by the local population. It also contains various censuses carried out by the municipal council.

Archivo Histórico Municipal (AHM), Cochabamba, houses notarial and trial records from the early colony to the late nineteenth century. Until 1984, when the archive was organized, very few of these documents were catalogued.

Juzgado Tiraque (JT), contains information on land and money loan litigations, lawsuits for perjury and libel, cattle rustling, and general disputes and conflicts. Most documents consist of loose papers thrown on the floor of a mice-infested room. I was obliged, therefore, to collect data somewhat "randomly." Although many documents are incomplete, they still provide rich information on the region.

Prefectura de Cochabamba (PC). The Notaría de Hacienda keeps incomplete and uncatalogued information on the Indian population of Cochabamba for the nineteenth century: Revisitas 1876–1880, or censuses of Indian tributaries, and land transactions in lands distributed to Indians after the last Revisitas (Libro de Indígenas). There are also general population censuses (Padrón de la Contribución Personal) and other notarial records. The Tesoro de Hacienda has a bound collection of undated cadastral censuses taken in every province of the department of Cochabamba in the early twentieth century.

Registro de Derechos Reales (RDR), Cochabamba. This office holds a wealth of historical and contemporary information (from 1888 to the present) on land transactions, organized in bound volumes by province and by year (Libro Principal del Registro de la Propiedad). The Libro de Gravámenes e Hipotecas contains information on sharecropping and lease contracts, land mortgages, and litigations. These data are also in bound volumes by province and by year. A third set of documents, registering former hacienda land allocated to colonos, may be found in the Libro de Propiedad Agraria (from 1960 to the present).

Servicio Nacional de Reforma Agraria (SNRA), La Paz. This office records all information on properties affected by agrarian reform. The documents, organized by cantón and province, provide rich and detailed information about colonos settled on haciendas, such as their number, place of birth, years on the hacienda, size of plots of land held in usufruct, and work conditions on haciendas. Each document also includes minutes of testimonies made during agrarian reform trials.

Published and Unpublished Works

Abercrombie, Thomas
1991 "To be Indian, to be Bolivian: 'Ethnic' and 'National' Discourses of Identity." In *Nation-States and Indians in Latin America*, edited by Greg Urban and Joel Sherzer. Austin: University of Texas Press, pp. 95–130.

Abu-Lughod, Lila
1990 "The Romance of Resistance: Tracing Transformations of Power Through Bedouin Women." *American Ethnologist* 17(1):41–55.

Adams, Richard N.
1970 "Brokers and Career Mobility Systems in the Structure of Complex Societies." *Southwestern Journal of Anthropology* 26(4):315–27.

Alberti, Giorgio, and Enrique Mayer (comp.)
1974 *Reciprocidad e Intercambio en los Andes Peruanos*. Lima: Instituto de Estudios Peruanos.

Albó, Xavier
1974 *Los mil rostros del Quechua*. Lima: Instituto de Estudios Peruanos.
1976 *Lengua y sociedad en Bolivia, 1976*. República de Bolivia. Ministerio de Planeamiento y Coordinación. La Paz: Instituto Nacional de Estadística.
1979 *Achacachi: Medio siglo de luchas campesinas*. La Paz: Centro de Investigación y Promoción del Campesinado.
1987a "From MNRistas to Kataristas to Katari." In *Resistance, Rebellion, and Consciousness in the Andean Peasant World, 18th to 20th Centuries*, edited by Steve Stern. Wisconsin: University of Wisconsin Press.
1987b "Por qué el campesino qhochala es diferente?" *Cuarto Intermedio*, Cochabamba, vol. 2:43–59.

Allen, Catherine J.
1988 *The Hold Life Has. Coca and Cultural Identity in an Andean Community*. Washington, D. C.: Smithsonian Institution Press.

Amin, S., and K. Vergopoulos
1977 *La question paysanne et le capitalisme*. Paris: Anthropos.

Anderson, Benedict
1983 *Imagined Communities: Reflections on the Origin and Spread of Capitalism*. London: Verso.

Appleton, Peter
1978 "Sistemas de comercialización para productos alimenticios." República de Bolivia, Ministerio de Asuntos Campesinos y Agropecuarios. Unpublished Working Paper No. 025/78.

Assadourian, Carlos S.
1982 *El sistema de la economía colonial.* Lima: Instituto de Estudios Peruanos.

Assadourian, Carlos S., Heraclio Bonilla, Antonio Mitre, and Tristan Platt
1980 *Minería y espacio económico en los Andes. Siglos 16–20.* Lima: Instituto de Estudios Peruanos.

Babb, Florence E.
1989 *Between Field and Cooking Pot: The Political Economy of Market Women in Peru.* Austin: University of Texas Press.

Barnes de Marschall, Katherine and Juan Torrico
1971 "Cambios socio-económicos en el Valle Alto de Cochabamba desde 1952: Los pueblos provinciales de Cliza, Punata, Tiraque, Arani, Sacaba y Tarata." *Estudios Andinos* 2(1):141–71.

Bartra, Roger
1974 *Estructura agraria y clases sociales en México.* México: Editorial Era.

Barrios de Chungara, Domitila
1978 *Let Me Speak!* New York: Monthly Review Press.

Bayly, C. A.
1988 "Rallying Around the Subaltern." *The Journal of Peasant Studies* 16(1):110–20.

Bernstein, Henry
1976 "Underdevelopment and the Law of Value: A Critique of Kay." *Review of African Political Economy* 6:51–64.
1977 "Notes on Capital and Peasantry." *Review of African Political Economy* 10:60–73.
1979 "African Peasantries: A Theoretical Framework." *The Journal of Peasant Studies* 6(4):421–41.

Bertero, Mauro
1986 "Crédito agrícola en Bolivia." *Debate Agrario* 4:7–56.

Blanco, Federico
1901 *Diccionario geográfico de la República de Bolivia*, 4 vols. Tomo 1. La Paz: Oficina Nacional de Inmigración,

Blanes, José
1983 *De los valles al Chapare: Estrategias familiares en un contexto de cambios.* Cochabamba: Centro de Estudios de la Realidad Económica y Social.

Boletín Agrario
1980 "Sindicalismo: Entrevista con Genaro Flores," vol. 1, p. 1. La Paz: Centro de Información y Documentación Obrera de Bolivia.

Bourdieu, Pierre
1990 *The Logic of Practice.* Stanford, Calif.: Stanford University Press.

Brass, Tom
1991 "Moral Economists, Subalterns, New Social Movements, and the (Re-) Emergence of a (Post-) Modernized (Middle) Peasant." *The Journal of Peasant Studies* 18(2):173–205.

Buechler, Hans C.
1966 "Agrarian Reform and Migration on the Bolivian Altiplano." Ph.D. Dissertation, Columbia University.

Buechler, Judith-Marie
1972 "Peasant Marketing and Social Revolution in the State of La Paz, Bolivia." Ph.D. Dissertation, McGill University.

Burke, Melvin
  1971 "Does Food for Peace Assistance Damage the Bolivian Economy?" *Inter-American Economic Affairs* 25:3–26.
Byres, T. J.
  1983 "Historical Perspectives on Sharecropping." In *Sharecropping and Sharecroppers*, edited by T. J. Byres. London: Frank Cass.
Cajka, Francis R.
  1979 "Peasant Commercialization in the Serranías of Cochabamba, Bolivia," Ph.D. Dissertation, University of Michigan.
Cancian, Frank
  1965 *Economics and Prestige in a Maya Community: The Religious Cargo System of Zinacantan.* Stanford, Calif.: Stanford University Press.
Cardona Carlos A.
  1979 *El desarrollo de la industria automotriz en un país de la periferia del capitalismo: Bolivia y el grupo Andino.* La Paz: Empresa Gráfica Visión.
Carter, William E. (comp.)
  1965 *Aymara Communities and the Bolivian Agrarian Reform.* Gainesville: University Press of Florida.
  1983 *Ensayos científicos sobre la coca.* La Paz: Editorial Juventud.
Chayanov, Alexandr V.
  1966 *A. V. Chayanov on the Theory of Peasant Economy.* Edited by Daniel Thorner, Basile Kerblay, and R. E. F. Smith. Homewood, IL: American Economic Association.
Chevalier, Jacques
  1982 *Civilization and the Stolen Gift: Capital, Kin, and Cult in Eastern Peru.* Toronto: University of Toronto Press.
Cipca (Centro de Investigación y Promoción del Campesinado)
  1979 *Estudio de la situación socio-económica de los productores de papa del Departamento de Cochabamba.* Cochabamba.
  1983 "Estudio de pre-factibilidad para la producción asociada de productos agrícolas en la zona de Tiraque, Sank'ayani, K'aspikancha y Koari Boquerón. Unpublished Manuscript. Cochabamba.
Clark, Ronald S.
  1968 *Land Reform and Peasant Market Participation on the Northern Highlands of Bolivia.* Land Tenure Center. Madison: University of Wisconsin.
Cobb, Gwendolin B.
  1949 "Supply and Transportation for the Potosí Mines, 1545–1640," *Hispanic American Historical Review* 29(1):25–45.
Collins, Jane
  1986 "The Household and Relations of Production in Southern Peru." *Comparative Studies in Society and History* 28(4):651–71.
  1988 *Unseasonal Migrations.* Princeton: Princeton University Press.
Comaroff, Jean, and John Comaroff
  1991 *Of Revelation and Revolution: Christianity, Colonialism, and Consciousness in South Africa.* Chicago: Chicago University Press.
Cook, Scott, and Leigh Binford
  1990 *Obliging Need: Rural Petty Industry in Mexican Capitalism.* Austin: University of Texas Press.
Corporación de Desarrollo Cochabamba (Cordeco)
  1980 "Análisis de problemas en el sector transporte." In *Análisis de problemas y potenciales en el desarrollo regional de Cochabamba*, vol. 2.

Crandon-Malamud, Libbet
1991 *From the Fat of Our Souls: Social Change, Political Process, and Medical Pluralism in Bolivia.* Berkeley/Los Angeles: University of California Press.
Cuadernos Justicia y Paz
1975 "La masacre del valle." La Paz: Cuadernos de Justicia y Paz.
Crummett, M. de los Angeles
1987 "Class, Household Structure, and the Peasantry: An Empirical Approach." *The Journal of Peasant Studies* 14(3):363–79.
Dandler, Jorge
1967 Local Group, "Community and Nation: A Study of Changing Structure in Ucureña, Bolivia (1935–1952)." M.A. thesis, University of Wisconsin.
1984 "La 'Ch'ampa Guerra' de Cochabamba: Un proceso de disgregación política." In *Bolivia: La fuerza histórica del campesinado*, edited by Fernando Calderón and Jorge Dandler. La Paz: Centro de Estudios de la Realidad Económica y Social, pp. 241–72.
Dandler, Jorge, and Juan Torrico
1984 "El Congreso Nacional Indígena de 1945 y la rebelión de Ayopaya (1947)." In *Bolivia: La fuerza histórica del campesinado*, edited by Fernando Calderón and Jorge Dandler. La Paz: Centro de Estudios de la Realidad Económica y Social, pp. 133–200.
Deere, Carmen D.
1971 "Bolivia: A Survey of Agricultural Credit." Unpublished Manuscript. La Paz: USAID.
1987 "The Peasantry in Political Economy: Trends in the 1980s." University of Massachusetts at Amherst. Program in Latin American Studies. Occasional Papers Series, No. 19.
1990 *Household and Class Relations. Peasants and Landlords in Northern Peru.* Berkeley/Los Angeles: University of California Press.
de Janvry, Alain
1981 *The Agrarian Question and Reformism in Latin America.* Baltimore: Johns Hopkins University Press.
Dunkerley, James
1984 *Rebellion in the Veins.* London: Verso.
Eagleton, Terry
1991 *Ideology. An Introduction.* London: Verso.
Ennew, Judith, P. Hirst, and K. Tribe
1977 "'Peasantry' as an Economic Category." *The Journal of Peasant Studies* 4(4):295–321.
Espejo Luna, Justo
1982 Contratos en compañía como forma de crédito en países de menor desarrollo negativo: El caso de Bolivia. Unpublished Manuscript. La Paz: USAID/Arizona State University.
El Heraldo
1882 "Cochabamba" (June 26).
1883 "Cuadro Jeneral del Catastro Departamental de Cochabamba" (July 1).
Estudio Integral del Transporte en Bolivia
1980 Costos del Transporte Automotor. La Paz: Preliminary Report.

Figueroa, Adolfo
  1982 "Production and Market Exchange in Peasant Economies: The Case of the Southern Highlands in Peru." In *Ecology and Exchange in the Andes*, edited by David Lehmann. Cambridge: Cambridge University Press, pp. 123–56.
Flores, Gonzalo
  1984 "Estado, políticas agrarias y luchas campesinas: Revisión de una década en Bolivia." In *Bolivia: La fuerza histórica del campesinado*, edited by Fernando Calderón and Jorge Dandler. La Paz: Centro de Estudios de la Realidad Económica y Social, pp. 445–545.
Folbre, Nancy
  1986 "Cleaning House: New Perspectives on Households and Economic Development." *Journal of Development Economics* 22(1):5–40.
Friedmann, Harriet
  1980 "Household Production and the National Economy: Concepts for the Analysis of Agrarian Formations." *The Journal of Peasant Studies* 7(2):158–84.
Geertz, Clifford
  1960 "The Javanese Kikaji: The Changing Role of a Cultural Broker." *Comparative Studies in Society and History* 2(2):228–49.
Gill, Lesley
  1987 *Peasants, Entrepreneurs, and Social Change. Frontier Development in Lowland Bolivia*. Boulder/London: Westview Press.
Glavanis, K. R. G.
  1984 "Aspects of Non-Capitalist Social Relations in Rural Egypt: The Small Peasant Household in an Egyptian Delta Village." In *Family and Work in Rural Societies: Perspectives on Non-Wage Labour*, edited by Norman Long. London: Tavistock Publications.
González de Olarte, Efraín
  1984 *Economía de la comunidad campesina*. Lima: Instituto de Estudios Peruanos.
Goodman, David, and Michael Redclift
  1981 *From Peasant to Proletarian: Capitalist Development and Agrarian Transitions*. Oxford: Basil Blackwell.
Gould, Jeffrey L.
  1990 *To Lead as Equals: Rural Protest and Political Consciousness in Chinandega, Nicaragua, 1912–1979*. Chapel Hill: University of North Carolina Press.
Gramsci, Antonio
  1975 *Selections from the Prison Notebooks*. New York: International Publishers.
Grieshaber, Erwin
  1980 "Survival of Indian Communities in Nineteenth-Century Bolivia: A Regional Comparison." *Journal of Latin American Studies* 12: 223–69.
Guha, Ranajit (editor)
  1989 *Subaltern Studies 6*. New Delhi: Oxford University Press.
Hall, Stuart
  1981 "Notes on Deconstructing the Popular." In *People's History and Socialist Theory*, edited by Raphael Samuel. London: Routledge and Kegan Paul, pp. 227–40.

1988 "The Toad in the Garden: Thatcherism Among the Theorists." In *Marxism and the Interpretation of Culture*, edited by Cary Nelson and Lawrence Grossberg. Urbana: University of Illinois Press, pp. 35–74.

Harris, Marvin
1964 *Patterns of Race in the Americas*. New York: W. W. Norton and Company.

Harris, Olivia
1982a "Households and Their Boundaries." *History Workshop Journal* 13: 143–52.
1982b "Labour and Produce in an Ethnic Economy, Northern Potosí, Bolivia." In *Ecology and Exchange in the Andes*, edited by David Lehmann. Cambridge: Cambridge University Press, pp. 70–96.

Harris, Olivia, and Javier Albó
1976 *Monteras y guardatojos: Campesinos y mineros en el norte de Potosí*. La Paz: Centro de Investigación y Promoción del Campesinado.

Harris, Richard
1978 "Marxism and the Agrarian Question in Latin America." *Latin American Perspectives* 5(4):2–26.

Hart, Gillian
1986 *Power, Labor, and Livelihood: Processes of Change in Rural Java*. Berkeley/Los Angeles: University of California Press.

Healy, Kevin
1979 Power, Class and Rural Development in Southern Bolivia. Ph.D. dissertation, Cornell University.
1983 *Caciques y Patrones: Una experiencia de desarrollo rural en el sud de Bolivia*. Cochabamba: Centro de Estudios de la Realidad Económica y Social.
1986 "The Boom Within the Crisis: Some Recent Effects of Foreign Cocaine Market on Bolivian Society and Economy." In *Coca and Cocaine. Effects on People and Policy in Latin America*, edited by Deborah Pacini and Christine Franquemont. Boston: Cultural Survival, pp. 101–43.
1989 *Sindicatos campesinos y desarrollo rural 1978–1985*. La Paz: Hisbol.

Heath, Dwight B., Charles J. Erasmus, and Hans C. Buechler
1969 *Land Reform and Social Revolution in Bolivia*. New York: Praeger Publishers.

Heyduk, Daniel
1971 *Huayrapampa: Bolivian Highland Peasants and the New Social Order*. Ithaca, NY: Cornell University Latin American Studies Program Dissertation Series, No. 27.

Hobsbawm, Eric J.
1983 "Introduction: Inventing Traditions." In *The Invention of Tradition*, edited by Eric J. Hobsbawm and Terence Ranger. Cambridge: Cambridge University Press, pp. 1–14.

Hoopes, Robert W., and Colin Sage
1982 *Overview of Potato Production and Consumption in Bolivia*. La Paz: Consortium for International Development.

Huizer, Gerrit
1972 *The Revolutionary Potential of Peasants in Latin America*. Lexington, MA: Lexington Books.

Hurtado, Javier
   1986   *El Katarismo*. La Paz: Hisbol.
Iriarte, Filemón
   1981   Análisis comparativo de los costos de producción del cultivo de la papa en el Departamento de Cochabamba. Tésis de Licenciatura, Universidad Mayor San Simón.
Iriarte, Gregorio
   1980   *Sindicalismo campesino: Ayer, hoy y mañana*. La Paz: Centro de Investigación y Promoción del Campesinado.
Isaacman, Allen
   1990   "Peasants and Rural Social Protest in Africa." *African Studies Review* 33(2):1–118.
Jackson, Robert
   1988   "Markets, Peasantry, and the Formation and Fragmentation of the Hacienda in Cochabamba." *Peasant Studies* 16.
   1989   "Decline of the Hacienda in Cochabamba." *The Hispanic American Historical Review* 69:259–81.
Jones, Jeffrey R.
   1980   Technological Change and Market Organization in Cochabamba, Bolivia: Problems of Agricultural Development Among Potato Producing Small Farmers. Ph.D. dissertation, University of California, Los Angeles.
Kay, Geoffrey
   1975   *Development and Underdevelopment: A Marxist Analysis*. London: Macmillan.
Kelley, Jonathan, and Herbert S. Klein
   1981   *Revolution and the Rebirth of Inequality: A Theory Applied to the National Revolution of Bolivia*. Berkeley/Los Angeles: University of California Press.
Klein, Herbert S.
   1969   *Parties and Political Change in Bolivia*. Cambridge: Cambridge University Press.
   1982   *Bolivia. The Evolution of a Multi-Ethnic Society*. Oxford: Oxford University Press.
Ladman, Jerry R., Glenn C. W. Ames, Thomas M. Dickey, David O. Hansen, and David C. Richardson
   1979   *Bolivian Rural Financial Market Assessment*. The Ohio State University for USAID.
Ladman, Jerry R., and José I. Torrico
   1981   "Informal Credit Markets in the Valle Alto of Cochabamba, Bolivia." In *Proceedings of the Rocky Mountain Council on Latin American Studies Conference*, edited by John S. Brasch and Susan R. Rouch. College of Business Administration, University of Nebraska, pp. 83–89.
Lagos, Maria L.
   1993   "'We Have to Learn to Ask': Hegemony, Diverse Experiences, and Antagonistic Meanings in Bolivia." *American Ethnologist* 20(1): 52–71.
Larson, Brooke
   1988   *Colonialism and Agrarian Transformation in Bolivia*. Princeton, NJ: Princeton University Press.

Latin American Bureau
1982 *Narcotráfico y política. Militarismo y mafia en Bolivia.* Madrid: Iepala Editorial.
Lavaud, Jean Pierre
1984 "Los campesinos frente al Estado." In *Bolivia: La fuerza histórica del campesinado,* edited by Fernando Calderón and Jorge Dandler. La Paz: Centro de Estudios de la Realidad Económica y Social, pp. 273–308.
Leeds, Anthony
1977 "Mythos and Pathos: Some Unpleasantries on Peasantries." In *Peasant Livelihood: Studies in Economic Anthropology and Cultural Ecology,* edited by Rhoda Halperin and James Dow. New York: St. Martin's Press, pp. 227–56.
Lehmann, David
1986 "Two Paths of Agrarian Capitalism, or a Critique of Chayanovian Marxism." *Comparative Studies in Society and History* 28(4): 601–27.
Lenin, V. I.
1899/1956 *The Development of Capitalism in Russia.* Moscow: Progress Publishers.
Leonard, Olen E.
1948 *Cantón Chullpas. A Socioeconomic Study in the Cochabamba Valley of Bolivia.* Washington D.C.: Foreign Agricultural Report, No. 27.
Leóns, Madeline B.
1977 "La economía política de la reforma agraria en Yungas, Bolivia." *Estudios Andinos* 7(13):93–221.
Long, Norman
1975 "Structural Dependency, Modes of Production and Economic Brokerage in Rural Peru." In *Beyond the Sociology of Development,* edited by I. Oxaal, T. Barnett, and D. Booth. London: Routledge and Kegan Paul.
1986 "Commoditization: Thesis and Antithesis." In *The Commoditization Debate: Labour Process, Strategy and Social Network,* edited by N. Long, J. D. van der Ploeg, C. Curtin, and L. Box. Wageningen, Netherlands: Agricultural University.
Long, Norman, and Bryan Roberts (eds.)
1984 *Miners, Peasants, and Entrepreneurs.* Cambridge: Cambridge University Press.
Los Tiempos
1984 Cochabamba.
Malloy, James M.
1971 "Revolutionary Politics." In *Beyond the Revolution: Bolivia Since 1952,* edited by James M. Malloy, and R. S. Thorn. Pittsburgh: University of Pittsburgh Press, pp. 111–56.
Marx, Karl
1852/1963 *The Eighteenth Brumaire of Louis Bonaparte.* New York: International Publishers.
1894/1977 *Capital.* Vol. 3. New York: International Publishers.
McEwen William J.
1975 *Changing Rural Bolivia.* New York: Research Institute for the Study of Man.

Mendoza, Domingo
  1982   Reactivación de la Asociación de Productores de Papa (APP). Unpublished Manuscript. Cochabamba: Centro de Estudios de la Realidad Económica y Social.
Mintz, Sidney
  1973   "A Note on the Definition of Peasantries." *The Journal of Peasant Studies* 1(1):291–325.
Mintz, Sidney, and Eric R. Wolf
  1950   "An Analysis of Ritual Co-Parenthood." *Southwestern Journal of Anthropology* 6:341–68.
Mitchell, Christopher H.
  1977   *The Legacy of Populism in Bolivia: From M.N.R. to Military Rule.* New York: Praeger Publishers.
Mitre, Antonio
  1981   *Los patriarcas de la plata.* Lima: Instituto de Estudios Peruanos.
Molinié-Fioravanti, Antoinette
  1982   *La Vallée Sacrée des Andes.* Paris: Société d' Ethnographie. Travaux de L'Institut Français des Etudes Andines. Tôme 18.
Montoya, Rodrigo.
  1982   "Class Relations in the Andean Countryside." *Latin American Perspectives* 9(3):62–78.
Murra, John V.
  1972   "'El control vertical' en un máximo de pisos ecológicos en la economía de las sociedades andinas." In *Visita a la Provincia de León de Huánuco, Perú en 1562*, edited by Iñigo Ortiz de Zúniga. Huánuco: Hermilio Valdezón, vol. 2.
Nash, June
  1979   *We Eat the Mines and the Mines Eat Us.* New York: Columbia University Press.
Orlove, Benjamin
  1977   "Inequality Among Peasants: The Forms and Uses of Reciprocal Exchange in Andean Perú." In *Peasant Livelihood: Studies in Economic Anthropology and Cultural Ecology*, edited by Rhoda Halperin and James Dow. New York: St. Martin's Press, pp. 22–35.
Painter, Michael
  1991   "Re-Creating Peasant Economy in Southern Peru." In *Golden Ages, Dark Ages: Imagining the Past in Anthropology and History*, edited by Jay O'Brien and William Roseberry. Berkeley/Los Angeles: University of California Press.
Patch, Richard W.
  1956   Social Implications of the Bolivian Agrarian Reform. Ph.D. dissertation, Cornell University.
Pearce, R.
  1983   "Sharecropping: Towards a Marxist View." In *Sharecropping and Sharecroppers*, edited by T. J. Byres. London: Frank Cass.
Pearse, Andrew
  1975   *The Latin American Peasant.* London: Frank Cass.
Peinado Sotomayor, Marcelo
  1971   Land Reform in Three Communities in Cochabamba, Bolivia. Unpublished, abbreviated version of Ph.D. dissertation. Madison: Land Tenure Center, University of Wisconsin.

Platt, Tristan
1982   *Estado boliviano y ayllu andino.* Lima: Instituto de Estudios Peruanos.
1983   "Conciencia andina y conciencia proletaria. Qhuyaruna y ayllu en el norte de Potosí." *Hisla, Revista Latinoamericana de Historia Económica y Social* 2:47–73.
Presencia November 29, 1973; July 13, 1980.
República de Bolivia
1900/1973   Censo Nacional de la Población de la República, 1900. Oficina Nacional de Inmigración, Estadística y Propaganda Geográfica. 2 volumes.
1950   Censo Agropecuario. Ministerio de Hacienda y Estadística. Dirección General de Estadística y Censos.
1950   Censo Demográfico. Ministerio de Hacienda y Estadística. Dirección General de Estadística y Censos.
1972   Reglamentación de la Resolución No. 49/71. Ministerio de Transporte, Comunicaciones y Aeronáutica Civil.
1973   *Gaceta Oficial de Bolivia* 13(649); February 2.
1977   Resultados del Censo de Población y Vivienda 1976. Vol. 2. Ministerio de Planeamiento y Coordinación. Instituto Nacional de Estadística.
1978   "Equivalencias de medidas típicas al sistema métrico utilizadas en las provincias de Cochabamba." Boletín Estadístico, No. 4. Ministerio de Asuntos Campesinos y Agropecuarios. Departmento de Estadística.
1980   "Boletín Estadístico." Gestión 1980. Banco Agrícola de Bolivia. Unidad Estadística. La Paz.
1982   "Boletín Estadístico." Gestión 1982. Banco Agrícola de Bolivia. Unidad Estadística. La Paz.
Reyeros, Rafael
1963   *Historia social del indio boliviano.* La Paz: Editorial Fenix.
Rivera Cusicanqui, Silvia
1978   "La expansión del latifundio en el altiplano boliviano: Elementos para la caracterización de una oligarquia regional." *Avances* 2:95–118.
1984   *"Oprimidos pero no vencidos." Luchas del campesinado aymara y qhechwa 1900–1980.* La Paz: Confederación Sindical Unica de Trabajadores Campesinos de Bolivia/Hisbol.
Robertson, A. F.
1987   *The Dynamics of Productive Relationships: African Share Contracts in Comparative Perspective.* Cambridge: Cambridge University Press.
Rodríguez Ostría, Gustavo
1983   "Expansión del latifundio o supervivencia de las comunidades indígenas? Cambios en la estructura agraria boliviana del siglo 19." Serie Historia, Instituto de Estudios Sociales y Económicos, Working Paper No. 1. Cochabamba: Universidad Mayor de San Simón.
Roseberry, William
1978   "Peasants as Proletarians." *Critique of Anthropology* 22:3–16.
1983   *Coffee and Capitalism in the Venezuelan Andes.* Austin: University of Texas Press.
1989   *Anthropologies and Histories: Essays in Culture, History, and Political Economy.* New Brunswick, NJ: Rutgers University Press.

Sánchez-Albornóz, Nicolás
  1965   "La saca de mulas de Salta al Perú, 1778–1808." *Anuario del Instituto de Investigaciones Históricas* 8:261–312.
  1978   *Indios y tributos en el Alto Perú.* Lima: Instituto de Estudios Peruanos.
Scott, James C.
  1985   *Weapons of the Weak. Everyday Forms of Peasant Resistance.* New Haven: Yale University Press.
  1990   *Domination and the Arts of Resistance: Hidden Transcripts.* New Haven, CT: Yale University Press.
Seligmann, Linda J.
  1989   "To be in Between: The Cholas as Market Women." *Comparative Studies in Society and History* 31(4):694–721.
Shanin, Teodor
  1973   "Peasantry: Delineation of a Sociological Concept and a Field of Study." *Peasant Studies* 1:1–8.
Sider, Gerald M.
  1980   "The Ties that Bind: Culture and Agriculture, Property and Propriety in the Newfoundland Village Fishery." *Social History* 5(1):1–39.
  1986   *Culture and Class in Anthropology and History: A Newfoundland Illustration.* Cambridge: Cambridge University Press.
Silverman, Sydel
  1979   "The Peasant Concept in Anthropology." *The Journal of Peasant Studies* 7(1):49–69.
Simmons, Roger A.
  1974   *Palca and Pucara: A Study of the Effects of Revolution on Two Bolivian Haciendas.* Berkeley: University of California Press.
Sindicato Mixto de Transportistas [Tiraque]
  1973   Libro de Actas, January 4.
Slater, Charles
  1969   Market Processes in La Paz, Bolivia. Research Paper No. 5, Latin American Studies Center. East Lansing: Michigan State University.
Smith, Carol
  1984   "Does a Commodity Economy Enrich the Few While Ruining the Masses? Differentiation Among Petty Commodity Producers in Guatemala." *The Journal of Peasant Studies* 11(3):99–108.
  1986a "Reconstructing the Elements of Petty Commodity Production." In *Rethinking Petty Commodity Production*, edited by Alison McEwen Scott. (Special Issue, *Social Analysis* 20:29–46.)
  1986b "Culture and Community: The Language of Class in Guatemala." In *The Year Left*, edited by Michael Sprinkler. London: Verso.
Smith, Gavin A.
  1986   "Reflections on the Social Relations of Simple Commodity Production." *The Journal of Peasant Studies* 13:99–108.
  1989   *Livelihood and Resistance. Peasants and the Politics of Land in Peru.* Berkeley/Los Angeles: University of California Press.
Smith, Waldemar
  1977   *The Fiesta System and Economic Change.* New York: Columbia University Press.
Stavenhagen, Rodolfo
  1975   *Social Classes in Agrarian Societies.* New York: Anchor Books.

Stern, Steve
1983 "The Struggle for Solidarity: Class, Culture, and Community in Highland Indian America." *Radical History Review* 27:21–45.
1987 "New Approaches to the Study of Peasant Rebellion and Consciousness. Implications of the Andean Experience." In *Resistance, Rebellion, and Consciousness in the Andean Peasant World, 18th and 20th Centuries*, edited by Steve Stern. Madison: University of Wisconsin Press.

Taussig, Michael
1979 *The Devil and Commodity Fetishism in South America*. Chapel Hill: University of North Carolina Press.

Thompson, E. P.
1976 "The Grid of Inheritance: A Comment." In *Family and Inheritance in Western Europe 1200–1800*, edited by Jack Goody, Joan Thirsk and E.P. Thompson. Cambridge: Cambridge University Press, pp. 328–60.
1978 "Eighteenth-century English Society: Class Struggle Without a Class." *Social History* 3(2):133–65.

USAID/Yacimientos Petrolíferos Fiscales Bolivianos
1969 Fertilizer Promotion Program. Unpublished Manuscript. La Paz.

Ustariz, Germán, and Domingo Mendoza
1982 *El fenómeno del "rescatismo" en la comercialización de la papa*. La Paz: Centro de Investigación y Promoción del Campesinado.

Viedma, Francisco de
1793/1969 *Descripción geográfica y estadística de la Provincia de Santa Cruz de la Sierra*. Cochabamba: Los Amigos del Libro.

Vincent, Joan
1977 "Agrarian Society as Organized Flow: Processes of Development Past and Present." *Peasant Studies* 6(2):56–65.
1978 "Political Anthropology: Manipulative Strategies." *Annual Review of Anthropology* 7:175–94.
1990 *Anthropology and Politics. Visions, Traditions, and Trends*. Tucson: University of Arizona Press.

Volmuller, J.
1954 "Transport in Bolivia." *Transport and Communications Review* 7(2): 14–27.

Warman, Arturo
1978 *. . . Y venimos a contradecir*. México: Editorial de la Casa Chata.
1980 *Ensayos sobre el campesinado en México*. México: Editorial Nueva Imagen.

Weismantel, Mary
1988 *Food, Gender, and Poverty in the Ecuadorian Andes*. Philadelphia: University of Pennsylvania Press.

Wennergren E. Boyd and Morris D. Whitaker
1975 *The Status of Bolivian Agriculture*. New York: Praeger.

Williams, Raymond
1973 *The Country and the City*. New York: Oxford University Press.
1985 *Keywords: A Vocabulary of Culture and Society*. Rev. ed. New York: Oxford University Press.
1989 *Marxism and Literature*. London: Oxford University Press.

Wolf, Diana
  1990 "Daughters, Decisions, and Domination: An Empirical and Conceptual Critique of Household Strategies." *Development and Change* 21:43–74.
Wolf, Eric R.
  1955 "Types of Latin American Peasantry: A Preliminary Discussion," *American Anthropologist* 57:452–71.
  1956 "Aspects of Group Relations in a Complex Society." *American Anthropologist* 58(6):1065–78.
  1957 "Closed Corporate Communities in Mesoamerica and Central Java." *Southwestern Journal of Anthropology* 13:1–18.
  1966 *Peasants*. Englewood Cliffs, NJ: Prentice-Hall.
  1983 "On Peasant Rent." In *Social Anthropology of Peasantry*, edited by Joan P. Mencher. Bombay/Madras/New Delhi: Somaiya Publications, pp. 48–59.
  1986 "The Vicissitudes of the Closed Corporate Peasant Community." *American Ethnologist* 13(2):325–29.
Wolf, Eric R., and Sidney W. Mintz
  1957 "Haciendas and Plantations in Middle America and the Antilles." *Social and Economic Studies* 6(3):380–412.
Wolfe, Patrick
  1991 "On Being Woken Up: The Dreamtime in Anthropology and in Australian Settler Culture." *Comparative Studies in Society and History* 33(2):197–224.

Index

University of Pennsylvania Press
The Ethnohistory Series

Lee V. Cassanelli, Juan A. Villamarin, and Judith E. Villamarin, Editors

Ronald R. Atkinson. *The Roots of Ethnicity: The Origins of the Acholi of Uganda Before 1800.* 1994

Christopher Boehm. *Blood Revenge: The Enactment and Management of Conflict in Montenegro and Other Tribal Societies.* 1987

Lee V. Cassanelli. *The Shaping of Somali Society: Reconstructing the History of a Pastoral People, 1600–1900.* 1982

James L. Giblin. *The Politics of Environmental Control in Northeastern Tanzania, 1840–1940.* 1992

Robert M. Hill II and John Monaghan. *Continuities in Highland Maya Social Organization: Ethnohistory in Sacapulas, Guatemala.* 1987

Maria L. Lagos. *Autonomy and Power: The Dynamics of Class and Culture in Rural Bolivia.* 1994

James McCann. *From Poverty to Famine in Northeast Ethiopia: A Rural History, 1900–1935.* 1987

Derek Nurse and Thomas Spear. *The Swahili: Reconstructing the History and Language of an African Society, 800–1500.* 1985

James A. Quirin. *The Evolution of the Ethiopian Jews: A History of the Beta Israel (Falasha) to 1920.* 1992

Norman B. Schwartz. *Forest Society: A Social History of Petén, Guatemala.* 1990

Lawrence J. Taylor. *Dutchmen on the Bay: The Ethnohistory of a Contractual Community.* 1983

This book was set in Baskerville and Eras typefaces. Baskerville was designed by John Baskerville at his private press in Birmingham, England, in the eighteenth century. The first typeface to depart from oldstyle typeface design, Baskerville has more variation between thick and thin strokes. In an effort to insure that the thick and thin strokes of his typeface reproduced well on paper, John Baskerville developed the first wove paper, the surface of which was much smoother than the laid paper of the time. The development of wove paper was partly responsible for the introduction of typefaces classified as modern, which have even more contrast between thick and thin strokes.

Eras was designed in 1969 by Studio Hollenstein in Paris for the Wagner Typefoundry. A contemporary script-like version of a sans-serif typeface, the letters of Eras have a monotone stroke and are slightly inclined.

Printed on acid-free paper.